Ros:

To salute a long
and pleasant professional
relationship. and my
best wishes

Paul

28.11.01

In Your Opinion

In Your Opinion:

Political and Social Trends in Ireland through the Eyes of the Electorate

TOWN
HOUSE
DUBLIN

First published in 2001 by

TownHouse and CountryHouse Ltd
Trinity House
Charleston Road
Ranelagh
Dublin 6
Ireland

1 3 5 7 9 10 8 6 4 2

A CIP catalogue record for this book is available from
the British Library.

ISBN: 1 86059 149 3

Cover Design: Terry Foley

Typeset: Typeform Repro

Printed: The Bath Press, Bath, England

Contents

List of Tables

List of Figures

Acknowledgements

This book, and the business which it recounts, would not have been possible without the unstinting generosity of the many, many people who co-operated on the *The Irish Times*/MRBI polls over 20 years, and my sincere thanks go to them.

The poll series was initiated by *The Irish Times* and I thank all of the people on the newspaper, with whom I have had such pleasant working relationships over the years.

A special thanks to my colleagues in MRBI: to Áine O'Donoghue, who reined in my prose when it tended to become overblown; to Marie Hobbs, the only person I know who could tame my manuscript and render it suitable to send to the publisher; and to Maura Murphy, who checked the many figures. My thanks to the current management team at MRBI, and at its new parent company Taylor Nelson Sofres, especially Ian McShane, managing director, who facilitated me in every way and who arranged the updating of the material on how we, the Irish people, view ourselves. My thanks also to John Bruton, Ken Casey, Fergus Finlay, Garret FitzGerald, Peter Green, Brendan Halligan, John Horgan, Shane Molloy, Sean O'Leary and Ruairi Quinn, and to all others who so kindly let me use their source material.

The help I received from the publisher, Treasa Coady and her team at TownHouse and CountryHouse was invaluable, as was that from John Gibson of the *Irish Times* library. The support of Dick Walsh, who has written the Foreword, and of Conor Brady, editor of *The Irish Times*, helped me reach the finishing line.

Jack Jones

October 2001

For Áine,
who made the business and the book a reality;
to the memory of my dear wife, Patty;
and for my only daughter, Finola.

Foreword

Éamon de Valera's reply to critics who questioned his Irishness was as bold a claim as he'd ever made: *"When I needed to know what the Irish people wanted,"* he said, *"I had only to examine my own heart..."*

Thirty years later party managers still believed they could "stay in touch with the grassroots" by turning up at cumann or branch and tuning in to the opinions of their members. Since Fianna Fáil and Fine Gael were catch-all parties, they couldn't go far wrong.

But leaders of the 1960s no longer spoke for their parties without fear of contradiction; and, by the 1970s, only fundamentalists – religious or political – would claim to know, without asking, what the people wanted. Politics had lost the certainty bred of civil war loyalties – certainty that once allowed two Donegal activists to join Ted Nealon on a hill above a polling station and identify the allegiances of the voters in the valley below. Nealon, as shrewd an observer as ever, marked a card, not doubting their count.

Now, though, the modernising challenges of Common Market membership, urban life and increasing exposure to outside influences have changed Irish society. Clearly our ways of assessing the needs and preferences of the electorate must change too.

The lead came, ironically, from one of de Valera's contemporaries. While Dev was examining his own heart, George Gallup, a professor of journalism lately recruited to a New York advertising agency, was exploring new ways of gauging public opinion. And when Franklyn D Roosevelt's landslide victory in 1936 proved the accuracy of his assessments and analysis, Gallup's name became synonymous with polling.

The names that have become synonymous with political polls in Ireland over the last 30 years are Jack Jones and MRBI. The Market Research Bureau of Ireland was set up in 1962; but Jack Jones, Áine O'Donoghue and their colleagues had already won a solid reputation for commercial research before their first, tentative test of the political waters in 1973.

The first *Irish Times*/MRBI Poll nine years later marked the start of a series that has provided a valuable public service – and added to the paper's burgeoning circulation. Here were dependable results produced by well-tried techniques, a narrative of political events with a commentary on the electorate's reactions to platforms and performances.

Of course, there are sceptics. But some obligingly answer their own criticism, though few as graciously as Dr Brendan Comiskey, Bishop of Ferns who began by writing (in the *Wexford People*) that *"in a choice between God and Gallup... for a Christian there could be no contest"* and ended, much later, with a private acknowledgement: *"If there is any error associated with the surveys, it seems to be an error of interpretation by people like myself who do not heed the... warnings of the polling organisations themselves."*

It's an example that some journalists and politicians, who still insist on misreading polls either for the sake of a headline or a note of encouragement to the troops, might follow.

Quite apart from misreading polls, politicians of various hues, from redoubtable ministers to impetuous opposition spokesmen have called, most recently in June 2001, for their restriction or prohibition – but only for public consumption. Presumably parties in or out of office would continue to make liberal use of them; it's only the public that can't be trusted with the information they supply.

It was suspicion of the parties, who were first to use market research, that made journalists reluctant to abandon conventional wisdom and accept the evidence of the polls. I was among those who believed that the rewriting of constituency boundaries was an unbeatable tactic in 1977. We were wrong. The polls, tracking the impact of the Fianna Fáil manifesto, were right.

Garret FitzGerald wrote of *"the naïve cynicism of most people in Ireland with regard to opinion polls"* and hoped that the 1977 result would *"encourage all concerned to take these polls more seriously in the future"*.

He too was right. In every election – local, national and European – and in every referendum over the following 25 years, the research of MRBI and of one or more of its competitors will chart the shifting ground of public opinion.

For MRBI the 1995 referendum on divorce was of special significance. First because, taken together, the seven polls in the *Irish Times*/MRBI series and three MRBI polls commissioned by the government drew such a precise graph of public support as to astonish observers at home and abroad. Support fell from 63 per cent to 50.3 per cent in little more than nine months so that, on polling day, the margin between supporters and opponents of divorce stood at little more than half of 1 per cent – 9,000 voters in a poll of 1.6 million.

There were complimentary comments by observers and experienced researchers in the High Court action that followed, and in which Jack Jones was a witness. Another witness, Gordon Heald, who had worked for 25 years with Gallup UK, said that he was:

> ...really quite surprised by the nature of the polling. This was a very sophisticated exercise... It was quite clearly very carefully thought-out... a kind of planning strategy for the government, not what you would normally find in ordinary opinion polls.

Not all of the arguments about polling have been settled. But if politics in Ireland has become more realistic since civil war divisions faded and our affairs took on a more modern form, I believe that research – and the researchers – deserves a share of the credit.

This is, indeed, a book with a cast of thousands – the citizens who agreed to co-operate with researchers over the years and answered, to the best of their ability, when asked for their opinions.

Dick Walsh
October 2001

Introduction

Growing up in pre-war Ireland in the small village of Suncroft, near the Curragh in south Kildare, where my father was the local schoolteacher, the term 'market research' was more distant than the stars. These I could see, but I had never heard of market research. Looking back to those boyhood days, I can now see that some of that local activity played a modest, but nonetheless identifiable, role in the evolution of the profession that was to become my second career.

As the eldest of a family of four, I was regularly dispatched up the hill to the village shop by my mother for the mid-week provisions. I was much too young to realise that my mother, the consumer, had no choice as to either brand or quality. It was life as we knew it, and she always appeared to be perfectly happy with the situation.

Many years later, I realised that the commercial activity of Suncroft in the thirties was eminently typical of what in marketing parlance, is now referred to as the pre-war *"seller's market"*.

The war came and went; we began to experience some of its more beneficial effects. Planned economic growth, coupled with innovation in product development and packaging design, was complemented by unprecedented developments in communications and distributive procedures – the face of Irish retailing was changing forever. I clearly remember, in the summer of 1960, visiting the lone centre-city supermarket where the main excitement was generated by the captivating appearance of the countless shelves of new products reaching out to the discerning and approving eyes of the hundreds of shoppers. The choices were innumerable, and it was a far cry from the slow trek up the hill in Suncroft a generation earlier. The *"buyer's market"* had arrived.

However, the transition, initially at least, brought new challenges for producers and manufacturers; providing choice meant being knowledgeable about consumer requirements and behaviour. The information gap needed to be bridged and market research was the vehicle.

Following its establishment in 1962, MRBI concentrated exclusively on commercial research for the first ten years of its existence. However, the techniques of market research are versatile, and one area where this versatility has been developed is that of political research.

Over many years, there has been considerable public and media interest in the political research conducted by the company and other media enterprises have consistently reported the findings. Today MRBI is widely acknowledged as an authoritative source of political information. The company has also conducted extensive research for political parties and much of this material has been utilised in this book. Some, however, must be maintained as confidential, in accordance with the ethics of our profession. This book tells the story of MRBI's political research and, in doing so, mirrors the great changes that have taken place in Ireland, North and South.

CHAPTER 1

Tír na nDall: The Land of the Blind

Shortly after 11 am on Tuesday 23th January 1996, I entered the witness box in Dublin's High Court, took the oath, and commenced giving evidence in answer to Mr Garrett Cooney SC, who was acting for the petitioner, Des Hanafin, in his case against the government. The petitioner's claim was that the divorce referendum of 24th November 1995 was null and void, as the outcome was materially affected by the government's print advertising campaign, which had been declared unconstitutional in the *McKenna* Supreme Court decision of 17th November 1995. I was appearing as the first expert witness for the petitioner, since MRBI had conducted three research surveys for the government during the campaign.

While I had been in court on previous occasions to provide research survey data as evidence in court cases, it had invariably been disallowed as hearsay. However, after lengthy legal argument, the findings of the MRBI research throughout the divorce referendum campaign were fully heard in court. It was a coming of age for opinion polling and was the impetus for me to chronicle the history of MRBI in this area. (The full story of the court proceedings is outlined in *Chapters 12* and *13*.)

IRELAND IN THE 1960s

The Ireland of the early 1960s was where it all started. The market research scene, when I first joined the Nielsen organisation in the spring of 1960, is tidily captured in the Irish *seanfhocal*:

"I dtír na nDall, is rí fear na leathshuile."
("In the land of the blind, the one-eyed man is king.")

There was a handful of people who had some understanding of marketing but terms such as scanning, barcodes and targeting were unheard of; the relevance of demographics and brand positioning were known to but a few; and, in market research terms, Ireland was very much the land of the blind.

There were, however, a few positive straws in the wind. The legendary pragmatist Seán Lemass, Taoiseach during the early 1960s, was alerting the captains of industry to the new competitive environment that lay ahead, through the various programmes for economic expansion. A few were already responding. Nielsen, which was established in the USA in the 1920s, had opened an Irish branch in the mid-1950s, and was servicing the information needs of a number of Irish manufacturers.

In the spring of 1958, having reached the rank of captain in the Irish Defence Forces, I noticed an advertisement by Nielsen for part-time interviewing work at weekends, relating to a national readership survey that the company was conducting. In sociological terms, I found survey interviewing novel and interesting, but the experience gave me my first taste of how people across all demographic groups live, think and express themselves. I also quickly became aware that the information I was collecting needed considerable further processing before the research findings would be meaningful to a client. The concept intrigued me and, on many occasions, I recall thinking through how interviews with a sample of people could provide realistic estimates of the behaviour of the total population.

A New Career

Two years later, I saw another Nielsen advertisement relating to the recruitment of executive staff for the Dublin office. At this stage, I was less than half way through my army career, having been commissioned as a lieutenant in the Army Cadet Class of 1945, and had successfully completed my staff course in the Irish Military College. Although I was comfortably settled with my family near the Curragh, my earlier experience of market research (and a description of the profession as *"the commercial equivalent of military intelligence"* in a book that I

2

had read) conveyed a message that the transition from a military to a market research career could be reasonably smooth.

I had also become aware that one of my cadet class colleagues, Padraig Ferguson, who had already retired to take up a commercial appointment, was doing very well in the advertising profession. Having carefully considered all aspects of the situation, I decided to respond to the advertisement, and I re-read the market research book that had been given to me by a close friend, Comdt Tom Maher, when he became aware of my interest in the subject.

Four months and two interviews later, on 1st July 1960, I found myself sitting at a new non-military desk at 36 Merrion Square, home of the Nielsen organisation in Ireland. My primary task was to establish and develop a consumer research division that would complement the conventional Nielsen retail audit service (in which Neilsen provided a measure of market share for a range of consumer products, by auditing sales through a representative sample of supermarkets and shops). On today's criteria, it would be unthinkable to appoint a person with no experience to manage a technical division in a market research company but, in the Ireland of the time, it was a logical option since there were very few even partially experienced researchers – or one-eyed kings – in the marketplace. My army training gave me the confidence and understanding to get on with the task. I also received full technical back-up from my colleagues Bernard Prendiville and Donal Stephens.

By the end of that first year, I felt I had come a long way. I was quite confident to take briefings from clients, assess the technical options and prepare proposals, though I continued to refer technical matters up the line and cleared all reports. On one such occasion, I was corrected by one of my superiors for using the phrase *"only 2 per cent"* in a report. I attempted to justify this by showing him the figure 2 per cent in the table. *"Yes,"* I was told, *"but where did the 'only' come from?"* I got the message, and my overall recollection after many years is that the Nielsen technical and ethical training at the time was first class.

In 1961, I found myself moving on to a much larger playing field, with even more scope than before. A new managing director had arrived and was concentrating primarily on the retail audit division. I had moved to the stage where I was now handling all services to clients and had developed the new consumer research department. I also began to realise that this land of the blind might hold the potential to embrace an Irish-owned market research company. In this regard,

I received considerable support from Padraig Ferguson, then in an executive position with Arks Advertising. Our paths had soon crossed in our new careers and his encouragement, along with that of my family, meant that the spark, which is now the 40-year-old MRBI, was ignited.

FOUNDING MRBI

In early discussions on a name for the new company, we felt the terms 'market research' and 'Ireland' were both descriptive and appropriate, but the composite title seemed to lack something. We also realised that one interpretation of the word bureau, as *"a business establishment for exchanging information"*, met the requirement, and the full title Market Research Bureau of Ireland was agreed upon. The company was formally incorporated on 25th April 1962; the two directors being Padraig Ferguson and myself. We had equal shareholding and I was managing director.

After a few weeks settling into our new offices at 11 South Frederick Street, I began the task of implementing our marketing plan. The first stage involved limited mailings of our brochure, though 'pamphlet' would be a more appropriate description. We had also decided to abbreviate the title for marketing purposes to MRBI Ltd. Before leaving Nielsen, I had decided not to tell any clients of my plans to establish an Irish company and, whether through loyalty or naïvete, I made no attempt to take any business with me. This, to some extent, was due to the fact that I always felt appreciative of the opportunities I was given in Nielsen to establish a new career, and I was also very much aware of the benefits of the technical and ethical training that I received there.

With the new MRBI brochure in my briefcase, I was working from a clean sheet. The fact that I was enthusiastic and committed, and had condensed considerably more professional experience into the previous 18 months than many would have thought possible, gave me some level of confidence to make the hundreds of contacts that were necessary at that early stage. I certainly needed that residual confidence because I spent a further five anxious months knocking at doors before the first project came on stream – a national survey of housewives. It was certainly a boost to our morale – and our finances. This gave us all the first real taste of what it was like to be working for ourselves, without the comfort of someone else further up the line carrying the can. That first survey put the company on its feet. At the end of the first year, I bought out the shareholding of Padraig Ferguson and my wife, Patty, became the other director and shareholder.

During these early years, the company's professional association with the public sector was first established and today, 40 years later, MRBI continues to have many semi-State clients on its books. The first specialised readership survey was commissioned as early as 1963, and the first radio listenership study in 1965, followed by a further monitoring one year later. Other notable projects at the time included surveys on air and rail travel, car ownership and quite a range of consumer characterisation studies for the manufacturing sector. By 1966, the company had grown to seven full-time employees with an interviewing force of 50.

Running the Business

As managing director, my role in the circumstances of the day was wide-ranging and demanding. I attended all client meetings, took briefs and prepared written proposals. When the go-ahead was given, I designed the questionnaire and briefed the staff who were to be involved. When the statistical analyses were put on my desk, I interpreted the findings and, at that time, wrote every report. In one respect, it was no different to today; client deadlines had to be met. We did not have computers and the procedures of the time meant that surveys took considerably longer to complete. Our first nationwide survey of 1,000 housewives in 1962 took two months from go-ahead to delivery of report. Today, the results of a national opinion poll of 1,000 electors for *The Irish Times* can, if necessary, be reported on within 48 hours. However, direct comparisons with 1962 are not really realistic.

Very soon after MRBI began to make its first impact in the marketplace, I realised the crucial importance of establishing a charter for the company. This worked on the axiom that a client must never be misled nor should we ever overstate, or understate, a situation.

Around this time, I was invited by the College of Commerce in Rathmines to lecture students of the Marketing Institute on market research, in preparation for the institute's examinations. I enjoyed the experience and continued teaching there for 12 years. The syllabus was detailed and I frequently introduced case histories from MRBI files, but without disclosing either client or brand identity. One of the characteristics, which I noticed at the time, was that many of our marketing clients left it very late to make contact, and only did so when the required information was crucially urgent. This led me to coin the first of many mixed metaphors that I used in my lectures, *"Why do marketing people wait until their backs are to the wall before they see the writing on it?"*

Expansion

Towards the end of the 1960s, we placed an advertisement for a senior research executive. Two of the criteria that we specified as desirable were: having an aptitude for mathematical procedures and an ability to work accurately under pressure. We received 24 replies, and I interviewed six people, but only one reply really interested me. Little did I realise at the time that I was about to take what was the most influential decision I have ever made in the annals of MRBI.

Áine O'Donoghue joined the company as a research executive. Her considerable skills and contribution to the company resulted in her promotion to research director and her intellectual talents and influence led to her joining the Board a few years later.

Fifteen years later, I can clearly remember being accompanied to the door of RTÉ by Paul Mulligan in 1984, after Áine had presented the MRBI proposal for the Joint National Media Research Contract to the JNMR Committee. Paul turned to me and said, *"Jack, that was a wonderful presentation, and Áine is the key."* MRBI was awarded the contract and the company has retained a national media contract since then.

Other Interests/Areas

I expect that many readers will share the view, frequently expressed, that the workload of MRBI rises and falls in line with elections and political events. Nothing could be further from the true situation. All of our political polling, both private and for publication, accounts for less than 5 per cent of our work in a normal year, and would not, even in an election year, rise to 10 per cent.

The core of the company's business is in the commercial market. There is hardly a household product in anybody's cupboard that has not been tested or evaluated by research – biscuits, coffee, tea, soups, soft drinks, alcoholic drinks, floor cleaners, washing powders – well-known brands and those that never made the breakthrough with consumers. We have examined tourism – within the country and abroad – train and bus travel, the postal service, the telephone service, banks, building societies and credit unions – it's almost a case of you name it, we've researched it. The phrase 'TAM rating' has entered everyday language. It relates to audiences for television programmes – the actual rating being a form of shorthand for the percentage of the population that views a particular programme. These ratings have implications for the cost of advertising during specific programmes. MRBI has, for many years, provided the equivalent ratings for radio programmes through the JNLR – the Joint National Listnership Research.

Ten Years in Business

But back to the toil and stress of the late 1960s, which saw the company moving towards a celebratory ten years in business and our thoughts turned to how we might honour the occasion. Our decision was a seminar – with a difference. The plan was to present three actual case studies to an invited audience, with three clients describing the brief given to MRBI, in the presence of a panel of marketing experts, with the entire operation chaired by a well-known marketing personality.

The seminar was held in Jurys Hotel, Ballsbridge, in April 1972, with Tom Garvey, general manager of the then Córas Tráchtála in the chair. The members of the panel were: Professor Tony Cunningham of UCD, who became a director of MRBI shortly afterwards, Archie Cook, marketing director of Irish Distillers Ltd, and the late Jim McMahon, managing director of Munster Chipboard Ltd and previously marketing director of CIÉ. The MRBI methodology was outlined by Áine and myself in turn and, finally, each client described how the research was acted upon.

The first case was put by the late Sean J White, public relations and publicity manager of CIÉ, who stated that the company had experienced a decline in rail travel. MRBI had been called in and a test market operation was undertaken on the Waterford–Dublin route. The survey identified the factors, including ticket pricing, that would influence potential travellers and, following the success of the localised project, the green light was given for a national CIÉ campaign.

Passenger traffic increased by 75 per cent, with a small increase in profits.

The second study was presented by the late Rev. Farrell Sheridan of the Holy Ghost Order, who stated that Vatican II, in changing the whole environment of the Catholic Church, also required religious orders to examine their own roles relative to the spirit of their founders. His order was primarily missionary but since, in Ireland, it also performed an educational role, he asked MRBI to conduct a survey to determine the image of the order among the general public. In technical terms, this was a very challenging undertaking, the main problem being to devise a methodology that would confirm that respondents were correctly identifying the religious order about which they were speaking.

Áine designed the MRBI approach. Since no comparative data was available, it was decided to compare the order, using agreed criteria, with two others – one exclusively missionary (SMA) and the other exclusively educational (Jesuits). The problem of the accurate identification of each of the three orders was highlighted by an early question that set out various locations in Ireland and asked respondents to identify the specific order that operated in these locations, e.g. the correct identification for Gardiner Street in Dublin would be the Jesuits. Those who did not identify the orders correctly were eliminated at analysis stage. Fr Sheridan concluded by saying that the research showed the public image of his order as, primarily, educational, which was not correct and that a campaign to change it was undertaken in a number of missionary magazines.

The third project was presented by Feargal Quinn, managing director of Superquinn Ltd, who outlined the research we had conducted among his customers. Quinn's commitment to customer service is ample evidence of the value he places on research.

Bob Kavanagh of the Department of Statistics at Trinity College, in an article on the seminar in *The Irish Times*, commented that it was a successful and innovative project both organisationally and in terms of content. He said that perhaps other market research companies might follow suit, as it *"would help fill the credibility gap that appears to exist at the present time"*. This was an interesting comment from an observant academic and, although we had not experienced a lack of credibility among MRBI clients, it was feasible that non-users of research could have credibility problems. After ten years, the land of the blind still needed more one-eyed kings.

8

CHAPTER 2

MRBI's First Steps in Political Research (1973–1977)

Having concentrated exclusively on research within the commercial sector over the 11 years since the company was established, early 1973 signalled the company's introduction to political research. On 5th February 1973, less than four years after coming into office, Jack Lynch dissolved the Nineteenth Dáil and a general election was called for 28th February. During that election campaign, Garret FitzGerald and Richie Ryan commissioned MRBI to undertake 400 interviews in marginal – as defined by Fine Gael – constituencies. No record exists, at the present time, of the findings of that research or of what precise use those two pioneers made of the data collected. However, on the day following the calling of the election, Liam Cosgrave and Brendan Corish, the respective leaders of Fine Gael and Labour, announced agreement on a programme for coalition in the event of the combined parties securing an overall majority. The two parties obtained 73 seats between them in the then 144-seat Dáil, and formed the new government. Fianna Fáil was five short of a majority, having obtained 46 per cent of the first preference vote; Fine Gael and Labour combined, had 49 per cent.

The more significant introduction of the techniques of market research to the political arena was the occasion of the presidential election of that year, and since it was the first time that research was used in a presidential campaign, it is relevant to look at the general background to the presidency up to that time.

THE PRESIDENCY

The first president, Dr Douglas Hyde, was born in Frenchpark, County Roscommon in 1860, and was an agreed candidate between the political parties. He was inaugurated as president on 25th June 1938, under *Articles 12* and *13* of the 1937 Constitution.

Following his retirement, in June 1945, the first election for the office of president took place. There were three candidates. The first was Seán T Ó Ceallaigh, who took part in the 1916 Rising and who was a co-founder of Sinn Féin and, subsequently, of Fianna Fáil. Second was General Sean Mac Eoin, also a participant in the 1916 Rising and, following the Anglo–Irish Treaty, the Chief-of-Staff of the Free State Army. The third candidate was Dr Patrick McCartan, a non-party candidate.

In the election, Seán T Ó Ceallaigh narrowly missed the quota on the first count, but was elected with a majority of 111,700 votes over General Mac Eoin after the elimination of McCartan. Ó Ceallaigh also served the full seven-year term, and was re-elected unopposed in 1952. After serving this second seven-year term, he retired on 24th June 1959.

There were two candidates in the ensuing election. General Mac Eoin and Éamon de Valera, one of the best-known Irish statesmen of the century. In addition to taking part in the 1916 Rising, de Valera was also a co-founder of Fianna Fáil, held ministerial appointments in three governments and had served as Taoiseach on three occasions. De Valera won the election with 56 per cent of the vote, and defeated Mac Eoin by 120,000 votes. He was inaugurated on 25th June 1959 and was 76 years old at the time.

Seven years later, there were again two candidates, de Valera, the outgoing president nominated by Fianna Fáil, and Thomas F O'Higgins on the Fine Gael side. O'Higgins was called to the Bar in 1938, was a TD from 1948–1973 and was Minister for Health from 1954–1957. The outcome of this presidential election was the closest in any up to that time; de Valera obtained 50.5 per cent of the vote, which represented a margin of 10,717 votes.

THE 1973 PRESIDENTIAL ELECTION

In early January 1973, at the end of de Valera's second term, the media were beginning to signal the onset of the presidential election, due to take place later in the year. Erskine Childers, then Tánaiste in Jack Lynch's Fianna Fáil government, stated that he had no wish to be a candidate. This followed media reports that Lynch wished him to run.

On 31st January, O'Higgins, then deputy leader of Fine Gael and still the recipient of favourable media comment as a result of his close run against de Valera in 1966, was again selected as that party's candidate.

Following the February general election, with O'Higgins still the sole candidate, Erskine Childers was finally nominated by Fianna Fáil on 4th April. The following day, the new government announced that the presidential election would be held on 30th May, and one day later – 6th April – Childers formally accepted the Fianna Fáil nomination.

Although he had appeared reluctant three months earlier, Childers had all the credentials for the post: he was son of Erskine Childers, one of the signatories of the 1921 Anglo–Irish Treaty, and had served as a government minister on four occasions. He had also been Tánaiste from 1969 until the defeat of the Fianna Fáil government in the February 1973 election. Because of his initial reluctance and the general election outcome, and also because of O'Higgins' performance against de Valera in 1966, the Fine Gael nominee continued to be the media favourite, and was tipped as the likely winner.

Although both candidates campaigned with notable decorum throughout, their respective supporters and activists did not. Right up to election day, much of the comment was hard-hitting, vigorous and, at times, disparaging.

It was against this background that, in early April, MRBI was approached by Fine Gael to undertake research. The objective of the study was to determine the attitudes of the electorate to the presidential election and to the role of the presidency, and to determine the image and impact of each candidate as a potential president. This information would form the foundation for the six-week campaign strategy. As this was the first occasion on which the company was commissioned to carry out a national political survey, we were very conscious of the challenge that we were undertaking. The project was scheduled for mid-April.

Research Methodology

In the circumstances, the MRBI technical approach was very much influenced by our experience in the commercial sector over the previous 11 years; i.e. to establish and agree the objective of the survey and structure the methodology accordingly. The statistical sampling was straightforward and was based on a controlled selection of a sample of 500 electors. The questionnaire, designed for personal in-home interviews, covered the following framework.

- The respondent's perception of the importance of the presidential election relative to a general election.
- The respondent's reaction to the role and powers of the president, and if these were likely to change.
- The extent to which each candidate was associated with specific relevant factors, and the rated importance of these factors.
- Whether or not the respondent's intent to vote would be based on a party or personal basis.
- The respondent's voting intentions at the time of interview.
- The respondent's reaction to other relevant political issues.
- The respondent's current party support (for cross-analysis of the data).

Whilst the general information emerging from the survey provided a very useful basis for the party to formulate its strategy for the rest of the campaign, the figures on candidate support showed Erskine Childers ahead with 55 per cent of the vote, with O'Higgins on 45 per cent (after allowing for the very considerable 43 per cent, who were then undecided). The situation was that MRBI's first political survey was producing figures that were fundamentally in conflict with all media estimates to date. This was not a comfortable position, but, having carefully rechecked the procedures and the data, we presented our report to the Fine Gael party, indicating that their candidate was behind.

It is now evident that the survey represented a very reliable picture of the state of play at the time, since – in the election – Erskine Childers confounded the media by winning on the first count with 52 per cent of the vote, with O'Higgins achieving 48 per cent. For MRBI it was reassuring to know that the methodologies we had developed over the first decade had proved to be appropriate and accurate. We were measuring *electorate opinion*, and not *media reaction*, and our first lesson was that they do not always concur.

	MRBI Poll (mid-April)	Election Result (30th May)
	%	%
Erskine Childers	55	52
Thomas F O'Higgins	45	48

Table 2.1: Comparison of the results of the MRBI poll and the 1973 presidential election

Mr Childers was inaugurated as the fourth president on 25th June, but died suddenly 17 months later on 17th November 1974. Cearbhall Ó Dálaigh, who had had a very distinguished legal career from 1946, both in Ireland and abroad, was chosen as the agreed candidate, and he assumed the presidency. However, his tenure was relatively short lived as, on the 22nd October 1976, he resigned suddenly from office following Minister for Defence Paddy Donegan's unparliamentary *"thundering disgrace"* speech given in Mullingar, which denounced the president's referral of the Criminal Law Bill to the Supreme Court.

The search was on for a new president and Dr Patrick Hillery was the choice of all parties. He was appointed without an election and served as president until 1990.

THE 1973 FINE GAEL/LABOUR COALITION

After winning the general election of February 1973, the new Taoiseach Liam Cosgrave (whose father, William, had been the first President of the Executive Council [1922–1932] following the foundation of the State) nominated what was seen as a well-balanced cabinet, given in *Table 2.2*, from the two coalition parties.

Taoiseach	Liam Cosgrave	FG
Tánaiste; Health and Social Welfare	Brendan Corish	Lab
Finance	Riche Ryan	FG
Foreign Affairs	Garret FitzGerald	FG
Education	Dick Burke	FG
Agriculture	Mark Clinton	FG
Justice	Paddy Cooney	FG
Defence	Paddy Donegan	FG
Local Government	James Tully	Lab
Transport and Power	Peter Barry	FG
The Gaeltacht	Tom O'Donnell	FG
Industry and Commerce	Justin Keating	Lab
Lands	Tom Fitzpatrick	FG
Posts and Telegraphs	Conor Cruise O'Brien	Lab
Labour	Michael O'Leary	Lab

Table 2.2: Members of the 1973 Fine Gael/Labour cabinet

During its four years in office, this government performed well, reflecting the fact that a majority in cabinet had considerable political experience; the journalist Raymond Smith described it as a *"team of all the talents"*. Its term, however, was not without problems, not all of which were of its own making. The first arose shortly after the government took office when the oil crisis of 1973 precipitated a very difficult economic climate in many western countries. In the following year, a Fine Gael senator, Billy Fox, was murdered, and, in July 1976, British Ambassador Christopher Ewart-Biggs and civil servant Judith Cooke were assassinated in Sandyford, south County Dublin.

Less than a year later, on the 25th May 1977, the Taoiseach, having weathered the storm of Cearbhall Ó Dálaigh's resignation, announced the dissolution of the Dáil and called a general election for 16th June.

THE 1977 GENERAL ELECTION CAMPAIGN

No monitoring research was conducted during the government's term of office, not even in the run up to the election in early 1977. Once the election was called, it was our view that, as there were less than three weeks remaining to polling day, it was far too late, at that stage, to begin assessing the views of the electorate. Nevertheless, immediately following the calling of the election, we were contacted by Richie Ryan, Garret FitzGerald and other members of the campaign committee, and, after a series of briefing meetings, MRBI was commissioned to conduct an immediate national survey, the primary objectives of which were to identify the major issues and to measure current voting intentions.

While we planned and implemented our survey, the campaign was getting underway. For the government, matters were pretty bad. Fianna Fáil, in opposition, had made very considerable preparations. Within a few days of the dissolution, it had published a manifesto that a majority of the electorate bought without reservations and, apparently, without any consideration as to when or how it would be paid for. This was not surprising since it contained such provisions as the removal of rates from residential property and the reduction of motor tax. Although the government responded to some extent, Fianna Fáil had taken the initiative and public reaction was very clearly reflected in the first opinion poll figures (see *Table 2.3*).

Our meeting with the governmental committee had been arranged for Saturday 4th June at 11 am and when we first saw the results, on the evening of Friday 3rd June 1977, and realised their full implication for our client (the government parties), we thought it wise to re-check our figures. We examined our methodology and analyses fully and, having done so, were satisfied that the figures were in order. From the government's viewpoint, the outlook was disastrous; Fianna Fáil support was in the high-fifties and a rout was on the cards.

Presentation of the Polls

When we arrived in Government Buildings, Garret FitzGerald, Richie Ryan, Michael O'Leary, Brendan Halligan, Jim Dooge, Conor Cruise O'Brien, Justin Keating and the late Senator Alexis Fitzgerald were waiting in a large conference room. I delivered the main message at the outset and reported that, unless immediate and constructive initiatives were taken on prices, inflation, taxation, and unemployment, the result of the election would be a landslide victory for Fianna Fáil, which, the poll indicated, had 59 per cent support. We showed Fine Gael at 25 per cent, Labour 10 per cent and Others 7 per cent. This was the first occasion on which a number of those attending had been presented with market research figures, and it appeared to me that much of what I said had been missed by many of those present, who appeared to be more focused on morning coffee! Brendan Halligan asked for everyone's attention and suggested that I repeat what I had just said. When I had done so, Conor Cruise O'Brien commented that the survey figures did not tally with the messages he was getting on the doorsteps, in Howth, to which Garret FitzGerald replied that he had long decided not to believe all he was told on the doorsteps.

I have no doubt that the vast majority of those at the meeting accepted the MRBI figures and, 20 years later, Brendan Halligan described that Saturday morning in Government Buildings as one of the most dramatic experiences of his career in politics, also commenting that the presentation left no room for ambiguity. Before we left, two further projects were commissioned: the first confined to Dublin and the second, a final national survey. The report for the latter survey was scheduled for Saturday 11th June, five days before the election, and showed: Fianna Fáil 51 per cent; Fine Gael 29 per cent; Labour 15 per cent; and Others 5 per cent.

Result of the Election

The result of the election, in first preference terms, was: Fianna Fáil 51 per cent; Fine Gael 31 per cent; Labour 12 per cent; and Others 6 per cent.

have, in the person of Maura Murphy, somebody committed to and capable of controlling this crucial aspect of surveys.

Of course, the role of the interviewers throughout the country, in carrying out the interviews, is also critical to the accuracy of the poll results and many people have travelled many miles in all weathers to ensure this.

Finally, the chance any individual has of being selected for interview on any particular survey is about one in 2,500. In answer to those who say they were never interviewed, I can only recount an occasion in Kilkenny where I was addressing a group of about 50 people. The first comment at the end of my address was not a question, but the inevitable statement, *"I was never interviewed."* In response, I asked if all those present who had been interviewed on an opinion poll or a research survey would raise their hand, and to the surprise of many, more than half did so.

Interpreting the Results

When the interviewing is completed, and the data computerised and analysed, it then needs to be interpreted – a critical area. To use Bill Clinton's comment after the US presidential election of 2000 – *"the people have spoken, it will take a little time to work out what they have said"*. The top-line figures on leader and party support can hide many underlying trends. A simple example of this is that consistently higher than average support, for a leader or party, in an older age group is indicative of a leader or a party whose popularity is in decline, while above-average support in the lower age groups, especially among those in the late-twenties and thirties, indicates a positive outlook. The political climate of the day will also influence interpretation – highs and lows will follow major events, purely because the polls are a measure of the state of opinion in the country on the day the interviews are conducted. Opinion can even have shifted before the findings are published.

Finally, at all times it must be remembered that the views of 1,000 people only provide an *estimate* of the state of opinion in the electorate as a whole. One can be 95 per cent confident that the result, if everybody in the country was interviewed, would lie within three percentage points – known as the statistical variation – either way of the poll figure.

Publishing the Results

When an MRBI poll is published, the ethical codes of our professional association – ESOMAR – ensure that we publish the following crucial information to allow readers to make an informed interpretation: the dates on which the interviews were conducted; the sample size; its distribution; and its attendant statistical variation.

The ethical codes of ESOMAR also place another obligation on the research company; that we maintain as confidential, not only every aspect of the findings of privately commissioned polls, but also the fact that a party or a candidate of such privately commissioned polls might even have considered the feasibility of undertaking research.

Happily all the polls in the *Irish Times*/MRBI series were conducted expressly for publication; the findings of many privately commissioned polls have already been released by parties and candidates to the media, and many former clients of MRBI have given me permission to publish here both the nature and content of our discussions along with their poll findings. However, in some instances, the confidentiality clause still applies.

CHAPTER 3

The FitzGerald–Haughey Era (1977–1981)

FINE GAEL IN 1977

At a Fine Gael parliamentary party meeting on 1st July 1977, Liam Cosgrave formally tendered his resignation as party leader, having indicated his intention to do so at a meeting a few days earlier. The brief period between the two meetings was used by senior party members to identify the sources and direction of support, and the eventual outcome of the meeting on 1st July was the unanimous election of Dr Garret FitzGerald as leader. During both the 1973 and 1977 election research, Fitzgerald was the main focus of the MRBI discussions and briefing sessions. He was also continually extrapolating from and re-analysing the research figures in his own characteristic fashion and, because of the professional relationship that had developed, MRBI was delighted with the news of his appointment.

Fine Gael had been demoralised by the scale of that year's election defeat and, in organisational terms, was in tatters. Without delay, FitzGerald set about confronting the very challenging and difficult task of regenerating the party. As might be expected, he needed a detailed understanding of the electorate – its views of and attitudes towards the political parties and party leaders. One of his first decisions was to commission an extensive national survey, the primary objective of which was to provide an informational basis for future planning. The survey was based on interviews with a nationwide sample of 2,000 electors and the findings confirmed the difficulty of the task he had to face.

In the area of political measurement, this was the first occasion on which a political party commissioned a large quantitative study designed to provide it with an in-depth understanding of the public's relationship with the political process. Today, much of that exploration is conducted in focus groups, i.e. discussions with groups of eight to ten people, that flesh out the basic information already available to all parties through the published opinion polls.

Twenty-five years on, it is interesting to reflect on the level of co-operation experienced by the interviewers in that survey, taken at a time when very few, if any, would have been aware of the term 'opinion poll'. With the extent and detail of the questioning, each interview would have lasted at least half an hour, considerably longer than today's polls.

Against the backdrop of Fine Gael having obtained 31 per cent of first preference votes in the election – its lowest return for 20 years – one of the most ominous indicators from the research was that the party's main support had come from older people and it was making little or no impact among the younger generation.

One of Garret FitzGerald's other immediate decisions was to appoint a new general secretary. This was Peter Prendergast. I had known Peter for about five years, during which time he was in practice as a marketing consultant with Marketing Partners. Peter was already a member of Fine Gael and had stood for the party in Dublin in the 1973 and 1977 general elections. His talents and potential were already well known to the new party leader and I saw him as an ideal choice. His executive skills were exceptional; and he had the ability to see the crucial issues in complex situations clearly. It was a bonus, from an MRBI perspective, to be reporting research findings to one who was so experienced in the use of research.

Around this time, in the autumn of 1977, the new party leader conducted a tour of all constituencies to assess the situation at local level and to set about re-establishing the morale of supporters on the ground. The respective approaches of the new leader and general secretary complemented each other to a remarkable extent, and, by the end of the year, the nucleus of a solid party structure was becoming apparent. In September, Ted Nealon was appointed Director of Press and Information Services, at which stage the party was home to three of the best political analysts in the country. Later, as a further development from the research, Dan Egan was appointed Assistant Organiser of the Youth Section.

EUROPEAN PARLIAMENT ELECTION

MRBI was soon given further evidence of the depth of the planning of Dr FitzGerald and his team. Although the next European parliament election was not scheduled to take place until June 1979 – a year down the road – MRBI was, in the summer of 1978, commissioned to undertake a very comprehensive research project, the main objective of which was to provide a basis for the overall planning of the pre-election campaign. While the research was initially commissioned by Fine Gael, the Labour Party joined with them at an early stage to share the project. Since that time, MRBI has continued to conduct research for the two parties and, as is the norm in a competitive situation, the company does not normally conduct research for other parties here. The European research consisted of four stages: qualitative group discussions; quantitative surveys by constituency; a national quantitative survey; and final quantitative surveys in each European constituency – all undertaken in a nine-month period from July 1978 (see *Table 3.1*).

Stage	Date	Research	Objectives
1	July–September 1978	Qualitative group discussions with the general public and in-depth interviews with farmers.	To identify the most appropriate type of candidate and to identify the issues of greatest importance to the electorate.
2	September–December 1978	Quantitative surveys in the constituencies comprising 2,000 interviews.	To measure support for potential candidates, assess the importance of the election, and measure ratings of the government and of the main political parties.
3	March 1979	National quantitative survey among 1,000 electors.	To measure importance of issues, and the ratings of the government, parties and party leaders on criteria relevant to the European election.
4	April 1979	Quantitative surveys in each European constituency comprising 1,550 interviews.	To measure the impact of the candidates, and the likely voting intentions in the June election.

Table 3.1: Structure of the research to determine Fine Gael's pre-election campaign in the run up to the 1979 European parliament election

The results of the research provided a very sound basis for campaigning in the lead up to the election. In assessing the potential of candidates in each constituency, MRBI developed and introduced the 'simulated ballot paper' technique, where each person interviewed marked a voting paper 1, 2, 3, etc., exactly as they would in a polling station. This allowed MRBI to conduct a full count (with elimination of some candidates and the distribution of the surpluses to others) to arrive at our final estimation.

In terms of candidate potential, the findings were very accurate for the Dublin, Leinster and Connacht–Ulster constituencies. In addition to indicating the most appropriate strategy for each, the findings also identified that Labour would get two seats in Dublin (Michael O'Leary and John O'Connell), and Fianna Fáil (Síle de Valera) and Fine Gael (Richie Ryan), one each. In the then Leinster three-seater, the three front runners, and eventual winners, were Mark Clinton (FG), Paddy Lalor (FF) and Liam Kavanagh (Lab). Similarly in Connacht–Ulster, three identified winners were Neil Blaney (Ind), Sean Flanagan (FF) and Joe McCartin (FG).

In Munster, two candidates TJ Maher (Ind) and Jerry Cronin (FF) were nominated subsequent to the completion of the research, and therefore were not taken into account in the research programme. Maher actually topped the poll, with Jerry Cronin being elected on the ninth count. The other three successful candidates (Munster was then a five-seater) Tom O'Donnell (FG), Eileen Desmond (Lab) and Noel Davern (FF) were all identified as likely winners in the research, as were Sean Brosnan (FF) and John Blair (FG), who subsequently lost out to the later nominees, Maher and Cronin. From the viewpoint of the two parties for whom the research was conducted, the outcome was very satisfactory, each obtaining four seats. Fianna Fáil won five and Independents two.

THE 1979 CORK BY-ELECTIONS

Following the European election, the endeavours of the new Fine Gael management team were beginning to convert the party into a much more professional organisation, and the main focus continued to be directed towards the next general election. This, however, was temporarily set aside by a new priority.

Over the summer, two TDs, Sean Brosnan (FF, Cork NE) and Pat Kerrigan (Lab, Cork City) died, and with the by-elections expected to take place after the summer recess, we were again approached by Prendergast to conduct research as a basis for campaign planning. Considering the very strong impact of Fianna Fáil just two years earlier, when the party obtained 59 per cent of first preferences in the Cork City constituency (where Jack Lynch had his seat), and 48 per cent in Cork North-East, it was obvious that Fine Gael was now facing a formidable challenge.

Peter Prendergast's brief reflected this. It was the most all-embracing specification we had ever received and, from a base of holding neither of the vacant seats, Fine Gael was now targeting victory in both. The general objective of the research was defined as *"maximising the prospects"* of achieving success in the two by-elections. The information covered by the surveys extended to the following topics.

- The government's rating – perceived strengths and weaknesses.
- The ratings of the main party leaders.
- The perception of the main issues requiring government attention.
- The perception of the relevance of the by-election, as a means of assessing the impact of the government to date.
- The perception of the type of candidate likely to succeed.
- The ratings of the potential candidates within specific criteria.
- The reaction to the overall result of the general election.
- The respondent's current voting intentions, if a general election was held.
- The respondent's current voting intentions in the by-election.
- How the respondent voted in the 1977 general election.
- How the respondent voted in the 1979 European election.

One of the crucial findings of the research was that Fianna Fáil would lose significant support relative to the 1977 general election and was unlikely to obtain the quota of 50 per cent in either constituency on the first count. In contrast, Fine Gael was on course to attract sufficient transfers to win possibly both seats. However, the fact that more than one in four were also undecided in each constituency meant that each party had a considerable amount of work to do before polling day.

As soon as the survey findings were presented, Peter Prendergast in an overall context, along with the two directors of elections – Austin Deasy and Fergus O'Brien – set in motion the process of candidate selection and began attempting to convert those who were undecided. The two chosen candidates were Liam Burke, a senator and former TD in Cork City, and Myra Barry, a daughter of Dick Barry, a former parliamentary secretary from the constituency.

MRBI learned an interesting lesson when we designed a simulated ballot paper that included the name of Myra Barry. As with all research, there was huge emphasis on confidentiality, so we had a moment of near panic when an interviewer reported back that one of the first people she selected for interview in Cork NE was, in fact, a relative of Myra Barry. Years later, a well-known journalist was considering standing in a general election and commissioned research. However, when told that if his name appeared on a simulated ballot paper, there was the potential for people in both politics and the media to learn of his intentions – he immediately withdrew from the research.

When the Cork by-elections were held on 7th November 1979, the result confounded the media, and also a few in Fianna Fáil, who had publicly expressed complete confidence in winning the seats during the final stages of the campaign. The respective first preference votes and the ultimate victors are given in *Table 3.2*.

Constituency	Candidate	Party	%
Cork City	J Dennehy	FF	36
	L Burke	FG	33
	T O'Sullivan	Lab	23
	L Burke was elected on the third count		
Cork North-East	M Barry	FG	39
	J Brosnan	FF	36
	J Sherlock	WP	23
	M Barry was elected on the second count		

Table 3.2: Results of the 1979 Cork by-elections

The Fine Gael victory was emphatic in both instances, and Peter Prendergast played an outstanding role in both the planning and implementation of the campaign. Reflecting on the three research projects – the post-election survey of July 1977, the strategic research in 1978–1979 for the European election and the research for the two Cork by-elections – it can be argued that Garret FitzGerald and Peter Prendergast were the pioneers in the constructive use of market research in the political arena in Ireland.

NEW LEADERSHIP IN FIANNA FÁIL

Following the 1977 general election, Jack Lynch had some reservations about his 20-seat majority, and felt that, in time, it would sow the seeds of instability. One comment attributed to him at the time was that *"if you are carrying a full jug, you have to tread carefully"*. After the European election of June 1979 – when the Fianna Fáil vote was down to 35 per cent from the 51 per cent of 1977 – backbenchers began to question some of his policy statements. Bill Loughnane, a party TD from Clare, accused the Taoiseach of not giving full information to the Dáil on certain security matters and Tom McEllistrim from Kerry also criticised him for agreeing to overflights by British forces across the border.

The results of the by-elections hit the airwaves when the Taoiseach was on the outward leg of a trip to the USA in early November 1979, and Dick Walsh of *The Irish Times*, who was among those accompanying Lynch, recalls that he appeared to be more concerned with the backbench speeches than he was with the results of the by-elections.

It is generally understood that Jack Lynch intended to step down early in the new year of 1980, but, on 5th December, some weeks after his return from the United States, he went public on the issue and announced his resignation as Taoiseach. The parliamentary party meeting to select a new leader was fixed for a few days later; the two nominees were George Colley and Charles Haughey. Cabinet members generally favoured Colley, while Haughey had the support of most backbenchers. When the vote was finally taken, the outcome was much closer than had been expected, Haughey won by six votes: 44 to 38. On

11th December he was elected Taoiseach – after a Dáil debate that included Garret FitzGerald's famous *"flawed pedigree"* speech – and Haughey appointed George Colley as Tánaiste.

In early January 1980, Charles Haughey, in a television address, brought everyone back to earth when he said that government spending would have to be curtailed; the level of government borrowing reduced and that we were all living beyond our means. While the irony of those words would not have been lost on those who had earlier questioned how the 1977 Fianna Fáil manifesto would be paid for, the fact that the new Taoiseach was now expressing himself precisely in accordance with its policies, created a serious headache for Fine Gael party strategists. Many wondered what the public reaction would be to Haughey's pronouncements – hence the requirement for another MRBI opinion poll, conducted in late January.

The findings brought little comfort to Fine Gael. Haughey had succeeded in creating a new mood of optimism among Fianna Fáil supporters, despite the by-election defeats of two months earlier, and had also made a very favourable impression across the electorate generally. In party support terms, Fianna Fáil was now back to its June 1977 level, and there was a full realisation that, if Haughey succeeded in maintaining this level of impact, the next election would present another difficult battle for Fine Gael. However, as time elapsed, it became apparent that Haughey was not implementing the policies he had advocated on television in early January. Furthermore, large street demonstrations calling for income tax reform for the PAYE sector, made both government and opposition realise that taxation would be one of the main issues at the next general election. The end of the year saw both unemployment and inflation increasing to very serious levels, while public spending had also gone considerably above the target set in the budget.

1981: Gearing up for Election

During the summer recess, Joe Brennan, the Ceann Comhairle died, and, after the resumption of the Dáil, the by-election in his Donegal constituency was fixed for 6th November. In October, Fine Gael commissioned a pre-election opinion poll in Donegal – the constituency at the time consisted of almost the entire county. In spite of the economic difficulties the government was experiencing, the findings showed that Fianna Fáil was in a strong position to take the seat, with 45 per cent of first preferences; Independent Fianna Fáil had 25 per cent, Fine Gael 20 per cent and Others 10 per cent. Although Fine Gael improved its position over the final stages of the campaign to 33 per cent, the Fianna Fáil candidate Clem Coughlan topped the poll with 39 per cent and was elected on the third count. This was a big turnaround from the two Cork by-elections a year earlier and, in spite of the result being flagged in the opinion poll, Fine Gael strategists were very disappointed, and realised that considerable work was still necessary if the party was to form a government after the next election.

The government experience since Haughey had taken over was a hit-and-miss affair, with public sector pay, exchequer borrowing and the national debt all increasing considerably. However, the Anglo–Irish summit between the Taoiseach and the British Prime Minister Margaret Thatcher on 8th December represented a positive breakthrough, as did the suspension two weeks later (which proved to be temporary) of the H-Block hunger strike.

Around this time, Garret FitzGerald decided to set up a new strategic committee to embody all planning for the general election that many felt would be called in 1981. The main people involved were Peter Prendergast, Ted Nealon, Shane Molloy, Derry Hussey, Sean Murray, Enda Marron and Jim Dooge. A further new development was the appointment of Sean O'Leary from Cork as Director of Elections.

January 1981 brought further election speculation, with the Fianna Fáil Ard-Fheis in early February expected by many to mark the informal launch of the campaign. However, the tragic Stardust disco fire on 14th February, in Haughey's own constituency, caused a postponement of the Ard-Fheis, and election preparations were put on hold.

The H-Block hunger strike in the Maze Prison had begun again in March and, on 5th May, Bobby Sands, one of the hunger strikers, died. The economic situation had not improved but, on 21st May 1981, the Dáil was dissolved and a general election was fixed for Thursday 11th June. The outgoing Dáil had 148 seats, and Fianna Fáil had won 84 in the 1977 election. The loss of the Cork NE by-election in 1979 left the party with 83, with Fine Gael on 45 (following the two victories in Cork) and Others on 20. Since the 1979 revision, the new Twenty-Second Dáil would have 166 seats.

THE 1981 GENERAL ELECTION:
FIRST PUBLISHED MRBI OPINION POLL

Shortly after the dissolution, MRBI was approached by the *Irish Independent* to conduct a national opinion poll for publication during the final week of the campaign. Despite extensive experience at this stage in private political research, this was the first occasion on which MRBI undertook a political survey where the sole objective was media publication. For the first time, MRBI highlighted the ability of the larger parties to maximise seats and sometimes to achieve majorities with less than 50 per cent share of the vote. The questionnaire was extensive; respondents were spread across all constituencies, and interviewing was conducted on Wednesday 3rd and Thursday 4th June 1981.

The main issues of concern to the electorate were found to be unemployment, inflation and prices, and there was a mixed reaction to the performance of Fianna Fáil under Charles Haughey over the previous 18 months – 41 per cent felt the government had not done well. However, the electorate was split down the middle on the question of which government would be the better for the country – one under Haughey or one under FitzGerald – although the latter was generally perceived as the more impressive leader. On the crucial issue of voting intentions, having allowed for a relatively small volume of undecided at 13 per cent, the net support figures were: Fianna Fáil 45 per cent; Fine Gael 38 per cent; Labour 11 per cent; and Others 6 per cent.

This showed that Fianna Fáil had a fight on its hands, with a FG/Lab coalition a possible outcome. The MRBI commentary stated that *"while Fianna Fáil would be the largest party in the new Dáil, it would not obtain sufficient seats to form a government on its own"*. The result of the election, in first preference terms, was: Fianna Fáil 45 per cent; Fine Gael 37 per cent; Labour 10 per cent; and Others 8 per cent. When converted to seats Fianna Fáil had 78, Fine Gael 65, Labour 15 and Others eight. The Others included two H-Block prisoners, Kieran Doherty (Cavan–Monaghan) who died on hunger strike on 2nd August, and Paddy Agnew (Louth). One of the main casualties of the election was the loss of his seat by Frank Cluskey, the leader of the Labour Party, in Dublin South-Central, to Dr John O'Connell who ran as an Independent.

The poll figures were remarkably close to the actual election outcome, bearing in mind that MRBI's estimates carry a statistical variation of plus or minus 3 per cent. In eliminating those who are undecided – 13 per cent on this occasion – we in effect make an assumption that those who are undecided will, when they eventually make up their minds, split in the same proportions as those who are decided. There is an argument that a supplementary question should be addressed to those who are undecided to attempt to discern which party or independent candidate they are leaning towards, and then make the distribution taking account of such leanings. However, MRBI has for many years adopted the more direct distribution, and the discussion over which methodology is the more reliable is of diminishing importance in the light of the more serious issue of falling voter turnout.

Some of the more interesting features of elections, which I became conscious of at that time, were the fact that fewer than 20 per cent of seats in the Dáil are filled at the end of first counts, and that the transfer patterns can yield bonuses in terms of numbers of seats, mainly to the larger parties.

The ratio of seats to votes that each party achieved in the 1981 election (given in *Table 3.3*) shows the bonus to Fianna Fáil and Fine Gael.

Party	Votes	Seats		Ratio
	%	%	Number	
Fianna Fáil	45	47	78	100:104
Fine Gael	37	39	65	100:105
Labour Party	10	9	15	100:90
Others	8	5	8	100:63

Table 3.3: Ratio of seats to votes for each party in the 1981 general election

The new Dáil met on Tuesday 30th June and, after a vote on Haughey's nomination was defeated, Garret FitzGerald was elected Taoiseach, on the votes of Fine Gael and Labour, along with one Independent, Jim Kemmy. Dr John O'Connell (Ind) had been elected Ceann Comhairle and the other Independents abstained. The H-Block TDs were absent. Fitzgerald formed a coalition government with Labour, under Michael O'Leary, and his full cabinet is set out in *Table 3.4*.

Taoiseach	Garret FitzGerald	FG
Tánaiste; Industry and Energy	Michael O'Leary	Lab
Finance	John Bruton	FG
Foreign Affairs	James Dooge	FG
Education	John Boland	FG
Agriculture	Alan Dukes	FG
The Environment	Peter Barry	FG
Defence	James Tully	Lab
Transport and Posts and Telegraphs	Paddy Cooney	FG
Trade, Commerce and Tourism	John Kelly	FG
Labour and Public Service	Liam Kavanagh	Lab
Health and Social Welfare	Eileen Desmond	Lab
Fisheries and Forestry	Tom Fitzpatrick	FG
Justice	Jim Mitchell	FG
The Gaeltacht	Paddy O'Toole	FG

Table 3.4: Members of the 1981 Fine Gael/Labour cabinet

CHAPTER 4

Interchanging Taoisigh (1981–1982)

For some time, prior to the 1981 general election, Garret FitzGerald, knew that the country's finances were in bad shape but, by all accounts, he and his finance minister, John Bruton, were horrified when, on taking office on 30th June 1981, they became aware of their true state. The new Taoiseach's immediate impression was that emergency action would be necessary. This situation represented a most unpalatable introduction to what turned out to be a crisis period in government, with limited options on every front and with no opportunity to introduce any of the tax reforming measures that the party had been working on while in opposition.

A further complication was the continuing H-Block hunger strike. By mid-July six prisoners had died, which precipitated a protest march and subsequent riot near the British Embassy in Ballsbridge. In the third week of July – after less than a month in office – John Bruton introduced an emergency budget that went some way towards bringing the State's finances under control. However, the continuing problems meant that it was crisis management all the way and there were occasions when the new Taoiseach must have been seriously tempted to go to the country with a financial package that would formally address the situation. Within six months, the opportunity arose in a manner that neither he, nor many others, could have expected.

THE 1982 BUDGET

Minister for Finance John Bruton had prepared his 1982 budget, which was due for delivery in the Dáil on Wednesday 27th January. In light of the financial situation, his plan included increasing VAT on all clothing and footwear, which had hitherto been zero-rated. Short-term social welfare payments were also to be taxed; food subsidies reduced and employee PRSI contributions increased. A new 1 per cent youth employment levy would apply to all incomes, and the entire package would go a long way towards balancing the books.

While its publication caused considerable dismay among Fine Gael backbenchers, the primary concern was the likely behaviour of the five TDs who held the balance of power – Jim Kemmy, Noel Browne, Neil Blaney, Joe Sherlock and Sean DB Loftus. One of these, Kemmy, had voted for Garret FitzGerald in the election for Taoiseach in June 1981. To carry the day with even the smallest possible margin, the government required the votes of two of the five, in addition to their own Fine Gael and Labour TDs. Dr John O'Connell was Ceann Comhairle and the two H-Block TDs had not taken up their seats. When the Dáil speeches were completed and the vote was taken, the result was a defeat for the government:

Níl/No	82	Fianna Fáil 78, J Kemmy, N Blaney, J Sherlock and Sean DB Loftus.
Tá/Yes	81	Fine Gael 65, Labour 15 and N Browne.

Not surprisingly for a politician as experienced in ministerial office as he is, John Bruton takes a very broad view of that Dáil defeat. His view is that one must go back to the budget of July 1981 and the financial situation the government inherited, where drastic action was necessary, and, had the government not been defeated in the Dáil vote of January 1982, it would have happened later in the year.

This was the first occasion on which a government had fallen as a result of being defeated in a budget vote. Following the defeat in the Dáil, Garret FitzGerald left for Áras an Uachtaráin to seek a dissolution; and, when he returned, he announced that the general election would take place on Thursday 18th February.

THE FEBRUARY 1982 GENERAL ELECTION

Within a short time, the *Irish Independent* had again contacted MRBI, commissioning us to conduct an opinion poll that would address reaction to the budget and the immediate political situation. The poll was undertaken on 4th February and was published a few days later.

Fifty per cent of respondents considered the budget to be the right approach to address the country's problems, compared with 38 per cent who felt otherwise. However, three in every four saw the imposition of VAT on clothing and footwear as unacceptable, and a similar number were critical of the adjustments to the subsidies on butter and milk. The proposed increases in the price of drink and cigarettes were heavily supported by three in every four, while the taxation of short-term social welfare benefits and the removal of a tax allowance on personal bank loans both received evenly balanced support.

It is clear that the primary adverse perception related to VAT on clothes and shoes. As this included children's clothing and footwear, the reaction must be seen as understandable. In the poll, Garret FitzGerald was heavily supported as being the more credible leader by a ratio of two to one over Charles Haughey, while a considerable majority – more than four in every five – saw the provision of a stable government as a major issue in the election. When the two leaders were assessed on the basis of which of them was the better person to handle specific issues, FitzGerald was positioned in front on controlling prices, the enforcement of law and order, reducing government spending and foreign borrowing, and handling Northern Ireland. Haughey was ahead on jobs for young people and reducing unemployment. Two weeks out from the election, the party support figures were: Fianna Fáil 47 per cent; Fine Gael 39 per cent; Labour 8 per cent; and Others 6 per cent – a finely balanced situation.

Considering the circumstances in which the election arose, the occasion represented a first-class opportunity for Fianna Fáil, under Haughey, to obtain another overall majority – although perhaps not of the same dimension as Jack Lynch had achieved five years earlier – and the MRBI figures were showing that this was a possibility. A further opinion poll for the *Irish Independent*, five days before the election, showed a non-significant movement in support for the two main parties. It also indicated that the state of the economy was now the dominant campaign issue, and a majority (54 per cent) saw a FitzGerald-led government as being better for the country than one led by Haughey. However, the ultimate selection of a Taoiseach is not the primary motivating factor in many people's voting intentions and, in the February 1982 election, Fianna Fáil received 47 per cent of first preference votes, with Fine Gael on 37 per cent, Labour 8 per cent and Others 7 per cent. This was very much in line with the opinion poll results. While it represented an increase of two points for Fianna Fáil relative to the previous election eight months earlier, Fine Gael also increased its vote by almost one point in spite of the unfavourable circumstances in which the party fought the election.

DUBLIN NORTH-CENTRAL

One of the most interesting and intriguing uses of MRBI research arose during that election. Within a day or so of it being called, the Director of Elections for Fine Gael in Dublin, Sean O'Leary, phoned to say that he wanted to meet Áine and myself at our office as soon as possible. When he arrived he looked at me with that impish look of his and said, *"Dublin North-Central. We're going for two seats. Look at 1981."*

In the 1981 general election, Fianna Fáil obtained 50.9 per cent of the first preference vote – 2.6 quotas – but just two seats. Charles Haughey had topped the poll with over 17,000 votes – 43 per cent of the total. The Fianna Fáil vote was, to put it mildly, unbalanced, and was certainly not as productive in the party's interests as it could have been. In short, if this pattern was repeated in the February 1982 election, it presented an opportunity for Fine Gael, and Sean O'Leary had a well thought-out and highly co-ordinated plan ready. It had to be so, since Fine Gael had obtained only 25.5 per cent of the vote in the 1981 election – 1.3 quotas. The co-ordination would involve MRBI with what he termed *"precision monitoring"*; knife-edge management of the canvassers on the ground and, finally, the full co-operation of the three Fine Gael candidates – George Birmingham, the incumbent TD who was elected in 1981 with 16 per cent of first preference votes; Richard Bruton nominated for the first time and Mary Byrne who also ran in 1981 and obtained 3 per cent of first preferences.

The MRBI Polls

The first MRBI monitoring survey was implemented without delay, the primary objective being to measure first and subsequent preference support for all candidates, with a view to confirming the Fianna Fáil positioning, and the relative support levels of the Fine Gael candidates, particularly Birmingham and Bruton. This first benchmark survey was crucial because, to win two seats, Fine Gael needed to position the two targeted candidates very precisely on voting day – not too close and certainly not too far apart, as Fianna Fáil had been in 1981.

After that first survey, using a simulated ballot paper, we looked on in awe as O'Leary conducted a count of the ballot papers, with all eliminations and distribution of surpluses, which told him exactly what needed to be done on the ground, and also by the candidates themselves. In fact, subsequent media reports commented that George Birmingham gained considerable stature by his selfless conduct during the campaign, when he arranged for some of his supporters to cast their first preference votes for Richard Bruton.

The second MRBI campaign survey provided the welcome information that the strategy was working and that the two had moved to an acceptable support level. It really was knife-edge management as O'Leary had described it and the rest is history. George Birmingham (sixth count) and Richard Bruton (eleventh count) won two seats for Fine Gael with 33 per cent of the vote – 1.6 quotas – and, as Fine Gael had expected, Fianna Fáil also won two seats with 51 per cent – 2.6 quotas. To copper-fasten the situation, the two young combatants held their seats in the November 1982 election with an increased vote of 37 per cent of first preferences.

THE FEBRUARY–NOVEMBER 1982 DÁIL

When the new Dáil assembled, it was agreed that Dr John O'Connell would remain as Ceann Comhairle, and Fianna Fáil, with 81 seats, needed the support of at least two others to form a government. With the support of Neil Blaney (Ind FF) guaranteed, Charles Haughey turned to Tony Gregory (Ind) who had just been elected in the Dublin-Central constituency for the first time. In return for specific expenditure in the north inner-city area, Tony Gregory agreed to back Charles Haughey for Taoiseach. As it happened, the three Workers' Party TDs (Proinsias de Rossa, Paddy Gallagher and Joe Sherlock) also voted for

Haughey, who was elected by 86 votes to 79. Fine Gael, the Labour Party and Jim Kemmy voted against. On his election as Taoiseach, Haughey announced his cabinet, shown below.

Taoiseach	Charles Haughey
Tánaiste; Finance	Ray MacSharry
Foreign Affairs	Gerard Collins
Education	Martin O'Donoghue
Agriculture	Brian Lenihan
Trade, Commerce and Tourism	Des O'Malley
Transport and Posts and Telegraphs	John Wilson
Labour and Public Service	Gene Fitzgerald
Health and Social Welfare	Michael Woods
Defence	Paddy Power
Justice	Sean Doherty
The Gaeltacht	Pádraig Flynn
Industry and Energy	Albert Reynolds
The Environment	Ray Burke
Fisheries and Forestry	Brendan Daly

Table 4.2: Members of the February 1982 Fianna Fáil cabinet

Within a few weeks, Ray MacSharry, the new Minister for Finance, presented the Fianna Fáil government's budget to the Dáil and, although it excluded some of the more difficult provisions of the Fine Gael budget (such as VAT on clothing and shoes), it was still structured to address the country's finances. As such, it included a number of provisions which did not find favour with many taxpayers, one of these being a large increase in PRSI.

THE 1982 DUBLIN WEST BY-ELECTION

Meanwhile, having organised the support of Tony Gregory prior to the Dáil vote for Taoiseach, Haughey lost little time in again displaying his machiavellian talents by embarking on a plan which, had it worked, could have made all the difference to the shelf-life of his new government. The position of EEC commissioner was vacant, Michael O'Kennedy having returned to win a seat in Tipperary North. The Haughey plan was to offer the appointment to the high-profile and experienced Fine Gael ex-minister and former EEC commissioner Dick Burke, who had also just won a seat in the Dublin West constituency. Fianna Fáil had a ready-made candidate for the by-election that would ensue, in the person of Eileen Lemass. She had previously won a Dáil seat in 1977, was the widow of Noel Lemass, a parliamentary secretary in the 1969 Fianna Fáil government, and daughter-in-law of the legendary Seán Lemass, who had shown all and sundry how to lead a stable government, with a majority of minus two, 21 years earlier.

On the other hand, Fine Gael had no obvious candidate available, and the pundits at large saw the plan as a masterstroke. However, in spite of the base position of the two parties, it turned out to be a much greater risk for the government party than was apparent to most observers when it first hit the headlines.

After some hesitancy, and an on/off relationship with the Fine Gael party, Dick Burke accepted the offer and left for Brussels towards the end of March. The episode stung the Fine Gael head office, and the party leader – aware that the unwelcome by-election would be a tough fight – selected a strong and experienced team to organise and run the campaign. John Boland was appointed the director of the election, with Jim Mitchell, the sitting TD for the Dublin West constituency, in charge of operations on the ground.

MRBI Polls in the 1982 Dublin West By-Election

The disadvantageous base from which Fine Gael was coming was very evident in the initial brief that MRBI received when the first research project was commissioned. The main objective, at that stage, was to identify the potential of no fewer than five possible party candidates using criteria similar to those in the Cork by-elections in 1979. The survey was also designed to identify the primary local issues in the constituency, along with prevailing party support levels. The outlook, as far as Fine Gael was concerned, was not improved when the survey findings indicated that none of the five assessed candidates was likely to win the seat – the initial MRBI figures showed Fianna Fáil substantially ahead. However, one finding from the research that turned out to be of considerable relevance, was that potential Fine Gael voters considered that the ideal candidate would be a local person who had had a successful business or professional career and who would have cross-demographic appeal. The search was on and the person eventually chosen by Fine Gael was unknown in political circles: Liam Skelly. Skelly lived nearby in Lucan and ran his own engineering business within, and contiguous to, the constituency. He had studied engineering at UCD and law at King's Inn. Since he was not a party member, he was recruited without delay and duly nominated.

A second MRBI survey was conducted subsequent to the close of nominations and, although Fianna Fáil remained in front, Skelly was beginning to make an impact, and the gap between the two main party candidates was closing. Of further significance, however, was the indication that Workers' Party votes garnered by Tomás Mac Giolla were not transferring to Fianna Fáil to the extent that the media were anticipating, and the fact that the three Workers' Party TDs voted for Haughey as Taoiseach just two months previously was not being replicated.

Both government and opposition were taking the by-election very seriously and each side was fully aware of the importance of the prize at stake. Government ministers were thick on the ground during the final weeks of the campaign – on one afternoon trip to the constituency I counted seven in the area. Fine Gael was no less determined to make the electorate aware of the party's new local candidate, and many high-profile senior party politicians were also concentrated into the Dublin West battleground.

The third and final MRBI survey showed a remarkable upturn in support for the Fine Gael candidate and, with little more than a week to go, the two main protagonists were running neck and neck, with Tomás Mac Giolla (WP) some distance back in third place. The two significant conclusions from the research were, firstly, that, with Lemass and Skelly locked together in the mid-thirties, the Fianna Fáil candidate was now unlikely to win the seat on the first count and, secondly, the strong indication was that the bulk of Mac Giolla's transfers were likely to go to Skelly. The actual result is given in *Table 4.3*.

First Count	Quota 21,531	
Eileen Lemass (FF)	17,095	39.7%
Liam Skelly (FG)	16,777	39.0%
Tomás Mac Giolla (WP)	6,357	14.8%
Others	2,789	6.5%

Second Count	Elimination of minor candidates	
Liam Skelly (FG)	17,736	
Eileen Lemass (FF)	17,571	
Tomás Mac Giolla (WP)	7,446	

Third Count	Elimination of Mac Giolla	
Liam Skelly (FG)	21,388	+3,652
Eileen Lemass (FF)	19,206	+1,635

Table 4.3: Result of the 1982 Dublin West by-election

Mac Giolla's transfers went to Skelly in the ratio of two to one, and Skelly was elected 2,182 votes ahead of Lemass, while being 143 short of the quota.

It was a well-planned and hard-fought campaign for Fine Gael, against considerable odds. Many people, but particularly Director of Elections John Boland, contributed to what was a highly significant victory. Significant to the extent that, had the Fianna Fáil candidate won – directly at the expense of Fine Gael, the Haughey government could have gone on to serve for a much longer period, with a very different outcome.

Analysis of the Results of the Dublin West Polls

What went wrong for Fianna Fáil in Dublin West? Many commentators have asked this question, and many still wonder how the assiduous

Fianna Fáil election machine came unstuck and was derailed by Fine Gael. The main opposition party devised and implemented what was a very successful campaign plan, and many people – from the party leader down – deserve all credit for turning the tables at a crucial stage on the new Haughey government. However, the extensive research commissioned by Fine Gael throughout the campaign showed that Fianna Fáil was actually fighting an uphill battle from the outset, and this can be attributed to decisions from within the party itself.

One of the most influential factors that can determine the outcome of an election is the perceived circumstance in which it is called. Observations, which became evident from the MRBI campaign research, indicated that many electors did not see the by-election as a requirement in the interests of the country. Many floating voters had similar feelings, and, having got 42 per cent of first preferences in the constituency in the previous general election, Fianna Fáil needed the floating vote if it was to get anywhere near the 50 per cent quota on the first count. It would appear that many Workers' Party supporters also held these opinions, as there was such a heavy transfer away from Fianna Fáil on the final count. Many commentators saw the Burke deal and subsequent by-election as a masterstroke, but the people who really mattered on the ground – those whose transfers were decisive on the final count – did not see it as such, and the result was evident long before polling day.

Many electors were also critical of the presence of so many Fianna Fáil ministers in state cars driving around the constituency – and felt that the country would have been better served had they remained in their offices in Government Buildings. A further observation from the campaign research was that the downturn in support for the Fianna Fáil candidate was in direct proportion to the increase in the number of photo-calls with the party leader. This became obvious as the campaign drew to a close, and it was no fault of Eileen Lemass that she lost the by-election.

THE FIRST *IRISH TIMES*/MRBI OPINION POLL

Around the time of the Dubin West by-election, a development that had a very pivotal effect on the future of MRBI, occurred. Jim Downey, then deputy editor of *The Irish Times*, met with me in the then MRBI offices in South Frederick Street. I recall Jim introducing himself by saying that he had a reputation for being *"a bit of a bastard"*, and I think he was really alerting me to the fact that the research assignment which he was about to discuss was an important and challenging one and that MRBI would be on trial. As I listened to his brief, I was disconcerted to learn that the proposed project would be in Northern Ireland, and would involve reaction to James Prior's proposals on a new consultative assembly, which had been introduced by the Northern Ireland Secretary of State at Westminster on 5th April 1982.

Northern Ireland at the time was difficult territory for market research, but MRBI agreed to prepare a proposal outlining a research plan for *The Irish Times*. This was accepted; the project was undertaken, the report delivered, and the findings duly appeared in the pages of *The Irish Times*. Although the project at the time was a one-off, it signalled the start of a long-standing professional relationship between *The Irish Times* and MRBI. Also I do not recall that Jim Downey lived up to the description with which he introduced himself. (The report on the Northern Ireland survey is addressed in *Chapter 14*.)

1982: AN UNEASY YEAR

Meanwhile, following the by-election defeat, the Fianna Fáil government began to re-focus on the financial situation. The PRSI increases that were introduced in the MacSharry budget were causing unrest to the extent that, during the final stages of the by-election campaign, a protest march had taken place. During the summer recess, the announcement of cuts in public expenditure caused further resentment from the trade unions. The main problem now facing the government was that the measures introduced in late summer were inadequate, and spending was running some 30 per cent above the target set in the budget.

A further unexpected problem arose when a man, wanted for murder, was found apparently residing in Attorney-General Patrick Connolly's apartment in south Dublin, and although he had no knowledge of the visitor's background, confusing reports to the media did not help the government. After Haughey described the incident as *"grotesque, unbelievable, bizarre and unprecedented"*, Conor Cruise O'Brien used the statement to introduce the new word – GUBU – into conventional usage. The term has frequently been used to describe the mishaps that have characterised the political arena in the recent past, and, indeed, some commentators described the administration of the time as the GUBU government.

The three Workers' Party TDs and at least one of the Independent members, who had supported the formation of the government in the early spring, were now becoming very uneasy, and, in early October, a number of Fianna Fáil backbenchers tabled a vote of no confidence in the leader. The motion was debated at length at a meeting of the Fianna Fáil parliamentary party on 6th October. Deep divisions emerged from the meeting but the motion was defeated by almost three to one and Haughey survived.

In mid-October, Fine Gael published its "National Plan", which addressed the nation's finances and which was really a preliminary manifesto for the inevitable election. In a matter of days, Fianna Fáil published a similar document and the countdown to an election was underway.

THE FIRST POLL IN THE *IRISH TIMES*/MRBI SERIES

At this juncture, we were commissioned by *The Irish Times* to conduct what turned out to be the inaugural *Irish Times*/MRBI opinion poll in the now longstanding series. The objective of the survey was to establish a benchmark in advance of the election being called. It was conducted on the 20th and 21st October and showed that Fianna Fáil and Fine Gael shared the lead with 42 per cent each, followed by the Labour Party on 8 per cent. This represented Fine Gael's highest impact in any opinion poll before or since. It was followed by two comparable campaign surveys, and the three-stage approach provided the first formal monitor leading up to an election.

Following the publication, in late October, of the findings of the first survey, an important development took place. Michael O'Leary, leader of the Labour Party, who favoured a pre-election coalition pact with Fine Gael, resigned – the party having postponed a decision on the issue – and was replaced by Dick Spring. The new Labour leader was 32 years old, had taken his father's seat in North Kerry in the 1981 election and was a Minister for State in the Department of Justice in the 1981–1982 coalition government under Garret FitzGerald. During the following week, Michael O'Leary joined Fine Gael.

THE NOVEMBER 1982 GENERAL ELECTION

For some time, Fine Gael strategists had been considering, not just the tabling of a motion of no confidence in the Fianna Fáil government, but the most appropriate timing for such a motion.

Garret FitzGerald in his autobiography, *All in a Life*, reflecting on his thoughts at the time, states that:

> *I believed that Labour would support me rather than Charles Haughey for Taoiseach, and I was buoyed up by the opinion poll published a week earlier, which, for the first time ever, showed Fine Gael level pegging with Fianna Fáil, each having the support of 42 per cent, with the Labour Party at 8 per cent.*

The no-confidence motion eventually materialised on 3rd November, when it was apparent that support for the government from the Workers' Party no longer existed and when Fianna Fáil would be without the votes of Jim Gibbons, who was ill, and Bill Loughnane, who had recently died. Following an acrimonious debate, the government fell by 82 votes to 80. The Twenty-Third Dáil was dissolved and the general election was fixed for 24th November – the third general election in less than 18 months.

The Second *Irish Times*/MRBI Poll

The November 1982 campaign was a bitter one and, with just three weeks to go, the second *Irish Times*/MRBI poll was scheduled for 12th November. This showed the Fine Gael vote remaining solid at 42 per cent, which was higher than the party had ever obtained in any general election. Fianna Fáil, however, was fighting back and regained some ground to 44 per cent – although this was still below the party figures for the previous seven general elections. Labour was also solid on 9 per cent. At this juncture – 12 days to go – Garret FitzGerald held more than a two to one lead over Charles Haughey on satisfaction ratings, and was also the preferred choice for Taoiseach of 55 per cent, compared with 32 per cent for Haughey. A FitzGerald-led government was also seen as the better to handle each of eight major issues – unemployment, government stability, crime, control of prices, taxation, living standards, control of public sector pay and Northern Ireland.

The Third *Irish Times*/MRBI Poll

The third and final opinion poll of the campaign was fixed for 20th November – four days before polling. It showed no significant change from that of a week earlier, although the Fine Gael share had slipped slightly to 41 per cent, and the MRBI conclusions, which were published in *The Irish Times* two days before the election, were:

- *Fianna Fáil will, again, be the largest single party, but is unlikely to obtain sufficient first preference votes to convert to a majority in the Dáil. It is also unlikely to be capable of forming a government solely with the support of the two independent deputies who voted with the party in the last Dáil.*

- *Fine Gael will very likely achieve its highest ever share of first preference votes.*

- *In spite of nominating marginally fewer candidates than in February, the Labour Party vote will hold and possibly increase.*

- *The first preference votes for the Workers' Party will also hold and possibly increase.*

  The overall conclusions from the survey is that the electorate's choice for Taoiseach will materialise in the form of a government under Dr FitzGerald, assuming that support from the Labour Party is forthcoming.

The conclusions provided a very reliable indication of the outcome of the November 1982 election and, after lengthy negotiations, Garret FitzGerald formed a coalition government with Labour, under its new leader Dick Spring.

It is worth noting that, even though the final poll somewhat overstated the first preference share of votes for Fine Gael, it indicated that the tide was running in the party's favour, and that it, and the Labour Party, would achieve a considerable bonus of seats (to first preference votes), with the help of the later transfers.

Party	Votes	Seats		Ratio
	%	%	Number	
Fianna Fáil	45	45	75	100:100
Fine Gael	39	42	70	100:108
Labour	9	10	16	100:110
Others	6	3	5	100:50

Table 4.4: Result of the November 1982 general election

The figures for each of the three campaign opinion polls are given below.

	First Poll (20th Oct)	Second Poll (12th Nov)	Third Poll (20th Nov)	
	%	%	%	
A. Satisfaction: Leaders				
CJ Haughey	31	26	31	
G FitzGerald	62	63	61	
M O'Leary/D Spring	33	32	42	
B. Preference for Taoiseach				
CJ Haughey	31	32	37	
G FitzGerald	53	55	52	
C. Voting Intentions (excluding undecided)				Election Result
Fianna Fáil	42	44	44	45
Fine Gael	42	42	41	39
Labour	8	10	9	9
Others	8	4	6	6

Table 4.5: Comparison of the results of the Irish Times/MRBI *polls and the general election result (November 1982)*

CHAPTER 5

Garret FitzGerald at the Helm
(1982–1987)

The 17-month period leading up to Garret FitzGerald's election as Taoiseach, for a second time, on 14th December 1982, was unprecedented in Irish politics. The electorate had experienced three general elections; FitzGerald had been Taoiseach for eight-and-a-half months, Haughey for a further nine, and the respective governments had fallen in circumstances which both would have preferred to forget.

Compared with his cabinet of 17 months earlier (June 1981), FitzGerald had a new young Tánaiste in Dick Spring, together with eight members of his previous administration (Peter Barry, John Bruton, Paddy Cooney, John Boland, Paddy O'Toole, Jim Mitchell and Alan Dukes – all Fine Gael – and Liam Kavanagh of Labour). The five new members were Austin Deasy, Michael Noonan, Gemma Hussey – Fine Gael – and Frank Cluskey and Barry Desmond – Labour. Peter Sutherland was again Attorney-General and Peter Prendergast was appointed Government Press Secretary. The full cabinet is given in *Table 5.1*.

The first formal task facing the new government was the publication of the 1983 budget by Finance Minister Alan Dukes on 9th February, and its contents clearly demonstrated a determination to address the nation's finances. It was one of the most severe and included such provisions as increasing the standard rate of VAT to 35 per cent; increasing road tax, telephone charges and petrol; a 1 per cent levy on gross incomes; increased PRSI; and the introduction of residential property tax.

Taoiseach	Garret FitzGerald	FG
Tánaiste; Environment	Dick Spring	Lab
Finance	Alan Dukes	FG
Foreign Affairs	Peter Barry	FG
Education	Gemma Hussey	FG
Agriculture	Austin Deasy	FG
Justice	Michael Noonan	FG
Defence	Paddy Cooney	FG
Labour	Liam Kavanagh	Lab
Industry and Energy	John Bruton	FG
Public Services	John Boland	FG
Trade, Commerce and Tourism	Frank Cluskey	Lab
Health and Social Welfare	Barry Desmond	Lab
Transport and Posts and Telegraphs	Jim Mitchell	FG
The Gaeltacht and Fisheries	Paddy O'Toole	FG

Table 5.1: Members of the November 1982 Fine Gael/Labour cabinet

Within a week, an *Irish Times*/MRBI opinion poll was undertaken and, not surprisingly, public reaction to the budget was very critical. On the standard assessment criteria of expected impact on living standards and perception of its benefit to the country, three electors in every four thought living standards were likely to fall as a result; half thought it was more difficult than expected and, within the more relevant criterion of whether or not it was good for the country, the electorate had very mixed views. In addition, a majority – 54 per cent – were dissatisfied with the government, then just two months in office. Although Fianna Fáil supporters comprised the bulk of this group, Labour supporters were also noticeably unhappy. At this juncture, with a long road ahead and many more difficult questions waiting to be addressed, the Taoiseach was valuing the cushion of his Dáil majority. One particular issue – abortion – probably the most bedevilling of all, would very soon return and displace the issue of State finances in commanding the attention of the government.

THE ABORTION ISSUE

In the early 1980s – as today – the abortion question was highly complex and confusing. The public at large, including those who could be described as experts, along with the politicians, who were faced with the responsibility for legislating on the subject, were widely divided on the issue. Against the growing liberal lobby, there remained a strong conservative element who were against abortion in all circumstances, whilst the Catholic Church and many medical professionals acknowledged the ethical acceptability of some life-saving operations on pregnant women, such as the removal of a cancerous womb or an ectopic pregnancy. Against this background, attempting to legislate was, and still remains, a political nightmare.

Background to the 1983 Debate

Abortion had been illegal since the passing of the Offences Against the Persons Act in 1861 but, since the provision was not embodied in the Constitution, the prohibition could at any time be repealed by the Oireachtas. This was one reason why party leaders came under pressure from anti-abortion groups to hold a referendum that would prohibit abortion in constitutional terms.

Prior to the 1981 election, Garret FitzGerald gave a commitment to hold a referendum when in government and the Fine Gael party included this provision in its election manifesto that year. When the party went into government with Labour, it set up a committee to review the Constitution but, by the time the government fell in January 1982, the issue, although heavily debated, had not been resolved.

In 1981, Charles Haughey had also committed Fianna Fáil to a referendum. During the February 1982 election campaign, both leaders were approached by the same anti-abortion groups and, shortly after being elected Taoiseach, Haughey undertook to hold a referendum guaranteeing the right to life of the unborn, during the life of the new Dáil.

The public debate extended over the summer months and, in early October 1982, the Minister for Health Dr Michael Woods announced that legislation would be introduced during the next Dáil term. The Fine Gael parliamentary party had also been actively debating the issue in the knowledge that a no-confidence motion in the Haughey government was imminent and the party could be back in power – and handling the hot potato again – within a short time.

Just prior to the no-confidence debate against Haughey in early November, the Fianna Fáil government published a proposed wording for a constitutional amendment, which read:

> *The State acknowledges the right to life of the unborn and, with due regard to the equal right to life of the mother, guarantees in its laws to respect and, as far as practicable, by its laws to defend and vindicate that right.*

This attracted both criticism and support in the run up to the fall of the Haughey government. While abortion was not primarily an election issue, it was not far from the minds of the main party activists, and most politicians accepted that the matter would have to be formally addressed sooner rather than later.

The First MRBI Poll

In late January 1983, the Attorney-General Peter Sutherland told Garret FitzGerald, the new Taoiseach, that, in his opinion, the Fianna Fáil wording was ambiguous, following which the Fine Gael ministers collectively withdrew their support for it. The Labour Party ministers had previously rejected it, and Michael Noonan, the Minister for Justice in the debate on the Amendment Bill on 9th February, indicated that the wording *"could be changed"*. This was the situation when, two days later on 11th February 1983, the *Irish Times*/MRBI opinion poll addressed the issue for the first time (in conjunction with the post-budget poll). At that stage, neither the date of the referendum nor the precise wording of the amendment had been agreed upon.

Two questions were put to respondents on the issue. The first related to the actual holding of a referendum and the second measured current voting intentions should a referendum be held. The Fianna Fáil wording was embodied in the second question.

As to whether or not a referendum should be held, a significant minority – almost two in every five – did not agree that it should and felt that the 1861 Act forbidding abortion should not be replaced, irrespective of its potential vulnerability. However, actual voting intentions, if there was a referendum, showed that there was very considerable support for the amendment, with 53 per cent in favour,

16 per cent against and 31 per cent undecided. The net figures, omitting the undecided, were 77 per cent in favour and 23 per cent against.

Re-wording the Amendment

In due course, Minister for Justice Michael Noonan prepared amendments to the Fianna Fáil text to meet the ambiguities which related to the child and mother having an *"equal"* right, and to the term *"unborn"*. When the proposed amendments were referred to Church leaders for their opinion, as Garret FitzGerald observes in his autobiography, the Protestant churches and Jewish community gave a reluctant and unenthusiastic acceptance, while the reaction of the Catholic Church was decidedly negative.

After considerable debate, during which a new proposal was put to the party, Fine Gael remained divided. Eventually, when the Fine Gael amendment was put to the Dáil in late April, it was defeated with some party members abstaining, and irony of ironies, the original Fianna Fáil wording when put to the house was carried substantially. The referendum was then fixed for 7th September, on the basis of the wording that had first seen the light of day way back in early November 1982, prior to the fall of the Fianna Fáil government.

Further *Irish Times*/MRBI Polls

The next *Irish Times*/MRBI opinion poll was fixed for a month later on 26th May, at which stage those against holding a referendum had increased to a majority (53 per cent). Many were obviously unimpressed with the divisive public debate and those who intended voting in favour if there was a referendum had dropped to 55 per cent, with 45 per cent against.

The final opinion poll was scheduled for a week before the referendum – Wednesday 31st August 1983 – and just a week before that, on 22nd August, the Catholic Church published a favourably disposed statement, indicating that the amendment would safeguard the life of both the mother and unborn child. This announcement would appear to have influenced many electors, since the opinion poll found that support for the amendment had substantially increased – to 69 per cent – and the MRBI commentary in *The Irish Times* read:

There are very significant indications that the amendment will be comfortably carried, and a majority in favour in the ratio of 2:1 can be expected.

The referendum result to insert the amendment in the Constitution was: Yes: 67 per cent; No: 33 per cent.

The campaign was unpleasant and divisive, and the final reference in the MRBI commentary read:

In endeavouring to evaluate and consider the various options, electors were not facilitated by the almost incessant and unparalleled divisiveness of the campaign, and the various claims, counterclaims and contradictions which emerged contributed to an unacceptable environment for exercising one's civic duty.

Divisive or not; ambiguous or not, the people had spoken and the right to life of the unborn and the equal right to life of the mother, was now a matter of constitutional law.

EVENTS IN 1984

The unexpected, and widely regretted, death of George Colley in London, following medical treatment, gave rise to a by-election in the Dublin Central constituency on 23rd November 1983, and the seat was held for Fianna Fáil by Tom Leonard.

Meanwhile, the government was getting on with the task of finalising its 1984 budget, and this was presented again by Alan Dukes, in mid-January. Although the correction of the State's finances remained its primary objective, the budget provisions were much less stringent than those of 1983. The old reliables – petrol, cigarettes, drink, car tax and VAT – were increased, these being offset to some extent by improvements in children's allowance and social welfare benefits.

Towards the end of January 1984, the next opinion poll found a much less critical and also less apprehensive electorate than was the case a year earlier. A small minority – compared with one in two previously – saw the budget as harder than expected, while half thought that their living standards would be unchanged, compared with a fifth in 1983.

However, in spite of this comparatively favourable reaction to the budget, satisfaction ratings of the Taoiseach, Tánaiste and other party leaders, and support for all parties, were down. A possible explanation for this was that, two months earlier, the government had awarded substantial salary increases to ministers, TDs and judges.

The 1984 European Parliament Election

The significant political activity at this time centred on a by-election and the second election of MEPs to the European parliament. On 14th June 1984, Brian Cowen (FF) won a by-election in Laois–Offaly, occasioned by the death of his father Bernard, who had been a TD from 1969–1973, and again from 1977 until his death the previous January.

The second European parliament election, which also took place on 14th June, resulted in significant gains for the two main parties. Fianna Fáil increased its representation to eight seats, and Fine Gael went to six.

In Dublin, where Labour lost its two seats, Richie Ryan (FG) was the only candidate to be re-elected, and was joined by Mary Banotti (FG). Fianna Fáil also won two seats through Eileen Lemass and Niall Andrews. In the Leinster three-seater, Mark Clinton (FG) and Paddy Lalor (FF) were re-elected, and were joined by Jim Fitzsimons (FF). In Munster, TJ Maher (Ind) and Tom O'Donnell (FG) were re-elected; the remaining successful candidates being: Tom Raftery (FG), Sylvester Barrett (FF) and Gene Fitzgerald (FF). In Connacht–Ulster, Joe McCartin (FG) and Sean Flanagan (FF) were re-elected, after Ray MacSharry (FF) had taken the first of the three seats. (In 1986 Chris O'Malley (FG) replaced Richie Ryan in Dublin and, in 1987, Mark Killilea (FF) replaced Ray MacSharry in Connacht–Ulster.) MRBI conducted limited research relative to the 1984 European parliament election, the focus of which was limited to a number of individual candidates.

The New Fine Gael National Plan

On 2nd October 1984, the FitzGerald government launched a new national plan, "Building on Reality", which set out the main aspects of economic policy for the following three years. In terms of timing, its promulgation preceded the Fine Gael Ard-Fheis by a few days, and the announcement of a new Fianna Fáil front bench, by just a week.

This was the background when MRBI, again on behalf of *The Irish Times*, measured public reaction to the plan just two weeks after its publication. In general terms, the government could not have been particularly happy with a satisfaction rating that had remained at the relatively low 28 per cent of five months previously, while those for both the Taoiseach and Tánaiste had actually dropped. Some clues as to the reason for this became apparent when it emerged that, although the plan had been unveiled to an audience of industrialists, trade unionists and farmers, many respondents did not feel sufficiently knowledgeable to rate it in any context. Furthermore, many people – two in every five – were also unsure and unwilling to comment on its likely impact, and finally, reaction was very mixed on perception of the government's ability to implement it.

The "New Ireland Forum Report"

Although a number of opinion polls had shown that the Irish electorate had not rated the Northern Ireland problem as important, both John Hume and Garret FitzGerald envisaged a potential resolution of the conflict, in the form of acceptable co-existence between nationalism and unionism, complemented by British and Irish co-operation in an environment of mutual understanding. The first constructive outcome of this philosophy was the publication of the "New Ireland Forum Report" on 3rd May 1984. The forum had been established in Dublin Castle a year earlier, during which period bi-weekly meetings were held between the three main political parties in the Republic, the SDLP from Northern Ireland and a number of other bodies. The report set out a framework for a new Ireland, presented proposals as to how unionist and nationalist identities could be accommodated and proposed three possible solutions to the Northern Ireland problem:

- **A unitary state:** With one government and parliament for the 32 counties.
- **A federation:** The two parts of Ireland each administering its own affairs, under a central Irish government.
- **A joint authority:** Joint rule over Northern Ireland from Dublin and London.

A week later, on 10th May, the next *Irish Times*/MRBI opinion poll measured public reaction in the 26 counties to the report. The first point of note was that, although the forum had been attracting national media attention over the previous year, an estimated 100,000 electors – equating with 4 per cent – claimed to be unaware of its existence. Surprisingly, general reaction to its usefulness was also mixed, with just one in two holding a positive viewpoint. While there was considerable support for the concept of a follow-through conference of political representatives from Britain, Northern Ireland and the Republic, a majority were of the opinion that this would never materialise.

Reaction to the three suggested solutions was measured at two levels: by the individual ratings of each and by overall preference. The rating analysis indicated that two suggestions – unitary state and federation – would have been broadly acceptable to the electorate, with majorities favouring each; while, in overall preference terms, the unitary state concept was significantly preferred to the other two. The respective figures in the survey are given in *Table 5.2*.

The analysis shows that, since support for the unitary state concept was not overwhelming, the public at large was not making an exclusive demand for a united Ireland, and was taking a broader and more tolerant stand on the issue. However, while there was considerable scepticism as to the usefulness of the forum, the research gave politicians an up-to-date appraisal of what was a radical and noteworthy initiative.

Although the New Ireland Forum was a unilaterally green operation, with only nationalist parties or interests participating, it nevertheless provided a fundamental focus for the constructive exchanges that took place at various levels between the Irish government, SDLP leaders and the British government, during the remaining months of 1984 and through to November 1985. While the fruits of these discussions became evident on the signing of the Anglo–Irish Agreement in November 1985, their impact at the time was masked by the media emphasis on the *"out, out, out"* comments of the British Prime Minister Margaret Thatcher at her press conference following the meeting between the two leaders, on 19th November 1984, at Chequers – the Prime Minister's weekend residence.

Considerable progress had been made during the six months leading up to the Chequers meeting; all cards and concepts had been put on the table including *Articles 2* and *3* of the Irish Constitution; there was a bilateral desire to find solutions, and each side knew where it and the other side stood. The Chequers meeting itself appeared to have been broadly successful, and, according to Garret FitzGerald in his autobiography, Mrs Thatcher in her press conference described it as *"the fullest, frankest and most realistic bilateral meeting I have ever had with the Taoiseach"*.

A. Rating of Each Proposed Solution

	Rating	Unitary State	Federation	Joint Authority
		%	%	%
In favour				
Very much	5	40	18	7
Somewhat	4	26	37	20
No opinion	3	10	13	13
Against				
Very much	1	8	13	34
Somewhat	2	16	19	26
Mean rating *		3.74	3.28	2.40

B. Preference (Choice of one only)	%
Unitary state	50
Federation	22
Joint authority	13
None of the above	15

* The average, based on the five-point scale, which shows the highest level of favourability for the unitary state but also reasonable support for the federal solution.

Table 5.2: Rating of the three proposals from the "New Ireland Forum Report"

The *"out, out, out"* problem arose at the end of Thatcher's press conference when she was taking questions, and, specifically, when she was asked by an Irish journalist if the British government had, for the foreseeable future, ruled out the three options in the forum report. In her reply she took and dismissed each option in turn by adding the phrase *"that is out"*. The impression created by Margaret Thatcher's public dismissal of the options, and also the unfortunate situation when, at his own press conference, Garret FitzGerald was not aware of what she had said, created a very difficult situation for the Taoiseach.

The matter was somewhat rectified at a further meeting in Dublin Castle on 17th November, when Mrs Thatcher took steps to restore relationships between the two governments. She admitted to having the weakness that *"when people ask me direct questions, I give direct answers"* and went on to add that the Chequers summit was constructive and that there was no rift between herself and FitzGerald. The general media impression was that, while some adverse public perception resulted from her rather blunt answers, both governments continued to be committed to seeking a new political framework for peace in Northern Ireland.

EVENTS IN 1985

Alan Dukes presented his third budget in January 1985. The *Irish Times*/MRBI opinion poll of 5th February found public reaction almost identical to that of a year earlier; almost half saw it being in line with expectations, and a similar volume felt that their living standards would not change as a result. In spite of this quite dispassionate reaction, government satisfaction ratings remained low, at 28 per cent and, in spite of the well-aired discussions on Northern Ireland, the rating of the Taoiseach had dropped seven points to 40 per cent, from the October 1984 opinion poll. What was also evident was that net support for Fianna Fáil was now at 52 per cent – its highest impact since the general election three years earlier – this was 11 points above the combined figure for the government parties.

Over the remaining months of 1985, three further polls in the *Irish Times*/MRBI series were conducted. In April and July, ratings for the government, Taoiseach and Tánaiste remained relatively low – in the mid-twenties, high-thirties, and low-thirties, respectively – while support for Fianna Fáil was still high at just over 50 per cent, with Fine Gael in the low-thirties. In the final opinion poll of the year in

November, following the signing of the Anglo–Irish Agreement, government satisfaction increased by ten points; that for the Taoiseach by a similar figure and for the Tánaiste by 11. Fine Gael support also improved by four points to 37 per cent. The government, Taoiseach and Tánaiste were now getting some credit for their efforts on Northern Ireland over the previous 18 months. Significantly, however, Fianna Fáil in opposition continued to command a solid 51 per cent and the omens for the re-election of the coalition government were not favourable.

NORTHERN IRELAND: THE ANGLO–IRISH AGREEMENT

In Northern Ireland, the early months of 1985 saw a continuation of the dialogue, at various levels, between the two governments and the SDLP. Matters were seen to have moved on, to the extent that they were now being referred to as negotiations, with chosen senior people involved on all sides – and the text of a proposed draft agreement now required an increasing degree of sensitivity. The outcome – the Anglo–Irish Agreement was signed by the Taoiseach, Garret FitzGerald, and the British Prime Minister, Margaret Thatcher, on 15th November 1985. The agreement moved away from the specifics of the New Ireland Forum, and set the scene for the future in the form of bilateral commitments by the two sovereign governments. (Its terms are set out in detail at *Chapter 14*.)

Public Reaction to the Anglo–Irish Agreement

Five days later, MRBI, on behalf of *The Irish Times*, conducted an extensive national poll to measure public reaction to various aspects of the agreement. A further poll, using identical criteria, was conducted on 3rd February 1986, two-and-a-half months later. Immediate and reflective reaction was, therefore, obtained.

	Dates of Polls	
	15th Nov 1985	3rd Feb 1986
	%	%
A. General approval of the agreement		
Approve	59	69
Disapprove	29	20
No opinion	12	11
B. Overall impact		
Will promote better relations between		
Republic of Ireland and Britain	66	69
Northern and Republic of Ireland	50	56
The two communities in Northern Ireland	42	50
Agreement will reduce violence	34	43
C. Will bring a united Ireland closer		
Yes: united Ireland closer	30	28
No: further away	13	13
No difference	53	54
No opinion	4	5
D. Will improve life in Northern Ireland		
For nationalists in Northern Ireland		
Yes	49	52
No	39	35
No opinion	12	13
For unionists in Northern Ireland		
Yes	31	28
No	52	51
No opinion	17	21
E. Reaction to Charles Haughey's criticism of the agreement		
Yes: he was right to criticise	32	26
No: he was wrong to criticise	56	63
No opinion	12	11

Table 5.3: Results of the Irish Times/MRBI *polls to assess the impact of the 1985 Anglo–Irish Agreement*

In interpreting these figures, it is relevant to assess them in context. In the post-forum survey of May 1984, a large majority (86 per cent) favoured follow-on meetings between representatives of the Republic of Ireland, Northern Ireland and Britain. The general level of approval for the agreement that emanated from these meetings – 59 per cent increasing to 69 per cent – was therefore not surprising (see *Table 5.3*), nor was the primary basis for this approval, i.e. the perception of a considerable majority (69 per cent) that the agreement would promote better relations between the Republic of Ireland and Britain.

In commenting on the perceived influence of the agreement on a united Ireland, it is also relevant to look at the general background. In the immediate post-forum research, support for the unitary state concept was by no means overwhelming, and a reasonable number (15 per cent) opted for none of the three forum solutions. In the MRBI 21st anniversary poll published in *The Irish Times* in May 1983, 40 per cent felt that Ireland would never be united, and a further 25 per cent put unification at least 50 years ahead. Viewed against this background, it is again not surprising that a majority (53 per cent and later 54 per cent) considered that the signing of the agreement would make no difference to unification.

The final question in the post-agreement research measured reaction to Charles Haughey's stand in criticising the agreement. The question was:

> *Mr Haughey, as leader of the opposition, has criticised the agreement. Do you think that Mr Haughey was right or not in the stand he has taken?*

In both the November and February surveys, majorities of 56 per cent and 63 per cent respectively, felt that Haughey was wrong, and it is evident that this negative reaction increased as time moved on. A closer look at the party support analyses showed that in the immediate post-agreement survey, a marginal majority (52 per cent) of Fianna Fáil supporters considered that Haughey was right, while a third (34 per cent) felt otherwise. A few months later in February, those agreeing with Haughey had dropped seven points to 45 per cent, whilst those who disagreed with him had increased by eight points to 42 per cent.

THE FOUNDING OF THE PROGRESSIVE DEMOCRATS

Whether or not the then leader of the opposition felt justified in his criticism is not known, but a month or so following the signing, a political tornado hit the scene and provided a new, unexpected challenge to all party leaders. The occasion was the formation of the Progressive Democrat party by two respected members of Fianna Fáil, Des O'Malley and Mary Harney, on Saturday 21st December 1985. The new party's immediate and short-term impact was very impressive, achieving – as it did – opinion poll support of 25 per cent of the committed electorate within two months. In the longer term, although this support eventually dropped to single figures, the party has played a very significant role in the formation of two governments; that of 1989 under Charles Haughey and, again, in 1997 under Bertie Ahern.

Irish Times/MRBI Poll

In February 1986, a special *Irish Times*/MRBI opinion poll measured the impact of the new Progressive Democrat party just two months after its formation and, at that stage, it had made serious inroads into both Fianna Fáil and Fine Gael support.

Extracts from the opinion poll (*Tables 5.4A–5.4D*) show the level of approval for the new party in February 1986, analysed by party supporters, at the time.

General approval of the establishment of the PDs							
	Total	Supporters					Undecided
		FF	FG	Lab	PD	Other	
	%	%	%	%	%	%	%
Approve	64	44	68	64	98	64	56
Disapprove	22	39	20	19	–	16	14
No opinion	14	17	12	17	2	20	30

Table 5.4A: Result of a poll to assess the general approval of the electorate to the formation of the Progressive Democrats

In terms of general approval (*Table 5.4A*), one of the most striking aspects of the survey, was that, in addition to the 21 per cent who would vote for the new party, considerable majorities of Fine Gael and Labour supporters (68 per cent and 64 per cent respectively) and 44 per cent of those who supported Fianna Fáil approved of the formation of the new party.

Party support following the formation of the PDs				
	February 1986		November 1985	Difference
	%	Excluding Undecided	%	%
Fianna Fáil	36	42	44	−8
Fine Gael	20	23	32	−12
Labour	4	5	5	−1
Progressive Democrats	21	25	−	+21
Others	5	5	5	−
Undecided	14		14	−

Table 5.4B: Results of polls showing Progressive Democrat support in 1986

Profile of PD support (from Table 5.4B)	
Voting behaviour general election of November 1982	**%**
Voted for Fianna Fáil	7
Voted for Fine Gael	10
Voted for Labour	1
Voted for Other parties	1
Non-voters	2

Table 5.4C: Profile of supporters for the Progressive Democrats relative to the 1982 general election

Approval of PD's coalition options in next election

	Total		PD Voters		FF Voters		FG Voters	
	Approve	Dis-approve	Approve	Dis-approve	Approve	Dis-approve	Approve	Dis-approve
	%	%	%	%	%	%	%	%
PDs and FF								
Under CJ Haughey	17	71	8	86	31	58	5	84
Under other leader	43	42	63	31	33	52	45	42
PDs and FG								
Under G FitzGerald	34	53	42	52	13	75	69	22
Under other leader	25	57	32	55	16	69	38	46

Table 5.4D: Result of a poll showing the approval rating of the various coalition options available to the Progressive Democrats

The Progressive Democrat profile based on prior political affiliations was measured on two criteria. The first relative to the figures from the previous opinion poll of November 1985 (*Table 5.4B*) and the second a comparison with voting behaviour in the general election of November 1982, three years earlier (*Table 5.4C*). The patterns are quite similar. Former Fine Gael supporters represented the majority of new Progressive Democrat voters. Of the 21 per cent who would vote for the new party, 12 per cent were previously Fine Gael and 8 per cent Fianna Fáil supporters (*Table 5.4B*). While on the other criterion (*Table 5.4C*), 10 per cent who would vote for the new party had voted Fine Gael in the November 1982 election and 7 per cent had voted for Fianna Fáil. At that early stage, the party had certainly brought a new dimension to Irish politics, and it was given a further impetus when two more senior Fianna Fáil people – Bobby Molloy and Pearse Wyse – also joined.

EVENTS OF 1986

The next poll in April 1986 showed the satisfaction rating of the new party leader, Des O'Malley, tying with that of the Taoiseach Garret FitzGerald on 44 per cent, two points behind Charles Haughey as opposition leader on 46 per cent, with Dick Spring on 27 per cent. Government ratings remained relatively low in the mid-twenties, while party support figures showed Fianna Fáil up six to 48 per cent; Fine Gael up three to 26 per cent; the Progressive Democrats down eight to 17 per cent; and Labour stable on 5 per cent. The settling down had already commenced, and Fianna Fáil and Fine Gael had recovered some of the lost ground. The next election would convey the real message.

The formation of the Progressive Democrats, and the consequent inroads into Fine Gael support, was only one of a number of factors that made 1986 the most difficult year that the government had to contend with. The recurring demands of each budget presented to date, and the desire that the final one would make a constructive and positive impact on the continuing difficult economic arena, meant that it was stress down to the wire. Garret FitzGerald acknowledges this in his autobiography, *All in a Life*, saying:

> *The most debilitating venture one can undertake in politics is identifying and deciding on cuts in public spending.*

Any cabinet reshuffle in the fourth year of a coalition government, comprising two strong parties with divergent ideologies, represents a potentially hazardous operation, and the reshuffle on which the Taoiseach embarked in the spring of 1986 turned out to be precisely that. FitzGerald acknowledges that *"the public impact of what was seen as a badly executed move was damaging"*.

The Divorce Debate

Then, to add to an already exhaustive agenda, the government decided to address again the question of divorce, a subject which was first raised within Fine Gael at the party's Ard-Fheis back in 1978, when delegates voted in favour of the removal of the constitutional ban on the dissolution of marriage. Later, both main party leaders in their role as Taoiseach – FitzGerald in 1981 and Haughey in 1982 – were pressurised to address the question and, in July 1983, after being returned to government the previous November, the coalition government – along with Fianna Fáil in opposition – established the Joint Committee on Marital Breakdown. Its objectives were to consider the protection of marriage and family life, and to examine the problems arising from marriage breakdown. Following the belated publication of the committee's report in 1985, the government decided to proceed with the referendum in 1986. Two reasons have been given for this decision. The first was to avoid the complication of it becoming an election issue, and, secondly, the opinion polls over the previous two years had shown a majority in favour of divorce in certain circumstances, and a smaller majority for amending the Constitution.

On 24th April 1986, the government held a press conference at which it was confirmed that a referendum would be held. The conditions that would apply to it were also published. The referendum was held on 26th June and will be remembered for the massive swing against the amendment that materialised during the final weeks of the campaign. It was defeated substantially by a ratio of two to one. (This subject is addressed in detail in *Chapter 6*.)

A June 1986 poll delivered the news that Charles Haughey continued to top the ratings among the party leaders with a 48 per cent satisfaction rating; Dr FitzGerald was on 45 per cent, Mr O'Malley 42 per cent and Mr Spring 24 per cent. Fianna Fáil support had also increased to 51 per cent, while Fine Gael was on 25 per cent, the Progressive Democrats 15 per cent and Labour 4 per cent. At that stage, Fianna Fáil appeared to have regained all ground lost since November – prior to the formation of the Progressive Democrats – whilst Fine Gael and Labour were down 12 and two points respectively.

Busy End to 1986

On the resumption of the Dáil in October, the Ministers with new portfolios were still settling in and many continued to be disappointed at the unexpected late swing and defeat for the divorce referendum. Tensions on a number of other issues had also surfaced and a few backbenchers were causing further problems for the Taoiseach. During the first week of the new session – on 23rd October – the government survived a vote of no confidence by two votes; a few weeks earlier the Progressive Democrats had published the party's tax policy document and Fine Gael had held its annual Ard-Fheis.

The next *Irish Times*/MRBI opinion poll – on 29th October – continued to deliver unfavourable news for the government; its ratings were down three points from June, and five from April. Those for all party leaders, however, remained stable with Haughey in opposition still marginally ahead of FitzGerald and O'Malley. Fianna Fáil support was 46 per cent, a slight drop; Fine Gael was on 29 per cent, a noticeable increase; the Progressive Democrats were stable at 15 per cent and Labour was on 5 per cent. The figures indicated that the election would be interesting with support for Fianna Fáil, Fine Gael and the Progressive Democrats remaining quite solid.

The government then received a boost when, in spite of Fianna Fáil opposition, the Dáil passed the Single European Act and the Extradition Bill – although the latter would not become effective for a further year. The narrow defeat of a Fianna Fáil motion to dissolve the Dáil was the final move before the Christmas break, but it was now evident that the countdown to the next election had commenced.

In attempting to reach agreement on the substantial cuts that the Taoiseach and Fine Gael ministers wished to introduce in the 1987 budget, an impasse had been reached between Fine Gael and Labour ministers, and it was decided to break for Christmas and review the situation in the New Year. When the parties met again in mid-January, the situation was accepted as hopeless and, on 20th January, the four Labour ministers resigned from cabinet. The Taoiseach allotted the vacated portfolios to existing Fine Gael ministers; duly dissolved the Dáil and fixed the general election for 17th February 1987.

THE 1987 GENERAL ELECTION

On Wednesday 21st January, the Taoiseach initiated the election campaign by offering the government's difficult budgetary proposals to the electorate, and within two days the first *Irish Times*/MRBI campaign opinion poll was under way. The general outcome strongly reflected the negative impact of these proposals. Fianna Fáil's core support remained solid, while that for Fine Gael had dropped by seven points from the previous poll in October. However, an exceptionally high volume of electors – one fifth – were undecided and, since many of these were identified as having voted for Fine Gael in the November 1982 election, it was apparent that the main reason for the indecision was the economic package that the government had put before the people. Grasping the nettle had cost the Taoiseach eight points in his satisfaction ratings. The poll positioned Des O'Malley ahead of the other four leaders and also confirmed the potential of the Progressive

Democrats, who remained solidly positioned at 15 per cent. The MRBI commentary concluded by stating that *"the survey confirms the Fianna Fáil position as the bookmakers favourite to lead the next government, but many hearts and minds have yet to be won over"*.

Towards the end of January, Fianna Fáil published its election manifesto, which attracted heavy criticism from both the Taoiseach and John Bruton, the Minister for Finance, for not committing itself to cuts in public spending and borrowing, and for not facing up to the challenge of correcting the nation's finances. When FitzGerald, commented on the poll forecast indicating that the Progressive Democrats could obtain up to 12 seats, Haughey replied that the Taoiseach was, in effect, conceding defeat.

The Second and Third Opinion Polls of the Campaign

The next opinion poll, conducted on 3rd February, indicated that many were still maintaining a wait-and-see attitude, with one in five still undecided. Fianna Fáil support remained solid while there was a marginal increase in that for Fine Gael. However, Des O'Malley's ratings of 53 per cent were considerably ahead of all other leaders, and it was now becoming apparent that the Progressive Democrats would deliver on its opinion poll impact.

The final *Irish Times*/MRBI campaign poll was timed for 11th February, six days before polling day, by which stage the undecideds had dropped to 16 per cent – still a substantial figure that indicated the election outcome could be different to the final poll figures. Fianna Fáil was positioned on a net of 48 per cent, a figure that had the potential to deliver a majority of seats. Fine Gael had again improved marginally and the Progressive Democrats were positioned on 16 per cent. The signs were clear, Fianna Fáil was definitely on course to form the next government. The Fine Gael vote was increasing as the campaign moved on, and the Progressive Democrat vote would almost certainly be in double figures.

The final outcome of the 1987 general election, in first preference terms, showed a general tightening of support for Fianna Fáil over the final days, while support for Fine Gael increased as the campaign concluded (see *Table 5.5*). The Progressive Democrats fulfilled expectations.

Party	Election Result First Preferences	Irish Times/MRBI Final Poll
	%	%
Fianna Fáil	44	48
Fine Gael	27	25
Progressive Democrats	12	16
Labour Party	6	6
Others	11	5

Table 5.5: Comparison of results between the 1987 general election and the final Irish Times/MRBI poll of the campaign

The ratios of seats to votes for each party are given in *Table 5.6*.

Party	Votes	Seats		Ratio
	%	%	Number	
Fianna Fáil	44	49	81	100:110
Fine Gael	27	31	51	100:114
Progressive Democrats	12	8	14	100:67
Labour Party	6	7	12	100:116
Other	11	5	8	100:45

Table 5.6: Ratio of seats to votes for each party in the 1987 general election

Some commentators have observed that the 1987 general election was the fourth occasion in which Haughey had failed to win an overall majority for the party. Although the statement is factually correct, it is unrealistic to imply that gaining a majority was possible, and I doubt if even the most ardent party supporter could have expected it.

Analysis of the Results of the 1987 General Election

As I saw the situation, a Fianna Fáil Dáil majority would not materialise unless certain relevant factors were in place and, in 1987, there was one crucial missing link. Admittedly, the party was coming from the advantageous base of being in opposition (this was the case in 1977 and again in February 1982), and full use was made of this by presenting what was to some electors, an attractive – albeit inappropriate – manifesto. The numbers were also in Fianna Fáil's favour, on the basis that the greater the number of candidates – particularly non-Fianna Fáil candidates – nominated, the greater the chances are of a large party, like Fianna Fáil, maximising its return of seats to votes. In the 1987 election, a total of 465 were nominated, of whom 344 were non-Fianna Fáil, and the party achieved an above average ratio of seats to votes 100:110 (44.15%:48.4%).

The final link in the chain, however, is that the party leader should, at that juncture, have the personal capability to attract transfers from the second and subsequent preferences of non-Fianna Fáil candidates. In the final two campaign opinion polls, Charles Haughey's satisfaction ratings were bogged down at the relatively low level of 43 per cent. When this is compared with the party's first preference vote in the election, of 44 per cent, it is evident that Haughey's impact among the electorate at large was inadequate to attract the final transfers that were necessary.

There is no doubt that the new Progressive Democrats played a crucial role by capturing 12 per cent of the first preference vote (14 seats) and that both main party leaders underestimated the potential of the new arrival. Relative to the November 1982 election, Fine Gael was down 12 percentage points, and Fianna Fáil one. The irony is that, if Fianna Fáil had received this 1 per cent, it would have obtained 83 seats, which, along with Neil Blaney and the Ceann Comhairle's vote, would have given it a workable cushion. As it happened, for an entirely different reason (which is identified in *Chapter 7*), the party managed very satisfactorily.

CHAPTER 6

Divorce: The People Decide (1986)

In keeping with its policy of addressing a number of the social issues of the day, particularly marriage breakdown, the coalition government of Fine Gael and Labour, under Taoiseach Garret FitzGerald and Tánaiste Dick Spring, had, in 1985, established a Joint Committee on Marital Breakdown. The committee published a report that set out a basis for action by the government to address the matter. On 24th April 1986, the government published a document entitled "A Statement of Intent with Regard to Marriage, Separation and Divorce", and FitzGerald announced that his government would hold a referendum on divorce. The document included the publication of the Tenth Amendment to the Constitution Bill 1986, and made provision for the referendum.

THE SITUATION PRIOR TO THE 1986 REFERENDUM

Back in September 1983, an *Irish Times*/MRBI opinion poll had addressed the question of divorce for the first time and, for the following three years, it measured public reaction on a regular basis. The developing situation can best be viewed by dividing the period into two distinct stages:

- **Stage I** September 1983 to April 1986
- **Stage II** 24th April 1986 to 26th June 1986
  (statement of intent) (referendum day)

Stage I: September 1983–April 1986

During Stage I, from September 1983 to April 1986, MRBI conducted seven national opinion polls for *The Irish Times*, which, in addition to the standard questions on political party support and government and party leaders' satisfaction ratings, included the following question on divorce:

> *Divorce is not legal in Ireland, but a legal separation where neither party is free to re-marry is permitted. Do you feel that divorce should be permitted in certain circumstances, or do you feel that it should never be permitted here in Ireland?*

Provision was made for agreement, disagreement or no opinion and, throughout Stage I, a substantial majority, extending from 65 per cent in September 1983 to 77 per cent in February 1986 (the last MRBI poll in the Stage I), stated that they were in favour of divorce in certain circumstances.

During this series – in May 1984 – a further question relating to the constitutional prohibition was also introduced:

> *As you probably know, the Irish Constitution contains an article prohibiting divorce. If a referendum was held to remove this article from the Constitution, would you vote to remove it and allow for divorce, or would you vote to keep the ban on divorce?*

Reaction to this constitutional aspect was much less favourable. In the May 1984 survey, 48 per cent stated that, if a referendum was held, they would vote to remove the ban. The most positive figures in favour of removing the ban were 52 per cent in April 1985 and a similar level again in February 1986. This general 25 per cent differential, between those who felt that divorce should be permitted in certain circumstances and those who would vote to remove the ban from the Constitution, precipitated the inclusion of a third question, which was structured to identify the reasons for the differential.

The findings clearly indicated that, whilst many favoured divorce in instances of family violence, hardship, alcoholism and suffering children they were equally committed to the concept that it should not be a 'free for all' situation. In my commentary to the *Irish Times*/MRBI January 1985 opinion poll, I addressed these issues in detail and concluded that *"many did not see the passing of the amendment as providing a guarantee that divorce would be introduced only in the circumstances which they envisaged".*

It was apparent, therefore, as early as January 1985 – some 18 months before the referendum – that many, who were in favour of divorce in certain circumstances, would not necessarily vote to remove the constitutional ban, unless the text of the amendment actually addressed the circumstances they had in mind. In my opinion, it would have been very difficult, if not impossible, to draft legislation to meet these perceived circumstances.

Stage II: April–June 1986

Stage II in the run up to a referendum began on 24th April 1986, when the government published its statement of intent, but had not, as yet, announced the actual date of the referendum. The statement included the following proposal:

Article 41.3.2° of the Constitution states:

> *No law shall be enacted providing for the grant of a dissolution of marriage.*

The proposed amendment to the Constitution would delete this and substitute a new *Article 41.3.2°* stating:

> *Where, and only where, such court established under this Constitution as may be prescribed by law is satisfied that—*
>
> - *a marriage had failed;*
>
> - *the failure has continued for a period or periods amounting to, at least five years;*
>
> - *there is no reasonable possibility of reconciliation between the parties to the marriage; and*
>
> - *any other condition prescribed by law has been complied with.*
>
> *The court may, in accordance with law, grant a dissolution of the marriage provided that the court is satisfied that adequate and proper provision having regard to the circumstances will be made for any dependent spouse and for any child of, or any child who is dependent on, either spouse.*

The first MRBI opinion poll in Stage II of the campaign was conducted on 27th April 1986 and was published on 5th May. It included for the first time a question based on the actual text of the proposed amendment. Having set out this wording, the question that followed was:

> *In the referendum, will you vote for or against this amendment?*

This survey indicated that 57 per cent intended to vote yes, 36 per cent no, and 7 per cent were undecided, and this represented an increase of 5 per cent, when compared to the 52 per cent of February 1986. This increase was not dramatic and, being aware of the reservations that many had previously expressed, it was very likely that the 21 points differential between the 'Yes' and 'No' voters would change over the four weeks of campaigning that remained. The commentary in *The Irish Times* on 5th May included the following caveat:

> *The campaign proper will not commence until the date of the referendum is known, and it would be unwise to assume that the outcome is, as yet, predictable. It must be emphasised that the results of this opinion poll cannot be taken as predicting the outcome of the referendum. Many potential voters will be influenced when the issues are more fully promulgated.*

Following the publication of this MRBI poll, a survey conducted by RSI for the *Sunday Press* on 3rd May saw the differential reduced to 16 per cent and, on 9th June the *Sunday Independent* published an IMS poll that showed a further downturn of four points, i.e. a differential of 12 per cent in favour.

On 14th June, MRBI, in a survey conducted on behalf of the government, identified the situation as evenly split. In retrospect, this represented the crossover point, since six days later on 20th June, the *Irish Times*/MRBI poll showed a majority of 55 per cent against for the first time – the differential was now a negative 10 per cent. My commentary in *The Irish Times* six days before the referendum included the following:

> *It is evident that a considerable swing has taken place against the amendment in the recent weeks of the campaign, which, if continued up to referendum day, could result in a further*

extension of last week's differential. It is clear that the amendment will not be carried.

In a final MRBI opinion poll conducted on behalf of one of the political parties on 23rd June, this trend was confirmed and showed a swing to 60%:40% against.

The outcome of the referendum, showing a defeat for the amendment at 63 per cent, represented an unprecedented swing over the two months between the 24th April and the 26th June, and was described by some commentators as more a political earthquake than a landslide.

Analysis of the Referendum Result

In its aftermath, many reasons were advanced to explain the remarkable turnaround during the referendum. There is little doubt that the anti-divorce campaign was the more co-ordinated and effective, and that issues such as succession rights, children's welfare and informal opposition by Fianna Fáil all made a contribution. In the final *Irish Times*/MRBI opinion poll of the campaign, Fianna Fáil supporters represented the only political party that recorded a majority (67%:33%) against divorce.

However, MRBI data identified two specific reasons for the defeat of the government proposal.

- The failure, or inability, of the legislation to come to terms with the actual circumstances that were envisaged by many who favoured the concept of limited divorce. This had become apparent in the early campaign polls.

- The influence of the Catholic Church, particularly during the final stages of the campaign.

Influence of the Catholic Church in the Divorce Referendum

In the MRBI 21st anniversary survey of May 1983 one area related to perceived sources of influences on society, and addressed the question of who has greatest influence on issues of family life, marriage and divorce. The relevant findings are given in *Table 6.1*.

The extent of the influence of the Church and the home on divorce and family life is evident from this extract and, when related to the referendum campaign, provides significant confirmatory data. The more detailed analyses of the survey show that those who claimed to be influenced by the Church to the greatest extent, in regard to divorce and family life, were rural people, mainly female aged 35+. Significantly, when a comparison was made between the *Irish Times*/MRBI campaign opinion polls of 27th April and 20th June, the greatest evidence of switching to a 'No' vote was among this same demographic segment.

Sources of influence	On Divorce	On Family Life
	%	%
The Church	40	31
The home	23	55
The media	17	7
Politicians	4	1
None of the above	16	6

Table 6.1: Results of a May 1983 survey showing the influences on attitudes towards family life and divorce

The Catholic Church, while formally advocating an informed conscientious approach, carried a clear anti-divorce message, particularly in the later stages of the campaign. There is little doubt that this was very influential in the final outcome.

It is evident, therefore, that six published opinion polls – four of which were conducted by MRBI – very accurately identified the downturn in support for the amendment right up to the referendum. In spite of this, some political and other commentators claimed that the opinion polls had been wrong, apparently based on the misinterpretation that the earlier campaign polls that showed a majority in favour, were inconsistent with the final result.

THE COMISKEY INTERVENTION

Writing in the *Wexford People* on 4th July 1986 – seven days after the referendum – Dr Brendan Comiskey, Bishop of Ferns, saw the MRBI contribution in the following context:

The opinion polls have brought further discredit on an already discredited trade. The polls have not only got it wrong about the outcome of the divorce referendum, but they were used to manipulate people... The truth is that we do not take our mandate from the polls or even from the people, but from the Gospel and from God. In a choice between God and Gallup, I suggest that for the Christian, there could be no contest.

The comments were also carried in *The Irish Times* a few days later. I had previously noted some journalists criticising opinion polls for what they saw as inaccuracies – based entirely on gross misinterpretations – but this was different. Here was an eminent churchman publicly criticising a profession that operates within very strict ethical and technical standards, and getting it completely wrong in the process. I discussed the matter with some colleagues and friends and my first decision was to do nothing for a few weeks. Eventually in mid-August – five weeks after publication – I wrote directly to Bishop Comiskey.

I congratulated him on the 25th anniversary of his ordination – which I had read about – and then drew his attention to what had appeared in the two newspapers. I explained that my delay was deliberate in that I wished to address the matter in a composed and restrained manner. I outlined details of the considerable research that the company had conducted for the Catholic Church – for religious magazines and newspapers and for various religious orders – and then set out the details of the accurate research undertaken in the political arena, particularly during election and referenda campaigns. I finally quoted from the last MRBI commentary that stated, *inter alia*, that the divorce amendment would not be carried. I concluded on the following lines:

On this basis, not only was MRBI not wrong, as you incorrectly claimed, but in common with the previous referendum and also all general elections since 1973, the company's record has been remarkably accurate.

In regard to manipulation, you have classified MRBI with a number of other interests. This should be taken up directly with these other interests. We value our professional independence, and would never undertake a project that we felt would be used to influence the public, and I do not accept, as you may have implied, that publication per se, *means manipulation.*

I would appreciate if you would now re-appraise the situation in the light of what I have said, and correct the false impression that you have published.

Four months later, in late December, I received a reply that was written on 26th December. The bishop admitted *"if there is any error associated with the surveys, it seems to be an error of interpretation by people like myself, who do not heed the advice and the warnings of the polling organisations themselves".*

Having commented on what he described as my restraint, he promised to attempt to set the record straight publicly at the first opportunity. He also undertook to send me a copy of his remarks. I responded to this letter on 20th January 1987, and I concluded by saying that I was anxious to have the record corrected publicly and that I was looking forward to this.

Not having heard further from the bishop within two months, I wrote again on 27th March 1987. I told him that I was surprised and disappointed not to have heard from him since December, and commented that there was now a hollow ring about his promise of *"setting the record straight at the first opportunity"*. I also said that I was not prepared to let the matter rest and, although I have waited a further 14 years to do so, I feel I am now justified in making the matter public.

CHAPTER 7

Charles Haughey Takes Over Again (1987–1992)

When the Twenty-Fifth Dáil met on 10th March 1987, Charles Haughey was elected Taoiseach on the casting vote of the Ceann Comhairle, Sean Treacy. He was supported by 81 Fianna Fáil deputies and Neil Blaney (Ind), and was opposed by 51 Fine Gael TDs, 14 from the Progressive Democrats, 12 from Labour, four from the Workers' Party and Jim Kemmy (DSP), also totalling 82. Tony Gregory (Ind) abstained. After the constitutional formalities, the new Taoiseach announced his cabinet.

Taoiseach	Charles Haughey
Tánaiste; Foreign Affairs	Brian Lenihan
Finance	Ray MacSharry
Education	Mary O'Rourke
Agriculture and Food	Michael O'Kennedy
Justice	Gerard Collins
Energy and Communications	Raphael Burke
Social Welfare	Michael Woods
Marine	Brendan Daly
Environment	Pádraig Flynn
Labour	Bertie Ahern
Tourism and Transport	John Wilson
Industry and Commerce	Albert Reynolds
Health	Rory O'Hanlon
Defence	Michael Noonan

Table 7.1: Members of the 1987 Fianna Fáil cabinet

CHANGES FOR FINE GAEL

The following day, Garret FitzGerald called a meeting of the Fine Gael parliamentary party and told them of his intention to resign as leader; having, by then, completed almost ten years in that capacity, including five as Taoiseach. The high points of his period of tenure were the 39 per cent support, which the party achieved in the November 1982 general election, and the signing of the Anglo–Irish Agreement in November 1985.

At a specially convened meeting of the parliamentary party on 22nd March, three candidates – Peter Barry, John Bruton and Alan Dukes – were nominated and, in the subsequent secret ballot, Alan Dukes was elected the new leader. At 42, he was the youngest ever leader of the party, and was also one of the few TDs to be appointed a cabinet minister (Agriculture) on his first day in the Dáil following the June 1981 general election.

Following his election, Dukes promised to continue to work for economic reform, and undertook to co-operate with the new government should it decide to target that objective. In saying this, he was restating Garret FitzGerald's commitment, given on RTÉ on the night of the election count, when he promised Fine Gael support to Fianna Fáil if the new government pursued similar policies to those that Fine Gael had presented to the people prior to the election.

RAY MACSHARRY AND THE 1987 BUDGET

When Ray MacSharry, the new Minister for Finance, presented the government's budget to the Dáil on 31st March 1987, it soon became evident that he, too, was committed to correcting the country's finances. He said that, while his message was unpalatable, it was a message that was critical to the revival of the nation's economic prospects. He then outlined his package:

- increased hospital charges;
- the abolition of housing grants;
- the imposition of a special withholding tax by State agencies;
- a reduction in mortgage interest relief;

- the abolition of duty-free allowances for those outside the jurisdiction for less than 48 hours;
- reduced farm grants; and
- a public sector pay freeze.

While the harsh provisions of his budget were surprising and dramatic, being, as they were, in direct contrast to the Fianna Fáil election manifesto, they illustrated in no uncertain terms Ray MacSharry's personal commitment to economic rectitude.

Irish Times/MRBI Poll

This period of political life was one of the most heavily monitored through opinion polls, with three to four conducted annually – the first of which focused on the budget. Finance Minister Ray MacSharry did not have long to wait before seeing what the electorate thought of his efforts. Within four days, an *Irish Times*/MRBI opinion poll carried the predictable message that the public at large saw it as harsher than expected, even more so than the previous three budgets. A considerable volume of people also believed their living standards would fall as a result.

However, the electorate's perception – and indeed tolerance – went further than this when, for the first time in post-budget surveys, a majority classified it as being good for the country. While MacSharry may have felt that his budget provisions were at least understood, if not formally appreciated, his mindset in the lead up to his taking up the finance ministry is very succinctly addressed in his book *The Making of the Celtic Tiger*, co-written with Padraic White.

When offered the portfolio by the Taoiseach, MacSharry hesitated to accept immediately for two reasons. Firstly, as an MEP, he saw his future in Europe and was happy there. Secondly, and very significantly, he was not impressed with what he described *as "the fast-and-loose approach to economic policy that the Fianna Fáil party had adopted in opposition"*. *"This,"* he said, *"had damaged the party's credibility, considering that the Fianna Fáil economic plan 'The Way Forward' had set out very clear budgetary guidelines which implied an acceptance of restraint – even in opposition."* He goes on to say that while he set no preconditions for his acceptance of the cabinet post, he felt there was a clear, if implicit, understanding between himself and the Taoiseach that he would be able to do what was necessary either in terms of expenditure cuts or tax reform, and that he could rely on Haughey's full support as Taoiseach.

When one considers the economic jigsaw that had to be assembled within a very short time span, the challenge facing the minister was of immense proportions. MacSharry's personal determination; the support and influence of the review group, which was set up shortly after the government took office; the economic consensus of the social partners; and, possibly most crucial of all, the political consensus in the form of support from the former and new leaders of Fine Gael and the Progressive Democrats, all contributed in a very constructive sense, to what MacSharry himself describes as "*a major turning point in our economic history*".

In the same April post-budget opinion poll, the government's satisfaction rating of 39 per cent was the highest of any government to date, and the MRBI comment in *The Irish Times* stated that "*it is apparent that the electorate is now prepared to accept a budget in the national interest whilst also recognising the immediate difficulties associated with it*".

It was evident that Charles Haughey, as Taoiseach, was benefiting from the spin-off from this budgetary policy. His satisfaction rating of 46 per cent represented an increase of three points relative to the previous poll when he was in opposition. However, the main beneficiary in terms of public impact was Alan Dukes, who, at 54 per cent, was positioned ahead of all other party leaders. He was followed in close proximity by Des O'Malley, leader of the Progressive Democrats, on 52 per cent. Dick Spring's 41 per cent rating as leader of the Labour Party was considerably above his pre-election figure, and Tomás Mac Giolla, leader of the Workers' Party, showed a marginal increase to 34 per cent. In interpreting satisfaction rating figures, it should be noted that leaders of small parties have a more difficult task in achieving high ratings, than with those of large parties, where a higher 'own party' support base applies.

In support terms, the Fianna Fáil figure was 46 per cent, up two points on the party's election result. Fine Gael on 27 per cent was identical to its general election figure, while the Progressive Democrats on 14 per cent and Labour on 6 per cent, each showed a marginal increase.

THE EUROPEAN DIMENSION

During this time, a significant European issue was on the horizon. The Single European Act, which was passed in the Dáil prior to the fall of the previous government, had yet to be ratified by the people, and the referendum that would give effect to this was fixed for 26th May 1987. Having joined the European Community in 1973, the ratification of the Single European Act was of fundamental importance to the government. It was an all-embracing mechanism that copper-fastened the concept of a new and full internal market. Notwithstanding the relevance of the act that was being put to the people, a very considerable volume – estimated by MRBI at the time to be of the order of almost 1 million electors (39 per cent) – were undecided as to how they would vote. Within this group, an estimated 670,000 (28 per cent) stated that they knew nothing about the provisions of the act and needed further information before deciding how they might vote.

These were some of the findings of the *Irish Times*/MRBI opinion poll conducted on 14th May 1987, 12 days before the referendum, and they reflected the inadequacy of the government's efforts to educate the public on the provisions of the constitutional amendment that they were being asked to ratify. The core and net voting intention figures in the up-coming referendum are given in *Table 7.2*.

	Core	Net
	%	%
Intend to vote 'Yes'	40	66
Intend to vote 'No'	21	34
Undecided	39	excluding undecided

Table 7.2: Core and net voting intentions derived from the poll on the Single European Act referendum

The MRBI commentary in *The Irish Times* concluded:

> *Having regard to the fact that the campaign had ten days to run when the survey was conducted; that the level of undecided is very high; and that the divergent interests will be taking varying courses of action as a result of the figures, the*

current indications are that the referendum will be carried with support in the region of 60–70 per cent.

The result of the referendum was:

- Voted 'Yes'   70%
- Voted 'No'   30%

The turnout, as indicated by the high undecided figure in the opinion poll, was very low, at 44 per cent, a massive 29 points below the 73 per cent in the general election three months earlier.

The same opinion poll continued to position Alan Dukes ahead of the other leaders, but government satisfaction had dropped eight points to 31 per cent and Fianna Fáil support was also down five points to 41 per cent; Fine Gael was up six to 33 per cent. The downturn in government ratings and Fianna Fáil support very likely reflected the delayed impact of the budget, although neither Alan Dukes nor his party were suffering as a result of their support for it.

THE TALLAGHT STRATEGY

Towards the end of the summer, the government received a considerable boost by the advent of what has become known as the Tallaght Strategy. The occasion was an address by Alan Dukes to the Tallaght Chamber of Commerce on 2nd September 1987, in which he elaborated on the Fine Gael policy of conditional support for the government in its efforts to address the economic problems of the country:

> *The resolution of our public finance problems is the essential key to everything we want to do in the economic and social fields...and when the government is moving in the right overall direction, I will not oppose the central thrust of its policy.*

This brief extract epitomises the policy that Alan Dukes wished to pursue. His unique initiative in the national interest should not have surprised many because, firstly, he knew precisely the problems that Ray MacSharry had to face, since he himself had presented four budgets as Minister for Finance in the previous administration and, secondly, the MacSharry budget mirrored the Fine Gael pre-election policy document in a number of respects. Dukes was entering uncharted territory politically and, in the opinion of some members of his own party, he was taking a considerable risk in sharing responsibility without sharing power.

This perception was possibly based on the fact that the Dukes strategy was unprecedented, and was in direct contrast to that of the Fianna Fáil leader in opposition when Alan Dukes was himself in government from 1982–1987. Almost every decision of the then FitzGerald government was opposed – to the extent that Ray MacSharry has described it as "*too much opposition for its own sake*". In commenting on the Tallaght Strategy, he goes on to say that:

> *As time moved on, the real significance of the Dukes speech became more apparent, and came to be seen as a landmark political development which served as a catalyst in redefining how politics was conducted in the Dáil. It signalled the end of opposition for its own sake, and ushered in a new era of greater co-operation and understanding between government and the opposition parties.*

This tribute from the Fianna Fáil Minister for Finance says it all, and illustrates that time has not given Alan Dukes the enormous credit to which he is entitled for this watershed decision.

The next *Irish Times*/MRBI opinion poll contained the not entirely surprising news that honourable decisions in the national interest do not always command universal support, even within one's own party, and that the policy of opposition for its own sake was alive and well. Since the previous opinion poll in May 1987, Alan Dukes' satisfaction rating had dropped by seven points to 44 per cent, but the real message was in the small print. Among his own and Labour Party supporters, his rating was down eight and 16 points, respectively, while among Fianna Fáil and Progressive Democrat voters it had increased by seven and ten points, respectively. The overall net downturn in his personal impact, caused mainly by Fine Gael supporters, shows that, at the time, traditionalists outnumbered innovative radicals. This, in the political world, is not particularly surprising.

For the record, Des O'Malley's ratings also dropped by four points to 43 per cent. Dick Spring was down by three to 33 per cent, as was

Tomás Mac Giolla, while Charles Haughey, as Taoiseach, remained static on 38 per cent.

THE PROGRAMME FOR NATIONAL RECOVERY

On 14th October 1987, the government held a special press conference, in conjunction with the social partners – the employers, trade union and farming organisations – at which the details of an extensive new economic agreement were announced. The Programme for National Recovery (PNR) followed months of negotiations that began shortly after the government had taken up office in March. It addressed the three years up to and including 1990 and, for the first time in an economic programme, represented a consensus with the social partners. This meant that Ray MacSharry had a much more constructive – albeit, in some respects, limited – framework within which to prepare his 1988 budget.

Political reaction was mixed and, on 6th November (three weeks after its publication), MRBI measured public reaction. The primary question was:

The government, employers, trade unions and farmers agreed last month on a Programme for National Recovery. In your opinion, will this programme contribute to economic recovery for the country?

As is usual in the economic mist that these situations create, a relatively large number, one in every three, had no opinion on the potential impact of the programme. However, among the 70 per cent who expressed an opinion, two in every three were favourably disposed. The basic figures are given in *Table 7.3*.

The government would have been happy with this reaction for two reasons. Firstly, it was generally much more favourable than that expressed by opposition spokespersons and, secondly, the reasons given by the minority who felt the programme would not contribute to economic recovery were varied and minimal, with no single criticism being mentioned to any significant extent.

The second question relating to economic matters also provided a boost for the government, with a majority (53 per cent) of electors saying that Fine Gael in opposition should continue to support the government's economic policies.

	Core	Net
	%	%
PNR will contribute to economic recovery	45	65
PNR will not contribute to economic recovery	24	35
No opinion	31	excluding undecided

Table 7.3: Reaction to the 1987 Programme for National Recovery

THE 1988 BUDGET

Ray MacSharry presented his 1988 budget on 27th January and, with heavy spending cuts already having taken place in 1987, the package represented a mixed bag of give and take. This attracted some media criticism suggesting he was juggling figures and moving money around, rather than producing a range of constructive and coherent measures. The electorate, however, did not concur and, in the *Irish Times*/MRBI opinion poll that followed on 1st February, reaction was, if anything, more favourably disposed than was the case following the 1987 budget.

In general terms, a majority (52 per cent) continued to hold the view that it was a good budget for the country and, at the same time, the highest majority ever (62 per cent) felt it concurred with what they expected. Those who believed their living standards would fall as a result (29 per cent) represented approximately half the volume of the previous year, while just 12 per cent felt it was harsher than expected, compared with 45 per cent in 1987. The main spontaneous criticisms related to the increases in petrol and cigarette prices, increased PRSI for farmers and the self-employed, and insufficient tax relief. The perceived benefits were the widening of income tax bands and the increases in social welfare benefits.

A considerable number – one in four of all electors – commented that the budget would bring the finances under control, and a similar volume collectively understood the government to be cutting public spending, reducing PAYE, and encouraging enterprise, and that there was no long-term alternative to what was being offered. It was apparent that the minister had got the balance right, and that operating within the parameters of the Programme for National Recovery was not causing any serious discontent among the electorate.

This was confirmed when, in the same opinion poll, government satisfaction ratings increased by 11 points to 40 per cent, those for the Taoiseach by eight to 46 per cent and support for Fianna Fáil also went up by four points to 44 per cent. Over the same period, Fine Gael support dropped four points to 28 per cent, while Alan Dukes' rating had increased by three points. This, however, was contributed to exclusively by Fianna Fáil supporters and, not for the first time, it was apparent that the Fine Gael leader's policy of supporting the Fianna Fáil government in the national interest did not appeal to many of his own party's voters.

EVENTS IN 1988

The next *Irish Times*/MRBI opinion poll appeared three months later on 14th May 1988, and the intervening period was characterised by a number of events, any one of which could have influenced public opinion in the short term. The main events were:

- the Gibraltar shootings;
- the expulsion of John Donnellan from Fine Gael;
- the Anglo–Irish Conference meetings; and
- the fishing-rod licence dispute in the west of Ireland.

The MRBI results provided a massive boost to the government, both in terms of increased satisfaction ratings for both Taoiseach and government, and a considerable upturn in Fianna Fáil support. My commentary in *The Irish Times* read:

> *The findings represent a comprehensive vote of confidence in the government on the implementation of its policies towards a solution of our economic problems. Although the adverse effects of these policies have attracted considerable media comment of late, the government now enjoys the support of*

almost half the committed electorate. Its satisfaction ratings reflect an all-time high at 42 per cent (two up on the February poll), while that of Mr Haughey as Taoiseach has increased by nine points to 55 per cent.

This latter positioning was just one point below that of Garret FitzGerald on taking up office in February 1983, and represented Haughey's highest personal rating to date. At that stage, against the background of such a favourable impact, commentators would have felt justified in anticipating that his minority government had the capacity to run for its full term, or thereabouts. Perhaps it might well have done so had Charles Haughey and his advisors not misread the situation one year later.

The Dublin Millennium

The Dublin millennium was celebrated in 1988 and was initiated during the tenure of Lord Mayor Carmencita Hederman. In the May survey, *The Irish Times* commissioned a special feature to measure attitudes, on a national basis, towards the capital city. The findings, which were analysed in two categories (Dublin and non-Dublin residents), are set out in *Table 7.4*.

Dublin was perceived to be a friendly city, particularly by residents, but was also seen to be unsafe and neglected and, while locals viewed it as a pleasant place in which to live and visit, the majority of non-residents would not like to live there.

A majority nationally did not see Dublin as having many attractions, the locals being most impressed by the friendliness of the people themselves. The perceived problems were, however, much more evident, and all respondents, irrespective of residence, saw unemployment, lawlessness and poverty as the main ones. A majority of residents also felt that Dublin had changed for the worse over the previous few years, the concept also being supported by non-residents.

In the same survey, Carmencita Hederman made a very favourable impression as Lord Mayor and, with her term of office due to terminate six weeks later, a majority – seven in every ten in Dublin itself – expressed the view that she should be re-elected. However, the law restricts the holding of the office of Lord Mayor to one year.

	Total	Dublin Residents	Non-Dublin Residents
	%	%	%
A. Image of Dublin			
Friendly	69	85	63
Unfriendly	20	11	24
United	37	45	33
Divided	46	46	46
Cared for	30	22	34
Neglected	57	69	53
Safe	17	25	14
Unsafe	74	66	77
B. Dublin – to visit			
Pleasant	84	92	80
Not pleasant	14	6	17
C. Dublin – to live			
Pleasant	49	91	32
Not pleasant	45	8	59
D. Dublin – Attractions			
History	38	42	37
People	30	53	21
Shops	25	10	31
Parks	22	27	20
Friendliness	20	43	10
Theatres	20	14	22
Pubs	14	22	11
E. Dublin – Problems			
Unemployment	73	86	68
Lawlessness	41	36	42
Poverty	34	39	32
Untidiness	14	21	12
Roads	13	32	5
Houses	13	13	13
Prices	10	25	5
F. Dublin – Past few years			
Changed for the better	39	41	38
Changed for the worse	46	51	44

Note: Pairs of figures do not add to 100 per cent due to some interviewees not expressing an opinion.

Table 7.4: Result of the 1988 national poll on people's attitude to Dublin

The Ongoing Problem of the Public Finances

When the next *Irish Times*/MRBI opinion poll was published in October 1988, the public had had ample time to experience the effects of Ray MacSharry's second budget and the general reaction could be described as one of stoical acceptance. The commentary to the poll interpreted the findings as a continuation of the vote of confidence that had been expressed in the previous survey in May. Many could be excused for forgetting that this was a minority government well into the process of tackling the difficulties of the nation's finances.

The crucial factor, however, was that the government continued to have the conditional support of the Fine Gael and Progressive Democrat parties. The all-time high satisfaction rating of Charles Haughey as Taoiseach was maintained, as was that for Alan Dukes. In party support terms, Fianna Fáil and Fine Gael were also maintaining their levels at 50 per cent and 26 per cent respectively, while support for the Progressive Democrats was, for the first time, down to single figures at 7 per cent. This represented a three-point drop on May, and a seven-point drop on February. On the other hand, the Labour Party, on 10 per cent, had achieved double figures for the first time and, with Dick Spring also moving up four points to 41 per cent, the seeds of the party's improved election impact in 1989, and its massive performance in 1992, were beginning to take hold.

At this juncture, a number of developments took place that resulted in changes in centre-stage personnel. Peter Sutherland's term as EC commissioner was due to expire on 1st January 1989 and, although media reports were very favourably disposed to his performance, the Taoiseach announced on 17th November 1988, that Ray MacSharry would be the new commissioner. This necessitated a limited cabinet reshuffle and, on 25th November, when nominating Albert Reynolds as Minister for Finance to replace MacSharry, Charles Haughey spoke of *"the need for unrelenting discipline in government spending and borrowing"*, thereby indicating a continuation of the fiscal policies that the government had implemented since MacSharry's appointment as Minister for Finance.

THE 1989 BUDGET

Albert Reynolds presented the 1989 budget to the Dáil on Wednesday 25th January and, while it again conveyed a mixed bag of give and take, the general message was one of continuing frugality. In the opinion poll that followed, the most noted adverse observations related again to price increases for cigarettes, drink and petrol, while the reductions in mortgage interest and life insurance relief, further health cuts, and increased PRSI also attracted unfavourable comment. On the credit side, increases in children's allowances, unemployment benefits and state pensions were the main positives. A substantial number – almost half, as was the case in 1987 and 1988 – saw the budget as being good for the country and, when further probed as to their reasons for saying so, a significant one in every three spontaneously commented that "*the government was tackling the national debt, was getting things done and was looking after the poor*". Since these viewpoints were held on a cross-party basis, it had become evident that the political consensus, which applied in the Dáil, now extended to the electorate itself.

In the broader context, when assessed within the other established criteria, reaction to this budget was remarkably tolerant and broadminded since, in spite of its being the third in a series of difficult budgets, seven in every ten felt it was as they would have expected. This represented a very notable increase on each of the previous two budgets, and, as a further boost to the government, just 15 per cent – compared with 50 per cent in 1987 and 29 per cent in 1988 – considered that their standard of living would fall as a result. On these criteria it was evident that Albert Reynolds, too, had got the balance right.

Concurrent with this budget reaction, the same opinion poll gave Taoiseach Charles Haughey a further massive boost by increasing his previous all-time high rating of 54 per cent by 13 points to 67 per cent, and that of the government by a similar figure to 49 per cent. Parallel with this, Fianna Fáil's net support (having adjusted for the undecideds) had also risen by four points to 54 per cent, the party's highest support level since political opinion polls were first introduced. This was a remarkable scenario, a minority government attracting such enormous support in an environment of severe financial constraint. There was little doubt that many senior figures in Fianna Fáil were visualising that the elusive overall majority was just around the corner. However, high ratings are subject to misinterpretation, and this is precisely what happened within the next few months.

THE 1989 GENERAL ELECTION

During its period in office to 1989, the government had been defeated on five occasions on private member motions, none of which warranted any extreme government reaction. However, when the Labour Party tabled a Dáil motion in late April, calling for the allocation of £400,000 for haemophiliacs, who had been infected with the Aids virus, Haughey – having just returned from an official visit to Japan – threatened a general election if the government's own motion, providing £250,000, was defeated. When this transpired, Charles Haughey described it as an attempt to undermine the authority of the government in the financial arena, and election speculation began to intensify. On 25th May, he dissolved the Dáil and nominated 15th June as the date for the general election – also the day of the European parliament election.

Many saw the Dáil defeat as an excuse rather than a justification for calling the election. When a Fianna Fáil press release announced that the election had been called with the express objective of obtaining an overall majority, the unfavourable reaction of the electorate was not surprising. While Haughey was not the first Taoiseach to go to the country prematurely, the big surprise was the extent to which the situation had been misread.

Satisfaction ratings mean no more, and possibly something less, than the semantics convey. In the wide open spaces of mid-term surveys, they convey the message that electors are generally satisfied with the performance of the party leader or government, and the criterion is far removed from providing any indication whatsoever of voting intentions in an actual election. In expressing satisfaction, electors are saying that they are happy with the administration and want it to continue in office, but they do not, in any context, imply that they want a general election. A Taoiseach who calls an election because of high opinion poll figures will pay the price of being perceived as having orchestrated the situation. When an election is called, the public are alerted to the fact that they will be given the opportunity to have their say in a few weeks' time, and a completely new political scenario arises. Many crucial elements in the electorate are invariably influenced by the circumstances in which an election is called, and the primary perception in 1989 was that it was unnecessary.

Irish Times/MRBI Polls

The first *Irish Times*/MRBI campaign poll indicated the extent of the electorate's disapproval of the new situation. Government satisfaction dropped six points from the previous poll in February, and Fianna Fáil support was down to 50 per cent. With 16 days of the campaign remaining, Fine Gael's support was up three points to 28 per cent; Labour up one to 9 per cent; Progressive Democrats down three to 5 per cent; with Others on 8 per cent.

Two other relevant findings also emerged. The first was that health cuts (83 per cent) were positioned in second place to unemployment (93 per cent) as an important campaign issue, and this was highlighted in the MRBI commentary in *The Irish Times*:

> *The survey shows that there is no ambiguity in regard to the issues which the electorate rates as of vital importance and any party, or politician, who ignores unemployment, health cuts, emigration, poverty or taxation, in that order, is taking a grave risk.*

The second was the mixed reaction, by voters of all parties, to the support given by Fine Gael and the Progressive Democrats, for the government's budgetary strategy to date. A majority (54 per cent) now felt that they did not want the political consensus to continue. This dichotomy illustrates one of the perils of the political profession when attempting to respond to the fickle moods of the electorate.

As the opinion poll was being conducted on Saturday 27th May 1989, Alan Dukes and Des O'Malley jointly announced a pre-election pact offering an alternative government. However, the announcement came too late to have any measurable impact on the poll findings.

The following two *Irish Times*/MRBI opinion polls – the first on 9th June, just a week before the election and the second on 4th July, three weeks later, but before the new government had been formed – identified a number of interesting developments, during what was an unprecedented four weeks in Irish politics.

The first evidence, which indicated that Fianna Fáil would be unlikely to meet its objective of an overall majority, came in the poll figures of 9th June, and showed the party down a further three points to 47 per cent, relative to the poll ten days earlier. During the 1987 election campaign, the party dropped eight points relative to its pre-campaign figure and now, with a week to go, it was already down seven points on the comparable pre-campaign level. Fine Gael support was stable at 28 per cent, three points above pre-campaign figures, Labour was hovering between 8 per cent and 9 per cent, and the Progressive Democrats and Workers' Party were each on 6 per cent. With Others likely to attract at least 6 per cent, the omens were not looking good for a Fianna Fáil majority. The MRBI commentary also made the point that, with fewer candidates nominated relative to 1987 (372 *vis-à-vis* 468), Fianna Fáil did not have the same mathematical capability of maximising its ratio of seats to votes as it had in the previous election.

> *Because of having fewer candidates ranged against them, the ratio of seats to first preference votes for Fianna Fáil is very likely to be below that of the last election and a realistic projection from a first preference base of 47 per cent would be of the order of 49 per cent of seats.*

The Health Issue

Of further significance was the fact that health cuts were *now* positioned as the primary issue at 86 per cent. Following the publication of the first campaign poll ten days earlier, when 83 per cent saw health cuts as very important (in second place to unemployment), the relevance of health as an election issue hit the media headlines. In a *Morning Ireland* programme on RTÉ radio, after I stated that the likely outcome would be another Fianna Fáil-led government (coalition was not yet in the Fianna Fáil vocabulary), the presenter put a final question to me that "*the main election issue will still be unemployment*". I disagreed, and said that health was now the crucial issue as it had emerged in the very recent past; that concern about it was very concentrated and intensive and, crucially, the government was being blamed for the problems in the health service.

During an RTÉ radio phone-in programme in the latter stages of the campaign, Haughey astonished many observers when he stated that he was unaware that health cuts had become a problem, but that he would now do something about it. When this situation is set against the expressed rationale for calling the election, i.e. the refusal of the government to allot £400,000 for haemophiliacs, one can only assume that the Fianna Fáil strategists seriously misread the situation on the health services in the lead up to the election and again during the campaign itself.

The Result

The fact that the opinion polls were both informative and accurate seemed to have escaped the attention of senior people in Fianna Fáil at the time; in particular those who continued to express public confidence in the party's ability to obtain an overall majority in the election. It is conceivable that the party's policy on health damaged its capacity to attract the necessary transfers from non-Fianna Fáil first preference voters, with the result that, in this election, the party obtained four seats fewer than in 1987. This outcome signalled the end of the prospect of a Fianna Fáil single-party government.

	1987		1989		Variation	
	Votes	Seats	Votes	Seats	Votes	Seats
	%	%	%	%	%	%
Fianna Fáil	44	81	44	77	–	–4
Fine Gael	27	51	29	55	+2	+4
Labour Party	6	12	9	15	+3	+3
Progressive Democrats	12	14	5	6	–7	–8
Workers' Party	4	4	5	7	+1	+3
Others	7	4	8	6	+1	+2

Table 7.5: Comparison of the results of the 1987 and 1989 general elections

Against this, however, the fact that the party again obtained 44 per cent of first preference votes – identical to the 1987 election figure – must be seen as a very creditable performance. In 1987, the party had two very relevant factors in its favour. Firstly, it was coming from opposition, the traditional launch pad for success and, secondly, the wide dispersion of candidates helped the party transfers. The variation in the volume of nominations between the two elections meant that, in 1987, the Fianna Fáil ratio of seats to first preference votes was 100:111, whereas in 1989 the comparable figures were 100:105. Since the two elections are inter-linked as part of the Haughey era, the respective figures make interesting reading (see *Table 7.5*).

Fine Gael would have been relatively happy with the outcome, an increase of four seats to 55, and 29 per cent of first preference votes. However, although the latter figure was up two points on 1987, it was below the party's performance for the previous three elections.

The Labour Party's performance since 1981 had been inconsistent, up and down, but remaining in single figures in each alternative election. This occasion, however, delivered one of the good results: its 9 per cent vote compared favourably with 6 per cent in 1987, and the 15 seats won represented an increase of three.

The big losers were the Progressive Democrats. Looking back, the first evidence of a downturn in support since the establishment of the party in December 1985, came in the MRBI figures in October 1988 when its position was 7 per cent. Its immediate pre-election poll figure was 6 per cent, and the election figure 5 per cent. This converted to six seats, down eight on 1987.

1989: POLITICAL IMPASSE

When the new Dáil met on 26th June 1989, it was obvious to most observers that, being seven short of a majority, Fianna Fáil would be unable to form another minority administration. Charles Haughey's nomination for Taoiseach was defeated by 86 votes to 78, and, following further defeats for the nominations of Alan Dukes and Dick Spring, a precedent had been established. For the first time the Dáil did not elect a Taoiseach immediately following a general election.

Mr Haughey addressed the Dáil briefly, referred to the impasse which had arisen and proposed an adjournment of a week to allow him time to consult further with the other leaders. This caused considerable surprise and concern among all opposition deputies, since it was widely understood that the Taoiseach had a constitutional obligation to resign. The relevant articles in the Constitution are:

28.10 *The Taoiseach shall resign from office upon his ceasing to retain the support of a majority in Dáil Éireann unless on his advice the President dissolves Dáil Éireann and on the reassembly of Dáil Éireann after the dissolution, the Taoiseach secures the support of a majority in Dáil Éireann.*

28.11.i *If the Taoiseach at any time resigns from office, the other members of the government shall be deemed also to have resigned from office, but the Taoiseach and the other members of the government shall continue to carry on their duties, until their successors shall have been appointed.*

When the constitutional position was put to the Taoiseach, initially by Dick Spring and then by the other party leaders, Haughey said that his legal advice was that he had up to a week before having to resign. *Article 28.10* does not support this: no time factor is mentioned and the implication in the phrase *"shall resign from office upon his ceasing to retain the support"*, etc. implies immediacy.

Having adjourned for two hours – again on a proposal by Dick Spring – to give Charles Haughey time to consider the position, the Taoiseach informed the Dáil of his intention to resign. He left for Áras an Uachtaráin with his letter of resignation, after telling the Dáil that he would not ask the president for a dissolution. On his return to the house as acting Taoiseach, in accordance with *Article 28.11.i*, Haughey proposed that the Dáil adjourn until 3rd July.

The situation that followed the three unsuccessful votes for Taoiseach was an untidy episode, as a Taoiseach had never before hesitated to resign having lost a Dáil vote. Two historic precedents had been created within a matter of minutes.

Fianna Fáil Abandons a 'Core Value'

Following the Dáil adjournment, the national media did not react kindly to the acting Taoiseach and accused him of erratic behaviour and of not coming to terms with the new realities. The party had lost four seats, but was acting as if nothing had changed. However, it very soon emerged that discussions had commenced between representatives of Fianna Fáil and the Progressive Democrats, and that the former had accepted the Progressive Democrats' "Framework for Dialogue" document, which stipulated no preconditions to talks. However, the discussions broke down almost as soon as they commenced, due to Fianna Fáil's refusal to consider Progressive Democrat participation in the cabinet.

When the Dáil met again on 3rd July, no agreement had been reached and the next session was fixed for three days later. *The Irish Times* immediately commissioned MRBI to conduct an opinion poll within that very limited timespan, to assess reaction to the situation that had arisen and to measure preferences between the main options. The primary message from the electorate – which was both timely and unambiguous – was that the relevant leaders should put their heads together to form a government and that the concept of another general election was unacceptable. The actual figures – 80 per cent preferring some new arrangement for government, 17 per cent another general election (primarily Fianna Fáil supporters) and just 3 per cent undecided – said it all. The poll supported the efforts of Alan Dukes and Des O'Malley to a greater extent than those of Charles Haughey and also indicated that, should another general election be called, Fine Gael and Labour would be likely to gain at the expense of Fianna Fáil.

Observers at the time commented that the results of the MRBI poll had motivated the relevant people to get on with the task of forming a government and, when the Dáil met again one day later, there was an air of optimism for the first time. The talks with the Progressive Democrats were reported to be making progress and the Dáil was adjourned again to allow the two parties further time.

When the Dáil finally met on the 12th July, Charles Haughey and Des O'Malley had agreed on a formula for a coalition government that provided for two cabinet posts and one minister for state post for the Progressive Democrats. Haughey was elected Taoiseach by 84 votes to 79: comprising Fianna Fáil 77, Progressive Democrats 6 and Tom Foxe (Ind). He was opposed by Fine Gael 55, Labour 15, Workers' Party 7 and by Jim Kemmy (DSP) and Tony Gregory (Ind). The composition of the new cabinet is given in *Table 7.6*.

Although the new cabinet represented a change in eight of the 15 portfolios, changes in personnel, compared with the out-going cabinet, amounted to just three. Des O'Malley and Bobby Molloy were given appointments at the expense of Brendan Daly and Michael Noonan, and Seamus Brennan replaced Michael Smith. While being part of a coalition government was a new experience for Fianna Fáil, it was arguably a more experienced government than the one which had just left office. Des O'Malley had held cabinet appointments in three previous Fianna Fáil administrations and Bobby Molloy had also been a minister.

Taoiseach; The Gaeltacht	Charles Haughey	FF
Tánaiste; Defence	Brian Lenihan	FF
Foreign Affairs	Gerard Collings	FF
Finance	Albert Reynolds	FF
Education	Mary O'Rourke	FF
Agriculture and Food	Michael O'Kennedy	FF
Marine	John Wilson	FF
Labour	Bertie Ahern	FF
Energy	Bobby Molloy	PD
Social Welfare	Michael Woods	FF
Justice and Communications	Ray Burke	FF
Environment	Pádraig Flynn	FF
Industry and Commerce	Des O'Malley	PD
Tourism and Transport	Seamus Brennan	FF
Health	Rory O'Hanlon	FF

Table 7.6: Members of the 1989 Fianna Fáil/Progressive Democrat cabinet

After publicly rejecting the coalition concept for many years, Fianna Fáil had now to live with the reality of being a partner in a coalition government and, not surprisingly, the concept did not find favour at all levels within the party. The new deal caused unrest in many rural constituencies, but Haughey was now back in government, and the presidency of the European Union would begin on 1st January 1990.

Heads Together

The next *Irish Times*/MRBI opinion poll conducted on 20th November 1989 – five months into the new government – brought favourable news. Back in July, before the government was formed, a majority of electors had told the politicians to put their heads together and form a government in the interests of the country. By November, the government's rating was at an all-time high of 52 per cent, and the Taoiseach up by six points. Satisfaction was widespread and the people were finding the Fianna Fáil-led coalition government considerably more acceptable than the minority government of 1987.

Whether this was because or in spite of the difficult budgets of that 1987 administration was not clear, but the essential point was that the FF/PD coalition government was now perceived by a marginal majority of electors to be performing satisfactorily. When asked if they approved or disapproved of the FF/PD coalition some observers saw the result as contradictory, with 46 per cent approving, 43 per cent disapproving and 11 per cent having no opinion. The responses were very much along party lines; Fianna Fáil and Progressive Democrat supporters approving, and those for the opposition parties not. However, I do not agree that a contradiction necessarily applied. It is quite logical to be satisfied with the performance of a coalition government and, at the same time, to disapprove of its composition. It might well have reflected a discerning electorate. In party support terms, after adjusting for 14 per cent undecided, the respective party support figures in the November 1989 poll were: Fianna Fáil 51 per cent; Fine Gael 28 per cent; Labour 8 per cent; Progressive Democrats 3 per cent; and Others 10 per cent.

EVENTS IN 1990

In January 1990, while Charles Haughey was taking over the presidency of the European Union, Albert Reynolds was presenting his second budget to the Dáil. Prior to publication there was considerable media speculation as to its likely content, particularly since it was the first in which the Progressive Democrats would have had an influence.

The *Irish Times*/MRBI post budget opinion poll brought the impressive news that the budget had made a more favourable impact among the electorate than any budget over the previous eight years. The reduction of the standard tax rate to 30 per cent, the upper rate to 53 per cent and VAT to 33 per cent were the main positive factors. Within the conventional criteria, one in four saw it as being less harsh than expected – this was considerably more favourable than any budget over the previous five years. At the same time, a massive 62 per cent – an all-time high – classified it as being good for the country. Finally, the extent to which people saw their standard of living rising or falling as a result was also considerably more favourable than any previous budget. Influence from the Progressive Democrats, or not, Albert Reynolds, in the eyes of the electorate, had got the balance right again.

The same opinion poll brought a further boost for the government in that its satisfaction rating of 54 per cent represented a new high, and with the figure eight points above the combined core support of the two government parties, it was apparent that satisfaction had extended across party divides. Whatever about the alleged dislike for the coalition concept among Fianna Fáil supporters, the reality of coalition was now working very well – in the short term at least – and the Taoiseach's rating of 56 per cent represented Haughey's third-highest ever impact. Fianna Fáil was positioned on 50 per cent; Fine Gael on 29 per cent; Labour on 10 per cent; Progressive Democrats 4 per cent; and Others 7 per cent.

Speaking at a party function in mid-February, Albert Reynolds made the point that "*the budget was a Fianna Fáil budget*" and he went on to describe the coalition as "*a temporary little arrangement*". This attitude was in direct contrast to that of the electorate generally, where a majority was expressing considerable satisfaction with the coalition government.

European Matters

Meanwhile, in the early spring, Charles Haughey began his duties as president of the European Union. It was a critical time for the union, since it followed the collapse of the communist regimes in eastern Europe. Although he saw that situation as one of his priorities, Haughey's most newsworthy undertaking was a formal visit to President Bush in Washington when he used the well-established Irish relationship to create a new structure for future European–US meetings.

On 21st May, five months into Ireland's presidency, the next *Irish Times*/MRBI poll measured public reaction to the Taoiseach and government, in the particular context of the EU presidency. Not surprisingly, considering the high profile that the appointment carried, Haughey's personal rating was up six points to 61 per cent and that of the government continued on the plateau of the previous six months. Fianna Fáil was on 51 per cent, maintaining its impact over the three previous polls, Fine Gael 23 per cent and Labour 10 per cent. With the Progressive Democrats up three points to 7 per cent – the party's highest impact for the previous two years – it was apparent that the junior partner in government was being given some credit for the satisfactory performance.

All Change

Following the summer recess and the resumption of the Dáil, the next opinion poll was conducted on 6th October 1990 and, in the anti-climatic environment of the post-European presidency, most figures represented a downturn from the previous poll of five months earlier. The government was down five points, the Taoiseach two, Fine Gael was up one and Labour two. In essence, the situation was relatively stable, but it was soon to change dramatically.

After John Bruton's budget was defeated in the Dáil vote, back on 27th January 1982, and Garret FitzGerald had left for Áras an Uachtaráin to seek a dissolution, a number of telephone calls were made by senior Fianna Fáil politicians in opposition, reportedly asking President Hillery to exercise his option not to dissolve the Dáil, thereby allowing Charles Haughey to form a government without a general election. While some of these facts were known in media circles, including the point that the president did not speak to any of the callers that evening, the episode had not surfaced in the public arena since 1982.

In May 1990, Jim Duffy, a UCD student working on an MA thesis on the presidency, interviewed Brian Lenihan on the basis – as stated in Brian Lenihan's book *For the Record* – that it was for academic purposes only, and not for publication. In his biography – *Lenihan, his Life and Loyalties* – Jim Downey states:

> *In September 1990, Jim Duffy published a series of articles in* The Irish Times, *and in one of them he wrote that telephone calls were made by Haughey and, at his insistence, by Brian Lenihan and Sylvester Barrett, two close friends of Hillery. The president angrily rejected all such pressure and, having judged the issue, granted Dr FitzGerald a dissolution.*

Brian Lenihan denied making the call on RTÉ's *Questions and Answers* programme in October 1990 and, subsequently, went on RTÉ news to state that, irrespective of what he said on the tape, his *"mature recollection"* was that he did not telephone the president on that occasion.

At this stage, the situation was contradictory and conflicting and, as far as the Progressive Democrats and some Fianna Fáil ministers were concerned, it was also damaging the credibility of the government. Heavy pressure was put on Brian Lenihan by the Taoiseach to resign as Tánaiste and Minister for Defence, but he held strongly to the view that he had done nothing wrong in either of these capacities, and refused to go. Again in *For the Record,* Lenihan reproduces a letter of resignation that Haughey asked him to sign. That he, again, refused to resign is by no means as startling as a sentence in the letter that reads:

> *This decision is mine and mine alone. I have not been subject to pressure from any quarter.*

On 31st October, seven days prior to going before the people as a candidate in the presidential election, Brian Lenihan was formally requested to resign as a member of the government, pursuant to *Article 28.9.4°* of the Constitution. He again refused, and was dismissed.

In his book, Brian Lenihan does not deny that he said on tape that he phoned President Hillery. He was very ill at the time, was on medication, and stated that he does not remember what he said. We will never know how he really felt, but some clues are evident in the following extract from *For the Record*:

> *In dismissing me, he [Haughey] succumbed to the political blackmail of the Progressive Democrats. It was a failure of nerve and political leadership on his part. Moreover he, above all others, was aware of the circumstances and happenings at the front bench meeting on 27th January 1982. He chaired the meeting. He made the moves.*

However, the next *Irish Times*/MRBI opinion poll, conducted on 3rd November during the final stage of the presidential election campaign, showed that the crisis had not had a negative impact on Fianna Fáil – both Fianna Fáil and Fine Gael showed small gains to 52 per cent and 26 per cent respectively, while most other parties showed minor losses.

IRELAND'S FIRST FEMALE PRESIDENT

During the summer, the eyes and minds of the three main party leaders were directed towards the presidential election, due to be held in November. Mary Robinson, the nominee of the Labour Party, was already on the hustings and had met large numbers of the electorate well in advance of the other two candidates, Brian Lenihan of Fianna Fáil and Austin Currie of Fine Gael. (The specifics of the election are addressed in *Chapter 8*.)

In the presidential election on 7th November 1990, Brian Lenihan topped the poll with 44 per cent of the votes, followed by Mary Robinson on 39 per cent with Austin Currie on 17 per cent. After Currie's elimination, Mary Robinson defeated Brian Lenihan by 53 per cent to 47 per cent. While the result was a watershed in that it signalled the arrival of Ireland's first female president – who would go on to make a highly impressive impact both nationally and internationally – it created serious problems for the two main parties and their respective leaders.

For Charles Haughey, it represented defeat in a presidential election for the first time in the party's history, this being compounded by the fact that the party's candidate had been dismissed from the Office of Tánaiste and Minister for Defence, just days before the election. For the party it was a political shambles.

In Fine Gael, matters moved faster. A number of deputies had earlier expressed disappointment at the poor showing of the party's candidate in the campaign opinion polls, and a few days after the election, Fergus O'Brien, who represented the party in Dublin South-Central, faxed a motion of no confidence in the party leader to the chairman of the parliamentary party. The meeting of the parliamentary party was fixed for the following Wednesday, 13th November, and, having taken soundings, Alan Dukes decided to resign. The following week John Bruton, then deputy leader, was elected unopposed as the new leader.

Although Alan Dukes attracted considerable support and admiration across the party divide for the conditional support he afforded the 1987 minority Fianna Fáil government in his Tallaght Strategy, and although he was seen to have been acting mainly in the national interest at the time, a number of his Fine Gael colleagues made it clear that they did not agree with the approach. After John Bruton's election, Alan Dukes declined to sit on the front bench of the party, but two years later in

October 1992, he accepted John Bruton's offer to be spokesman on environment.

Three months after Brian Lenihan's dismissal, at the party's Ard-Fheis on 9th March, against the background of the presidential election defeat, Haughey predicted that he would lead Fianna Fáil into the next election.

CONTROVERSIES AND DROPPING STANDARDS IN 1991

The next *Irish Times*/MRBI opinion poll on 16th April, showed a three-point drop to 56 per cent in the Taoiseach's ratings, while John Bruton was on 42 per cent – up six points on Alan Dukes' most recent rating. Dick Spring (Lab) on 65 per cent was now in first position, with Des O'Malley on 52 per cent, four points below Haughey. In party support terms, Fine Gael, Labour and the Progressive Democrats were all stable on 23 per cent, 11 per cent and 6 per cent, respectively, while Fianna Fáil was down two points to 49 per cent. A June poll in the run up to the local elections, where Fianna Fáil fared badly, showed a further drop in support for the party.

The reasons for the downturn in the ratings for the government and Taoiseach, and in Fianna Fáil support, had been evident over the previous few weeks. On 13th May – a month before the June opinion poll – a *World in Action* programme on ITV made a number of allegations about the Goodman Group claiming, *inter alia*, tax evasion and selective and favourable treatment from the government on export credit insurance. This resulted in a series of questions in the Dáil from Dick Spring, Barry Desmond and Tomás Mac Giolla. Around the same time, the Greencore – formerly Siúicre Éireann – financial disclosures had also surfaced, and these, coupled with the convoluted purchase of the Carysfort site from the Sisters of Mercy, all contributed to a situation where Haughey and the government were very much on the defensive. The poor ratings were not surprising.

In light of the controversy about export credit insurance, the Oireachtas, on 31st May 1991, established the Beef Tribunal under Justice Liam Hamilton, to investigate practices in the beef industry, relating to the export insurance and related matters. The fallout, during the course of the tribunal, caused serious problems for one government, and the publication of its report in July 1994 led to the break-up of another.

Following the sedative of the summer recess, the next *Irish Times*/MRBI poll was conducted on 10th October, and published on the 15th, the day before the resumption of Dáil business. It brought alarming news for the government, the Taoiseach and Fianna Fáil. The impact of what were now widely referred to as the financial scandals, had spread to all corners of the country. The government rating was down a massive 15 points to 29 per cent. The Taoiseach's rating had disintegrated – a further drop of 19 points to 33 per cent, and Fianna Fáil support was down by a further four points to 41 per cent. Labour had gained four to 15 per cent and Fine Gael was up one to 26 per cent.

The government's rating was the lowest of any over the previous ten years. Then the really bad news – three in every four electors agreed that there had been a drop in standards in Irish politics, and at least four in every five of these held the view that Haughey and his government were responsible for it.

It was clear that nearly 60 per cent of the electorate blamed Charles Haughey and his government for the drop in standards. Finally, the compelling corollary: a highly significant 63 per cent – two in every three electors – considered that Haughey should now resign from the leadership of Fianna Fáil, this being favoured by 40 per cent of Fianna Fáil supporters.

However, the more informative news from the opinion poll was that, in spite of all that had arisen, the electorate at large – seven in every ten – did not want a general election. For those with reasonable memories, Haughey's misreading of the situation in 1989, when he called a general election, came sharply into focus. A change of leader in Fianna Fáil, Yes! But a change of government, No! In retrospect, this was one of the most compelling research projects conducted by MRBI for *The Irish Times*. Within two weeks, media reports of anti-Haughey Fianna Fáil members openly campaigning for his removal and replacement by Albert Reynolds appeared.

The final *Irish Times*/MRBI opinion poll of 1991, on 11th December, wrapped up an *annus horribilis* for Fianna Fáil, and all the provisions of the disastrous October poll were confirmed. The government's and Taoiseach's ratings, and Fianna Fáil support, were each down by a further point to 28 per cent, 32 per cent and 40 per cent respectively, two of these being all-time low levels, and the third – Fianna Fáil support – equalling a previous all-time low. Fine Gael and Labour remained stable at 26 per cent and 15 per cent, respectively, and the

Progressive Democrats were up one to 8 per cent. Others, on 11 per cent, included the then Workers' Party 4 per cent; the Greens 3 per cent; and Independents 4 per cent. Dick Spring on 62 per cent continued to lead the field on satisfaction ratings; followed by Des O'Malley on 53 per cent; Proinsias de Rossa on 42 per cent; John Bruton a 37 per cent; and Charles Haughey a 32 per cent.

A few weeks earlier when the pressure was on Haughey to resign, he stated that he himself would decide when to go, and this poll included a question on when that should be. The outcome was:

- Immediately   46%
- After the 1992 budget   9%
- Before the next general election   18%
- When he himself decides   27%

Among the general electorate, the favourite to replace him was Bertie Ahern (24 per cent) followed by Albert Reynolds (15 per cent) and Brian Lenihan (13 per cent). Among Fianna Fáil supporters the figures were Bertie Ahern (23 per cent), Brian Lenihan (19 per cent), Mary O'Rourke (15 per cent) and Albert Reynolds (10 per cent). All indications from the opinion poll were that the curtain was about to come down, and this happened early in 1992.

A CHANGE OF LEADERSHIP IN FIANNA FÁIL

To set the final scene, it is necessary to go back to 1982 when Sean Doherty was Minister for Justice under Charles Haughey. In January 1983, just a month after the new FG/Lab coalition government had taken office, Michael Noonan, the new Minister for Justice, announced that the previous minister, Sean Doherty, had had the telephones of two journalists – Geraldine Kennedy and Bruce Arnold – tapped. Shortly afterwards, Mr Doherty issued a statement saying that he had ordered the tapping because of his concern for the security of the country, and then, in answer to a question, added that Charles Haughey was not aware of what had been done. Later, on RTÉ, Sean Doherty confirmed that Haughey did not know the phones had been tapped.

However, in January 1992, again on an RTÉ programme, Sean

Doherty changed his story and gave the impression that others knew of the phone tapping. A short time later, in late January, at a specially convened press conference, he told the assembled journalists that he actually gave the transcripts of the taped phone calls to Haughey in 1982, and that the Taoiseach had known all along about what had happened. Although Haughey denied it, his denial did not satisfy the Progressive Democrats. They demanded Haughey's head and got it. On 6th February 1992, Charles Haughey resigned and, on 11th February, Albert Reynolds was elected as Taoiseach and the new leader of Fianna Fáil.

Taking an overview of Charles Haughey's performance as Taoiseach and leader of Fianna Fáil, in my opinion, the best decision made in the interests of the country, the party and himself was his appointment of Ray MacSharry as Minister for Finance following the general election of 1987. MacSharry's unwavering determination and commitment to put in place measures that would contribute towards the eventual rectification of the country's financial problems, was crucial. Rectification would, of course, not have been possible without the unprecedented, albeit conditional, support of Alan Dukes.

The negative side of the coin is considerably less clear-cut, and a number of situations vie for the red card. The debacle of the Dublin West by-election following Dick Burke's acceptance of Haughey's Brussels job in 1982 is one, and another more cogent example is starkly recalled by Jim Downey in *Lenihan, his Life and Loyalties*:

> *Notwithstanding the findings of the McCracken Tribunal, and notwithstanding all the allegations, true or false, launched against him throughout his long career, he [Haughey] never did anything worse in his life than to betray Lenihan.*

I look beyond these instances. Although, in the longer term, it ironically turned out to be in the national interest, in my opinion, the worst decision Haughey ever made relative to his own and his party's interest was the calling of the 1989 general election.

For the party, it meant the end of a very coherent and successful minority government and, although a great deal more is known today about his mindset in 1989 than was the case at the time, he took an enormous risk in shooting for a Dáil majority. Unfortunately for Haughey and his party, the only option – apart from opposition, which we now know was definitely not on his agenda – was to negotiate a partnership with his erstwhile colleagues in the Progressive Democrats, and he must have realised that whenever controversy arose, he would be under severe pressure to deliver to their wishes, irrespective of his personal orientation.

The risk in calling an election was much greater than continuing in the successful minority government for another year or so, when the statutory time limitation would have been on the horizon, and the decision would no longer have been seen as opportunist. If the 1987 situation had continued, Charles Haughey would not have been under the same pressure when the Brian Lenihan problem surfaced in late 1990, and there might conceivably have been a less dramatic and unpleasant solution. Both senior and grassroot party members were unhappy with coalition from the outset and, in time, the consequences of his initial decision brought him under pressure, not only from his partners, but also from certain influential interests in his own party. It was unlikely that Fine Gael would have risked precipitating an election by pulling the plug while Haughey was seen to be acting in the national interest; the possibility of their losing votes in the ensuing election would have been a deterrent. While much of this may be hypothetical, it is set out merely to illustrate that all aspects of the situation were not considered when the 1989 election was called. The concept of a Dáil majority was a naïve and unrealistic one.

The circumstances that flowed from Haughey's decision to call the 1989 election aggravated a series of personal and political difficulties when they arose, and sowed the seeds of his eventual resignation.

Finally, and ironically, the formation of the FF/PD coalition government fitted into what has now become the European democratic norm. Fortunately, this turned out to be very much in the country's interest. The financial situation was still being addressed and the high ratings continued until the crisis of June 1991. From then on, ratings plummeted and Haughey began his slow walk off the playing field and, reluctantly, started to remove his captain's armband.

However, having regard to the revelations that have since emerged from the McCracken, Moriarty and Flood tribunals, the crucial point is that, had the desired objective of a Dáil majority materialised for Haughey's Fianna Fáil, it would have been potentially catastrophic for the political establishment and, by extension, for the country.

CHAPTER 8

The Presidential Election: A Watershed (1990)

BACKGROUND TO 1990

When Erskine Childers died suddenly on 17th November 1974, he was the first president to die in office. He was replaced by Cearbhall Ó Dálaigh, whose unopposed inauguration on 19th December was the first since Dr Douglas Hyde in 1938.

Cearbhall Ó Dálaigh was a barrister and had served, with distinction, as Attorney-General, Chief Justice, President of the Supreme Court and, later, as a judge of the Court of Justice of the European Community. However, his tenure as president of Ireland was short lived. He resigned on 22nd October 1976, following an irreverent comment made by the then Minister for Defence, Paddy Donegan, regarding Ó Dálaigh's referral of the Criminal Law Bill to the Supreme Court to determine its constitutionality.

Donegan's remark was made when addressing members of the Defence Forces in Columb Barracks, Mullingar. There was only one journalist present and he quoted the words used as *"thundering disgrace"* – others present described it in more *lingua militaire* terms, and Garret FitzGerald in his autobiography acknowledges – with some diffidence – that "'*thundering disgrace' may have been a euphemism for the words actually spoken*". In any event, *Article 134* of the Constitution states that the supreme command of the Defence Forces is vested in the president, and it follows that any public criticism of our first citizen, in the presence of troops, would have serious repercussions.

Following the resignation of Ó Dálaigh, Dr Patrick Hillery was nominated by Fianna Fáil for the presidency and was the first nominee of a political party to be appointed unopposed. Hillery had had a distinguished political career, having served as a minister in four government departments – Education, Industry and Commerce, Labour, and Foreign Affairs – and finally as Ireland's first commissioner in the then EEC. He was inaugurated on 3rd December 1976, served his seven-year term, and was re-appointed, again unopposed, in 1983. Following his statutory retirement on 2nd December 1990, the scene was set for the first contested presidential election since 1973.

THE SITUATION IN 1990

In the early spring of 1990, there were no signs that the scheduled presidential election would be the most eventful in the history of the State. Candidates nominated by Fianna Fáil had won the four elections to date, and many saw this as the likely outcome again. On all other occasions, a candidate had been agreed, and some party leaders may have been looking to this expense-saving device as the way to proceed.

However, Dick Spring and his close advisors had other ideas, and the Labour Party's initial approach to Mary Robinson in February, lit the fuse that later injected a new buzz into the presidential election, and also, in the opinion of many, into the presidency itself.

Mary Robinson was a barrister and Reid Professor of Constitutional and Criminal Law, and lectured on European law at Trinity College Dublin. She had also been a senator, and member of the Labour Party, from which she resigned in 1985, having disagreed with aspects of the Anglo–Irish Agreement. She was the first woman and, at the time, the youngest person to be nominated for president. In short, she had the credentials to bring a new impetus and image to the appointment.

News of the proposed nomination first appeared in early April and, on 26th April, it was confirmed by the Labour Party, supported by the Workers' Party. The campaign was formally launched four days later. While the new candidate had got away to a flying start, one of the surprising features was that she was running on a non-party basis. In strategic terms, it turned out to have a crucial influence on the outcome, as it enabled her to attract very considerable cross-party support. The increasing inroads that she made among supporters of all parties, particularly those of Fine Gael, as the campaign developed are shown in *Tables 8.7* and *8.8* (see *pages 123* and *124*), while her capture of 77 per cent of Austin Currie's transfers on the second count speaks for itself.

Mary Robinson sowed the seeds of her success during the summer months when she, her husband and her chosen advisors travelled the length and breadth of the country meeting people and promoting her candidacy.

MRBI Opinion Polls

At this stage, Mary Robinson's potential to perform very well had not been realised and opinion polls on the subject had not yet appeared. Later, during the three months prior to the election on 7th November, MRBI conducted five national opinion polls, three for Fine Gael and two, including the final campaign poll, for *The Irish Times*.

Emily O'Reilly, in her book *Candidate, the Truth Behind the Presidency* quotes extensively from the MRBI/Fine Gael research, which positions the material in the public arena, along with *The Irish Times* polls.

When Alan Dukes approached MRBI in June 1990 and set out his requirement in a very comprehensive brief, our immediate impression was that he had given considerable thought to the situation, and that he was being very assiduous in his quest for the informational framework that he saw as necessary. He sought to have every angle covered at that early stage. The requirement included:

- electorate perception of the personal characteristics of a good president;
- the rated importance of a number of factors relating to the presidency; and
- a measure of the extent to which each of six potential candidates – including three from Fine Gael – were associated with each of these factors.

As it happened, the six people who were assessed included the three who later contested the election. The brief also included a measure of positive and negative perceptions relating to the six potential candidates, which meant that the Fine Gael leader had access to very relevant and crucial information, prior to planning the election campaign.

As time moved on, we noted that there had been little evidence of the implementation of the findings, or on how the campaign plan was developing, and the reasons for the delay became apparent when Alan Dukes telephoned some time in mid-September to say that the party's candidate would be Austin Currie. I was very surprised because Currie had not emerged well on the research – he was far from being the Fine Gael front runner.

A short time later, Dukes commissioned the second opinion poll on behalf of his party. Its objectives were:

- to measure relative support for each of the three candidates – Austin Currie, Brian Lenihan and Mary Robinson – who had been nominated at that stage;

- to measure current transfer patterns; and

- to rate the importance of a number of factors relating to the presidency and the association of each candidate with these factors.

The survey was conducted on 29th September. Brian Lenihan emerged in a very strong position and the indications at the time were that his first preference vote could be very close to the quota, with Mary Robinson also well positioned in second place. The figures are given in *Table 8.1*.

Candidate	Core	Net
	%	%
Brian Lenihan	42	49
Mary Robinson	29	33
Austin Currie	15	18
Undecided	14	excludes undecided

Table 8.1: Result of the September MRBI opinion poll for Fine Gael

The opinion poll also indicated that, with less than six weeks remaining, the transfer patterns from the Fine Gael candidate were running three to two in favour of Mary Robinson.

Stage Two of the Campaign

On 4th October, Mrs Robinson gave an interview to *Hot Press* magazine, aspects of which also appeared in the national newspapers. The interview was wide ranging and covered literally every controversial subject on the public agenda. Her advisors were very concerned that the Robinson campaign might be damaged as a result of the interview but, on 6th October, the next MRBI opinion poll for *The Irish Times* showed that her support level had dropped by a mere point to 32 per cent. The figures are given in *Table 8.2.*

Candidate	Core	Net
	%	%
Brian Lenihan	42	49
Mary Robinson	27	32
Austin Currie	17	19
Undecided	14	excludes undecided

Table 8.2: Result of the October Irish Times/*MRBI opinion poll*

This poll showed Brian Lenihan holding his strong position at 49 per cent, with Austin Currie improving marginally and Fine Gael transfers still holding three to two in favour of Robinson.

Later in October, the now well-documented RTÉ *Question and Answers* programme, with Brian Lenihan and Garret FitzGerald, as two of the panellists, went on air and in the next opinion poll on 22nd October conducted for Fine Gael, Brian Lenihan had dropped a significant five points. Mary Robinson was up four and Austin Currie up one. The figures are given in *Table 8.3.*

This opinion poll also showed a further move in transfer potential, in favour of Mary Robinson, from the three to two ratio in the previous poll to three to one. If this trend was to continue, it would give Robinson a strong chance of winning on the second count, providing Brian Lenihan's first preferences did not swing back to the earlier level of 49 per cent.

Candidate	Core	Net	Difference
	%	%	
Brian Lenihan	39	44	−5
Mary Robinson	31	36	+4
Austin Currie	17	20	+1
Undecided	13	excludes undecided	

Table 8.3: Result of the second MRBI opinion poll for Fine Gael (October)

The circumstances of Brian Lenihan's dismissal, after refusing to resign as Tánaiste and Minister for Defence (see *Chapter 7*), were such that he was likely to attract a level of sympathy and, according to the *Irish Times*/MRBI opinion poll of 3rd November, this materialised among Fianna Fáil supporters where his support increased from 29 per cent to 32 per cent. However, the trend was offset by a downturn among Fine Gael and Labour voters from 5 per cent to 2 per cent (see *Table 8.7* on *page 123*). The overall figures in this final campaign poll are given in *Table 8.4*.

Candidate	Core	Net	Difference
	%	%	
Brian Lenihan	39	43	−1
Mary Robinson	39	43	+7
Austin Currie	13	14	−6
Undecided	9	excludes undecided	

Table 8.4: Result of the final Irish Times/MRBI opinion poll

Finally, a further significant finding was that Currie's second preferences had moved substantially in favour of Robinson and were now four to one in her favour. The MRBI commentary in *The Irish Times* two days before the election stated that:

> *It is now almost certain that no candidate will be elected on the first count, and that the distribution of Austin Currie's second preference votes will decide the outcome. As of now,*

Mary Robinson would be elected on Currie's transfers and it would take a swing back to a level of 47 per cent or better for Brian Lenihan to be in contention, based on the 20 per cent of the Currie transfers which the poll indicates.

The result of the election is given in *Table 8.5*.

First Count: First Preferences	
Candidate	%
Brian Lenihan	44
Mary Robinson	39
Austin Currie	17

Second Count: Austin Currie eliminated	
Candidate	%
Brian Lenihan	47
Mary Robinson	53

Table 8.5: Result of the 1990 presidential election

Analysis of the 1990 Presidential Election Result

Relative to the final opinion poll figures, the slight swing back to Brian Lenihan in first preference votes continued until election day, but it did not reach the level that was necessary to grant him victory.

The fact that Mary Robinson's actual first preference vote was below the level indicated in the final poll is probably due to the extent of the turnout on election day. This was one of the first indications of the difficulty being experienced nowadays on all polls, where a significant number of respondents, when interviewed, opt for a front runner or best-known candidate or party, but their support is quite weak and, ultimately, many of these people do not turn out to vote.

The campaign opinion poll figures relative to the final first preference results are given in *Table 8.6*.

121

Candidate	Dates of Polls				Election Day
	29 Sept	6 Oct	22 Oct	3 Nov	7 Nov
	%	%	%	%	%
Lenihan	49	49	44	43	44
Robinson	33	32	36	43	39
Currie	18	19	20	14	17

Table 8.6: Results of MRBI opinion polls taken during the 1990 presidential election campaign

THE NON-PARTY FACTOR

Mary Robinson's choice to be described as a 'non-party' candidate was one of the factors that had a crucial influence on her success since, as already commented, it enabled her to attract votes from supporters of all parties and none. Looking at *Table 8.8* (see *page 124*), the first campaign poll on 29th September showed that, at that stage, 79 per cent of her first preference support was coming from supporters of parties other than Labour. The comparable figures for Brian Lenihan and Austin Currie were 24 per cent (non-FF) and 53 per cent (non-FG), respectively. In other words, almost all of Lenihan's support was coming from Fianna Fáil and half of Currie's from Fine Gael. The level of non-Labour support for Robinson actually increased as the campaign developed, and was at its maximum in the poll of 22nd October. At that stage, 87 per cent of Robinson's first preference support was from non-Labour supporters. It stabilised somewhat after that and in the final campaign poll, non-Labour accounted for 82 per cent of her support. There is, therefore, a strong argument that, had she rejoined the Labour Party and been nominated as a Labour Party candidate, Robinson would not have attracted such massive non-Labour support, and in all probability Brian Lenihan would have won.

Survey Date	Candidate	FIRST PREF %	FF	FG	Lab	PD	Other	Un-decided
29 Sep 1990	B Lenihan	42	31	5	1	–	1	4
	M Robinson	29	8	5	6	–	3	7
	A Currie	15	3	7	2	–	1	2
	Undecided	14	1	3	–	1	1	8
	Totals	100	43	20	9	1	6	21
6 Oct 1990	B Lenihan	42	30	4	2	1	2	3
	M Robinson	27	6	6	5	2	4	4
	A Currie	17	2	9	2	1	2	1
	Undecided	14	4	1	1	–	1	7
	Totals	100	42	20	10	4	9	15
22 Oct 1990	B Lenihan	39	29	3	2	–	2	3
	M Robinson	31	9	9	4	1	4	4
	A Currie	17	3	10	1	–	1	2
	Undecided	13	4	–	–	2	1	6
	Totals	100	45	22	7	3	8	15
3 Nov 1990	B Lenihan	39	32	1	1	1	–	4
	M Robinson	39	8	11	7	3	4	6
	A Currie	13	2	9	–	–	–	2
	Undecided	9	2	1	1	–	2	3
	Totals	100	44	22	9	4	6	15

Base: All electors   *Source: MRBI*

Table 8.7: Presidential election 1990: cross-party support for candidates during the campaign

Table 8.7 shows the picture from a different perspective – that of the *all-elector* base. In the opinion poll of 29th September, Mary Robinson had 29 per cent basic support against Brian Lenihan's 42 per cent and

Austin Currie's 15 per cent. In Robinson's case, 23 per cent was coming from parties other than her nominating party, with the corresponding figure for Lenihan and Currie 11 per cent and 8 per cent, respectively. After increasing in the two intermediate opinion polls, the final poll situation on 3rd November showed Robinson on 39 per cent, of which 32 per cent came from non-Labour supporters. In the cases of Lenihan and Currie, at that late stage, the corresponding non-nominating party support figures were 7 per cent and 4 per cent, respectively.

Survey Date	Candidate	FIRST PREF %	FF	FG	Lab	PD	Other	Un-decided
					← %			
29 Sep 1990	B Lenihan	42:100	76	12	2	–	2	8
	M Robinson	29:100	28	17	21	–	10	24
	A Currie	15:100	20	47	13	–	7	13
6 Oct 1990	B Lenihan	42:100	71	10	5	2	5	7
	M Robinson	27:100	22	22	19	9	15	15
	A Currie	17:100	12	53	12	6	12	6
22 Oct 1990	B Lenihan	39:100	74	8	5	–	5	8
	M Robinson	31:100	29	29	13	3	13	13
	A Currie	17:100	18	59	6	–	6	12
3 Nov 1990	B Lenihan	39:100	82	3	3	3	–	9
	M Robinson	39:100	21	28	18	8	10	15
	A Currie	13:100	15	69	–	–	–	16

* Party support based on stated voting behaviour in the 1989 general election

Base: Each candidate support level   *Source: MRBI*

Table 8.8: Presidential election 1990: cross-party support for candidates during the campaign

IMPACT OF THE ELECTION RESULT

In a number of respects, the presidential election of 1990 was a watershed. Firstly, there was the capacity of Mary Robinson to attract massive support from all parties – the final opinion poll disclosure that more than eight in every ten of her supporters were non-Labour can only be described as comprehensive. Other criteria are no less impressive.

She was the first woman to be nominated and elected president. She injected a laudable buzz into the campaign from the early stages, when she, her husband and her retinue first moved into the highways and byways three months before either Fianna Fáil or Fine Gael had put their campaign plans together. She also put across a new message that was succinctly epitomised in an *Irish Times* editorial after the election:

> *Electing Lenihan would be to elect a man enmeshed in a set of attitudes and values from which the State must escape. The Robinson choice would be committing Ireland to a vision of the country as one which can be open, tolerant, pluralist and generous.*

For Fianna Fáil and Charles Haughey, it was also a comprehensive watershed because the party had not lost a presidential election on any of the previous four occasions – in 1945, 1959, 1966 and 1973. Considering the Fine Gael reaction to the result, Haughey must be considered lucky to have lasted a further 15 months as leader, only to make his exit for an entirely unrelated reason.

Finally, a comprehensive watershed would hardly be an adequate description of what happened to Alan Dukes. Although Fine Gael candidates had been defeated in the four previous presidential elections, on no occasion was the party leader given the red card as Alan Dukes was. I have no knowledge of what goes on at parliamentary party meetings, and I have no direct knowledge as to whether or not Dukes was previously given a yellow card; what I do know from the MRBI relationship with him, is that his approach was committed, clear, professional and impressive, and that he did everything he possibly could in his party's interest to win the election. The people who had the potential to perform well did not wish to run, while those who apparently agreed to run did not have the capacity to win. This may be an oversimplification, but it represents the situation.

After a very successful tenure, Mary Robinson resigned from the presidency on 12th September 1997, three months before the completion of her first term, to take up the post of United Nations Commissioner for Human Rights, which she had been offered three months earlier.

CHAPTER 9

Four Referenda and an Election (1992–1994)

The early spring of 1992 provided a number of indications that the coming year would be a busy one in political research. The Maastricht Treaty was signed on 7th February; Charles Haughey resigned as Taoiseach on the 10th, and was succeeded by Albert Reynolds, who appointed a cabinet very much in line with his own political vision (see *Table 9.1*). The Beef Tribunal was ongoing and the *X-Case* – in which a pregnant teenager, the victim of rape, was refused permission to leave the country to have an abortion – had just surfaced. Prior to this, Fianna Fáil had experienced a consistent decline in support, but the mid-February changes brought what appeared to be a new impetus for the main government party.

Political and media comment at the time indicated a keen interest in the outcome of the next opinion poll and, after a short delay to give the electorate time to reflect, the first poll of the year for *The Irish Times* was undertaken on the 24th and 25th February. The information covered was rather more extensive than usual and included: government and party leader ratings; reaction to the composition of the new cabinet; perception of government priorities; the abortion issue; and the possibility of another referendum.

The findings gave considerable satisfaction to Fianna Fáil showing a significant upsurge in support from the December 1991 poll. This had positioned Fianna Fáil at 40 per cent net, and the government satisfaction rating at 28 per cent was the lowest for any Fianna Fáil-led government for the previous ten years.

127

Taoiseach	Albert Reynolds	FF
Tánaiste; Defence	John Wilson	FF
Finance	Bertie Ahern	FF
Foreign Affairs	David Andrews	FF
Education	Seamus Brennan	FF
Agriculture and Food	Joe Walsh	FF
Industry and Commerce	Des O'Malley	PD
Labour	Brian Cowan	FF
Tourism, Trade and Commerce	Máire Geoghegan-Quinn	FF
Marine	Michael Woods	FF
Environment	Michael Smith	FF
Energy	Bobby Molloy	PD
Health	John O'Connell	FF
Justice	Pádraig Flynn	FF
Social Welfare	Charlie McCreevy	FF

Table 9.1: Members of the 1992 Fianna Fáil/Progressive Democrat cabinet

Now, immediately following Mr Reynolds' appointment as Taoiseach, Fianna Fáil support was up 13 points to 53 per cent, government satisfaction had also increased by 17 points to 45 per cent, and Reynolds' personal rating of 60 per cent was supported by majorities in all parties. Furthermore, the new cabinet also received a notable seal of approval. The MRBI interpretation of the findings reported in *The Irish Times* on 28th February, stated that:

> ...there is no denying that the new figures are highly satisfying and comforting for Fianna Fáil, the temptation to rejoice – or in opposition terms to agonise – on the basis of a 'one-line' interpretation, should be resisted.
>
> A more in-depth and logical interpretation of the data indicates a number of scenarios:
> - that the Taoiseach and his new cabinet have been given a clear vote of confidence by the electorate;

- *that this, after just two weeks in office, encapsulates a high level of expectation; and*

- *that the current level of 53 per cent support does not necessarily reflect a Fianna Fáil majority in the next general election, as 'mid-term' figures are no more than estimates of the current mood of the electorate.*

The survey also set out the challenges to the government by presenting the priorities perceived by the electorate. Significantly, while unemployment was positioned ahead of all others, the next in line were: making business more enterprising; more open government; and restoring confidence in politics.

This was 1992, long before the recent tribunals were established, and the result reflected the people's reaction to the ongoing Beef Tribunal. The opinion poll had other interesting messages for Albert Reynolds and his new government, particularly on abortion. In the light of the controversy surrounding the *X-Case* and the threat of suicide by the young girl at its centre, it was not surprising that two-thirds wanted the constitutional provision on abortion either removed or amended, and, among those aged under 34, the figure rose to three in every four. Among Progressive Democrat supporters (who were in government with Fianna Fáil), the figure was also higher than average at almost 80 per cent.

The Maastricht Treaty Referendum

The next opinion poll for *The Irish Times* was conducted on Tuesday 5th and Wednesday 6th May 1992, just two-and-a-half months after the last poll, and three months following the formation of the new Reynolds administration. The main messages were that the electorate continued to be well satisfied with both the government and Fianna Fáil, while the Progressive Democrats were also benefiting, with their support increasing from 4 per cent to 9 per cent. The honeymoon appeared to be ongoing and I again drew attention to the fact that *"whether or not these levels of support would remain firm up to the next general election would depend on a number of factors, not least important being the perceived circumstances in which the election is declared"* – comments that turned out to be very relevant six months later.

The May survey was also the first occasion on which electors were asked by MRBI how they intended to vote in the referendum on the Maastricht Treaty (which was signed by the EU Member States on 7th February 1992). At that stage, whilst almost a third were undecided, the indications were that it would be carried comfortably.

By the time the next opinion poll was taken on 8th June, the referendum on the Maastricht Treaty had come into focus and, at this juncture, ten days before the referendum, support for ratification had tightened considerably. With a third still undecided, the figures were: in favour 67 per cent; against 33 per cent. (This compared with an 80%:20% situation a month earlier.)

The final pre-Maastricht referendum opinion poll (and the fourth since the new Reynolds government was formed) took place on Monday 15th June, three days before the referendum. Not surprisingly, the undecideds had dropped significantly and the net figures on voting intentions were: in favour 64 per cent; against 36 per cent.

This represented a slight drop, by four points, amongst those in favour from the 67 per cent of a week earlier. Based on the trends over this and the two previous polls, it was realistic to be confident that Maastricht would succeed and the general conclusion was that "*it would be carried in the ratio 2:1*". The actual result of the referendum was: in favour 69 per cent; against 31 per cent.

Although government ratings and Fianna Fáil support remained solid throughout the referendum campaign, a marginal majority of electors thought the government had handled the campaign badly. After ratification, the houses of the Oireachtas adjourned for the summer recess.

Crucial Autumn Opinion Poll

The next opinion poll for *The Irish Times* was not taken until Thursday 24th and Friday 25th September 1992. This was also the first poll conducted after Des O'Malley gave his startling evidence to the Beef Tribunal back in late June, where he criticised the manner in which some of his predecessors – as ministers for industry and commerce – had handled the Export Credit Insurance Scheme. This poll was perhaps the most extensive of the year, in informational terms, and provided many messages for the government. Whether or not some of these messages were taken into account is not apparent. However, bearing in mind what was to transpire on 25th November, it would appear that the views of the electorate were, in many respects, ignored.

Since its formation seven months earlier, the coalition government of Fianna Fáil and the Progressive Democrats under Albert Reynolds had maintained high satisfaction ratings, and the Fianna Fáil party had averaged 53 per cent support over the four *Irish Times*/MRBI opinion polls during the period. In the background, the Beef Tribunal continued and provided a political smoking gun for the government. Not for the first time, the media were indicating that the time could be at hand for Fianna Fáil to dissolve the coalition and go for the elusive overall majority and single-party government. Against this background, one of the new questions introduced in the September opinion poll was:

> *Some politicians and commentators are talking about a general election. The present coalition was three years in office in July. In your opinion, is it time for a general election or not?*

Seventy-five per cent did not agree that the time was right to hold an election – a massive 83 per cent of Fianna Fáil supporters did not want one. Other questions related to:

- government satisfaction ratings;
- leaders' satisfaction ratings;
- current party support;
- reaction to the holding of the Beef Tribunal;
- reaction to the issue of cabinet confidentiality;
- voting intentions on the right to travel to have an abortion;
- voting intentions on the right to information on abortion;
- reaction to having a constitutional ban on abortion;
- reaction to the Maastricht Treaty – in retrospect; and
- reaction to the retention of *Articles 2* and *3* in the Constitution.

Perhaps not surprisingly, against the background of the Beef Tribunal, the survey results gave the first indication of a downturn in support for the government. Mr Reynolds' personal rating was down three points, which, although not significant if taken in isolation, was consistent with other figures in the poll. The government rating was down eight points and Fianna Fáil had dropped four to 49 per cent.

Dick Spring, the Labour Party leader in opposition, was the highest rated of the five party leaders at 62 per cent. There was mixed reaction to the establishment of the Beef Tribunal, Maastricht got the all clear in retrospect, and a majority felt that cabinet discussions were unduly secretive. There were many messages for the government, the most important of which was that the electorate did not want a general election.

Considerable tension was evident between the two parties in government after the return from the summer recess. After Des O'Malley, Minister for Industry and Commerce, had given his evidence to the Beef Tribunal on 30th June, the Taoiseach, Albert Reynolds, stated that he would respond at an appropriate time. This materialised on 28th October when Reynolds described O'Malley's evidence about him as *"reckless and dishonest"*. The Progressive Democrats were outraged, and called on the Taoiseach to withdraw the allegation or dismiss O'Malley. Reynolds repeated the charge and the Progressive Democrats threatened to withdraw from government. When they did so, on 4th November, and a government confidence motion was defeated in the Dáil, a general election became inevitable and was fixed for 25th November 1992 – 21 days later.

An *Irish Times*/MRBI opinion poll, the first in the formal campaign, was undertaken on Monday 9th November, 16 days before polling day. Since many people in the September poll did not agree that an election was necessary, the crucial relevance of the circumstances in which an election is called came clearly into focus and I recalled, whilst awaiting the survey results, the number of occasions on which politicians had been warned against over-reacting to high mid-term figures. When I saw the new data I was not surprised. Not only was the political honeymoon well and truly over, but all indications pointed to the fact that Fianna Fáil would have a real fight on its hands.

Government satisfaction ratings and Fianna Fáil support had each plummeted nine points over the previous six weeks; Mr Reynolds' personal rating as Taoiseach had dropped a massive 29 points from 60 per cent over the same period. A strong majority (71 per cent), including an even greater majority of Fianna Fáil supporters, were not in favour of holding the general election and, most significantly of all,

Albert Reynolds was perceived by most electors to have been primarily responsible for the calling of the election. In essence, to win a general election, the floating vote, or an adequate share of it, must be won over, and this recent survey showed that Fianna Fáil was very unlikely to do this. I made the further point that when a government, and particularly a coalition government, is perceived to be performing well and is maintaining high satisfaction ratings, the main body of electors, including the potential floating voters, want that government to continue in office.

THE ISSUE OF ABORTION

In all of the polls throughout 1992, the issue of abortion was included. In May, the survey showed that, since the previous poll in February, attitudes towards the legalising of abortion had broadened and those against had fallen by ten points. The 80 per cent in favour were not all without reservations, as the figures show in *Table 9.2*.

Options	%
Should be available for all	16
In special circumstances only	46
When there is a threat to the mother's life	18
Not in any circumstances	20

Table 9.2: Result of an Irish Times/MRBI *poll showing the electorate's attitude towards the issue of abortion (May 1992)*

Support continued to hold up in the June poll, but there were tensions within the government, and between the government and the opposition parties, regarding the proposed wording of an amendment on the availability of abortion. The Progressive Democrats favoured legislation to deal with the matter, but a cabinet sub-committee rejected this. In making his point, Des O'Malley for the Progressive Democrats referred to the September *Irish Times*/MRBI opinion poll and he suggested that *"the electorate and all political parties share a consensus on how this emotive and divisive issue might be resolved*", specifically referring to the fact that the poll showed that 58 per cent were against holding a referendum to ban abortion.

On 8th October, the proposed wordings of the three amendments were published. Amendment One covered the right to travel outside the country for an abortion; Two, the right to information about abortion; and Three, the substantive issue of availability of abortion. The third amendment sought to draw a distinction between a right to abortion where a mother's health, as distinct from her life, was threatened. Opposition TDs and some Fianna Fáil ministers expressed concern that women might regard the distinction between their lives and their health as an unacceptable insult. There was considerable public debate on the issue, and many wanted the specific threat of suicide to be included as grounds for an abortion.

When the Dáil resumed on 10th October after the summer recess, there were conflicting accounts given by senior members of the government regarding the interpretation of the proposed amendment. At this stage, five parties – Progressive Democrats (in government), Fine Gael, Labour, Democratic Left and Workers' Party – all opposed the proposed wording. However, the die was cast and, when the confidence motion in the government was defeated on 4th November, the referendum on abortion was fixed for 25th November 1992 along with the general election.

Because the abortion referendum was being held on the same day as the general election, the polls included four specific questions relating to the issue:

- The voting intentions of the respondent on the right to travel for an abortion.

- The voting intentions of the respondent on the right to information about abortion.

- The respondent's personal opinions on availability of abortion.

- The voting intentions of the respondent on abortion, having been presented with the actual wording which would appear on the ballot paper.

Confusion over the Wording of the Amendment

Both the right to travel and the right to information were heavily supported as they had been since May and, with almost two weeks to go, I had no doubt that both would be carried. However, the wording for amending the Constitution on the substantive issue appeared to be causing considerable confusion.

This is best illustrated by setting out the two relevant questions in the survey, and the associated responses.

QA. Which of the phrases on this card comes nearest to your own opinion about the availability of abortion in Ireland? [The four options were then put to respondents with the sequence of presentation of the four options varied.]

Option	%
Should be available for anyone who wants it	19
Should be available if a threat to the life of the mother	33
Should be available if a threat to the life of the mother including suicide	21
Total in favour of some access to abortion	73
Should never be available in any circumstances	20
No opinion	7

QB. The wording on the ballot paper on the right to life/abortion issue will be: "*It shall be unlawful to terminate the life of an unborn unless such termination is necessary to save the life, as distinct from the health, of the mother where there is an illness or disorder of the mother giving rise to a real and substantial risk to her life, not being a risk of self-destruction.*" Will you vote 'Yes' to put this amendment into the Constitution, or 'No' not to put it in?

Decision	%
Will vote 'Yes'	48
Will vote 'No'	30
No opinion	22

The proposed amendment gave the electorate two options:

- to provide for abortion where there was a real risk to the life of the mother through illness or disorder other than suicide; or
- to leave matters as they were.

Leaving matters as they were was the crux of the problem in that, in 1983, an amendment to the Constitution was believed to have enshrined a ban on abortion. However, a Supreme Court interpretation in the *X-Case*, in 1992, ruled that abortion was permissible in the case of the young girl who was threatening suicide.

Question B:	Total	Should be available to everybody		Available on threat to physical life of mother		Available on threat to physical life and suicide		Never in any circumstances		No opinion	
Voting intentions: amendment	100%	19%		33%		21%		20%		7%	
	% Group	%	Group	%	Group	%	Group	%	Group	%	Group
Will vote 'Yes': limited abortion	48	10	B	21	C	11	E	5	F	1	A
Will vote 'No': hold the 1983* constitutional ban)	30	6	C	6	D	6	C	11	G	1	A
Don't know/ No opinion	22 A	3		6		4		4		5	

* The 1983 ban was undermined by the Supreme Court interpretation.

Table 9.3: Voting intentions in the abortion referendum, analysed by personal attitudes to abortion; illustrating the level of confusion on this issue

The survey, two weeks prior to the referendum, showed that 73 per cent favoured abortion in varying circumstances (of which 33 per cent did so in the case of a risk to the life of the mother as stated in the amendment); 20 per cent said it should never be available and 7 per cent were undecided. While the amendment was undoubtedly based on legal advice and represented two logical options, the survey showed that, when presented with the proposed wording of the amendment, respondents became confused to the extent that many intended to vote in direct conflict with their personal views on the issue. This confusion was identified when we cross-analysed the data from the two survey questions. *Table 9.3*, which was included in my commentary in *The Irish Times*, highlights the groups who were confused or inconsistent.

Examining the groups shows the inconsistencies in people's thinking, as shown in *Table 9.4*.

Group	Inconsistencies
A	This group (24%) admit to their confusion, i.e. don't know/no opinion.
B	This 10% are voting 'Yes', i.e. for restricted abortion, although they feel that it should be available to all.
C	This group (6% + 21% + 6%) are reasonably consistent in attitudes and voting intentions.
D	This group (6%) should be voting 'Yes' if they are to be consistent.
E	These people (11%) are voting 'Yes' to change the existing situation, with which they agree.
F	The amendment will permit abortion in limited circumstances, while they (5%) do not want it at all.
G	This group (11%) is reasonably consistent.

Table 9.4: Analysis of results of abortion referendum poll, showing the level of confusion among different groups

MRBI's published commentary in *The Irish Times* addressed the primary conclusions that many electors were confused to varying degrees; that many did not understand what was being put to them and that only a minority intended to vote in a manner that was consistent with their personal convictions. We saw this as an unacceptable reflection on the politicians who had referred the matter to the people, and suggested that an authoritative source should attempt to clarify the situation and rectify some of the confusion. It was apparent that the democratic process could be potentially prejudiced when many members of the electorate did not understand the nuances about which they were being asked to vote.

Final *Irish Times*/MRBI Poll

The next, and final, MRBI survey of the campaign was conducted on Tuesday 17th and Wednesday 18th November, six days before polling day. It again addressed two main areas: the political situation and voting intentions in the general election; and the three abortion issues in the referendum – all scheduled for Wednesday 25th November 1992.

Taking the abortion issues first, support for both the right to travel and for information had held firm since the previous poll nine days earlier and the conclusion given in *The Irish Times* was that both would be carried comfortably. However, on the actual abortion issue, a remarkable swing of 18 points had taken place against the amendment over nine days, and it was now apparent to me that this provision would be defeated, and I said so in my commentary in *The Irish Times*. I referred readers to the previous survey, which showed extensive confusion among the electorate on the right to life issue, to the extent that many had intended to vote in a manner which was in conflict with their own personal opinion. I claimed it was evident that the downturn had taken place against this background of confusion, and it could be assumed that:

> ...*many people were reacting negatively towards being confronted with a choice in a constitutional referendum that they did not understand, and they were now referring the matter back to the politicians.*

During the final week of the campaign, the government issued an information publication that addressed some of the questions and also advocated a 'Yes' vote in all three referenda. However, it was either too late, or inadequate, or both. In all three referenda the indications presented in the survey were confirmed. The right to travel and to information were passed by the electorate, and the right to life/abortion issue was defeated quite significantly 65%:35%. The messages were clear. The 'No' vote represented continuing resistance by the electorate to what was being offered. The survey of 9th November had shown that there were four segments of opinion relating to abortion – those who thought it should be:

- available to anyone who wants it;
- available in the event of threat to life including suicide;
- available in the event of threat to life excluding suicide; and
- not in any circumstances.

When only some of these options were addressed in the wording, and in a language which many misunderstood (the undecided had increased to 25 per cent or approximately 600,000 in the last campaign survey), it is hardly surprising that people were confused, and decided to vote no on the day.

THE 1992 GENERAL ELECTION

Looking now to the outcome of the general election, the final campaign survey of 18th November also provided unpleasant news for the government. The satisfaction rating for Albert Reynolds as Taoiseach had dropped another three points to 28 per cent since the previous poll nine days earlier. This reflected a total downturn of 32 points from September. In party support terms, Fianna Fáil remained on 40 per cent, identical to that of nine days earlier but down nine points from September. Fine Gael's 25 per cent represented the party's highest positioning for almost a year. The real mover, however, was Labour. Having increased its support by five points to 17 per cent in the previous poll, the party had now made further inroads into the floating vote, and its 22 per cent represented possibly its highest ever support. The Progressive Democrats were also satisfactorily positioned on 6 per cent, and the smaller parties continued to be stable at their normal levels.

On the publication of this MRBI opinion poll, an interesting aside arose when a senior member of the Fianna Fáil government was reported in the print media as saying *"the published figure (40 per cent) flew in the face of the party's private polls, which showed Fianna Fáil on 42 per cent going on 43 per cent"*. When asked to comment on campaign opinion polls by the Marketing Society, I confined myself to saying that the industry guidelines state that, when figures from private opinion polls are released to the media, the name of the company that conducted the poll must be stated, in addition to the sample size and date of the project, and that, in disclosing the figure in isolation, the party and the research organisation had broken these guidelines. A few days later, a national Sunday newspaper stated that it had contacted all four Irish market research companies that conduct opinion polls and none had conducted the poll from which the figure was quoted. On the following day, a Fianna Fáil panel member on RTÉ's *Questions and Answers* programme, on being asked who conducted that private poll, after some hesitancy claimed that *"we did it ourselves"*. The position is that a political party, like anybody else who wishes to release figures to the media, is obliged to conform to professional standards, and if a party conducts its own polls, this should be stated if the findings are being quoted. While the matter could perhaps have been dealt with in a more direct fashion, it was put to rest when I received a telephone call from a senior person in the party asking me to let the matter drop. On the basis of his attitude and comment I drew my own conclusions.

But back to the MRBI poll. Having studied the figures, and the ever-changing political background – which included a Fianna Fáil press conference in Dublin on Saturday 14th, an appearance by the Taoiseach on *This Week* on Sunday 15th and again on *The Pat Kenny Show* on Tuesday 17th – I scripted the following conclusions in *The Irish Times* during the final week of the campaign.

> *With less than a week remaining, Fianna Fáil has not succeeded in making any inroads into the crucial floating vote. While it will again be returned as the largest party, it will not obtain a Dáil majority and may have to settle for its lowest first preference vote for many decades.*
>
> *It is also evident that many floating voters intend to vote Labour and, consequently, the party will show a significant increase in its Dáil representation.*
>
> *It is evident that Irish politics is moving towards the European mould where a number of coalition options will be on the post-election agenda!*

The points made in the MRBI conclusions accurately represented the outcome of the election. The overall message was that the new government would almost certainly be a coalition in the European pattern. The results of the general election are given in *Table 9.5*.

Party	First Preference	Seats		Seat:Vote Ratio
	%	%	Number	
Fianna Fáil	39.1	41.0	68	100:105
Fine Gael	24.5	27.1	45	100:111
Labour Party	19.3	19.9	33	100:103
Progressive Democrats	4.7	6.0	10	100:128
Democratic Left	2.8	2.4	4	100:86
Others	9.6	3.6	6	100:38

Table 9.5: Result of the 1992 general election

Although the Fianna Fáil/Labour aggregate of 100 seats (Pádraig Flynn (FF) had resigned on 4th January on being appointed a European commissioner) would have been a considerable factor in a movement to form a government, it was not until 12th January 1993, almost seven weeks after the election, that Albert Reynolds was re-elected Taoiseach. Negotiations between the two party representatives took some considerable time, and the Dáil had met on four occasions before the new FF/Lab coalition was voted into power.

After the final poll had been conducted, I was invited to lunch by one of the first secretaries in a large foreign embassy. As soon as we met, he said he wanted to thank me for giving him such an accurate steer on the composition of the new government, and he elaborated by saying that his country's administration had expressed surprise at the news saying that the Irish embassy, with which they had made contact, were of the opinion that Fianna Fáil and Labour would not form a government.

The 1992 Fianna Fáil/Labour Coalition

Although the numbers added up, I had not explicitly stated before the result that the coalition would consist of Fianna Fáil and Labour, primarily because the body language of the two party leaders over the previous two years indicated that this was unlikely. I was also influenced by the fact that, before the election, Albert Reynolds had been blamed by most electors for calling an election that a majority did not want, and his ratings had dropped by almost 30 points over the two-month period leading up to the election.

However, the irony of politics came clearly into focus when, against the background of Fianna Fáil obtaining its lowest first preference vote since 1927, the composition of the new coalition ensured that Albert Reynolds was elected Taoiseach by a massive Dáil majority of 42, reportedly the largest in history. The new government was on its way, with "A Programme for Government" that had been agreed between the two parties. The cabinet announced by the Taoiseach is given in *Table 9.6*.

Taoiseach	Albert Reynolds	FF
Tánaiste; Foreign Affairs	Dick Spring	Lab
Finance	Bertie Ahern	FF
Education	Niamh Bhreathnach	Lab
Agriculture, Food and Forestry	Joe Walsh	FF
Social Welfare	Michael Woods	FF
Justice	Máire Geoghegan-Quinn	FF
Enterprise and Employment	Ruairi Quinn	Lab
Health	Brendan Howlin	Lab
Tourism and Travel	Charlie McCreevy	FF
Transport and Trade	Brian Cowen	FF
Defence and Marine	David Andrews	FF
Environment	Michael Smith	FF
Equity and Law Reform	Mervyn Taylor	Lab
Arts, Culture and The Gaeltacht	Michael D Higgins	Lab

Table 9.6: Members of the 1992 Fianna Fáil/Labour cabinet

With the large Dáil majority and the well-aired programme for what was termed 'partnership government', some commentators were predicting that Albert Reynolds' new administration could last until the millennium. However, many were also aware that the contrasting personal characteristics of the two party leaders had the potential to cause political fallout at any time, or at the very least that it could prejudice a balanced approach when problems arose. For these reasons, and also because of the circumstances in which the election was called, the publication of the next opinion poll was awaited with considerable speculation. It should also be remembered that expectations on the performance of the new government were high.

THE 1993 SCENARIO

On 1st March 1993, the next poll was undertaken and, before commenting on the outcome, it is relevant to set the background. The Beef Tribunal was ongoing; devaluation of the punt had just taken place; the job losses at Digital had brought unemployment to the top of the political agenda; and, of course, the new government's first budget had just been published.

On almost every criterion, the impact of the government and its constituent parties was disastrous. In the first instance, the new satisfaction rating of 22 per cent was the lowest for any government for over six years, which meant that it was lower than that for the FF/PD government of December 1991, just a month before Haughey's resignation. Albert Reynolds' rating as Taoiseach at 37 per cent, while above the pre-election nadir, was 23 points down on his February 1992 figure when he took over as Taoiseach. The big loser, however, was Dick Spring, whose ratings plummeted from his immediate pre-election figure of 71 per cent to 36 per cent, a drop of 35 points. Des O'Malley, as leader of the Progressive Democrats, topped the ratings on 47 per cent. In more direct terms, 46 per cent, equating with 1.2 million electors, disapproved of the new partnership government, among whom were 42 per cent of Fianna Fáil supporters, 22 per cent of Labour's, and, not surprisingly, 57 per cent of Fine Gael's.

Furthermore, following the publication of the budget, and indeed also the media hype on partnership government, a majority of two electors in three held the view that unemployment was not being reduced because the parties were not working together towards solving the problem. The budget itself also took a hammering. Seventy-five per cent were unimpressed and identified aspects that they saw as hurtful in personal terms; the most negative related to increases in VAT, the 1 per cent levy and general cost of living increases. While the minister in his budget speech had said that it was framed with the objective of creating more employment, a heavy majority of electors – three in every five – saw it as leading to more job losses, a viewpoint that was held by a majority of supporters in all parties.

The new partnership government had had a very poor take off, probably the worst in history; one of the most damaging aspects being that criticism was wide ranging and extensive, and came from all directions.

The Tax Amnesty

Although the public at large was not impressed with what it had seen of the government to date, the proposal for another tax amnesty brought further criticism from many quarters. The proposal permitted heavy tax evaders to have their tax arrears written off, the main apparent benefit – from the government viewpoint – being that it would bring considerable capital back from overseas. However, the cabinet cleared the proposal in spite of considerable media criticism, many commentators recalling that a similar amnesty had been enacted just five years earlier.

This was the cue for another *Irish Times*/MRBI opinion poll which was implemented on 2nd July 1993 and, in addition to the usual questions on political issues, it also measured reaction to the introduction of the amnesty and perception of which party was the more influential in the coalition government. On the amnesty, among those who expressed an opinion (and 7 per cent did not), the balance was 54 per cent to 46 per cent against its introduction. The highest incidence of disapproval was evident in Dublin and urban areas generally, among those aged 35 upwards, among working-class electors and among supporters of all parties, except Fianna Fáil. Interestingly, the highest approval levels were in farming homes and among Fianna Fáil supporters.

The ratings of the Taoiseach and Tánaiste were identical on 40 per cent, which was considerably below the average for each over the previous three years. Two in every three electors continued to be dissatisfied with the government, and its satisfaction level of 30 per cent was almost identical to the pre-election level of November 1992. Overall, a very unsatisfactory impact. Des O'Malley, as leader of the Progressive Democrats, continued to top the party leader ratings on

44 per cent, with John Bruton down to 23 per cent. Fianna Fáil's core support of 36 per cent was marginally up on the three previous polls, but considerably down on its average for the previous three years. Labour had improved its position by two points, while Fine Gael had, for the second opinion poll in succession, lost two points.

Fianna Fáil, not surprisingly, was perceived by three in every five to be the more influential party in government. The omens were not good, but the welcome summer break had arrived and a temporary respite was on the horizon.

The October 1993 *Irish Times*/MRBI Poll

Three months later, the next *Irish Times*/MRBI opinion poll, conducted on 1st October, showed that the electorate at large remained unimpressed with the continuing performance of the government. Three in every ten considered that it was making no impact on unemployment – a view particularly held by young people, while many felt that taxation was too high and unfair, and that domestic affairs were largely being ignored. Government ministers were also perceived to be looking after themselves too well and to have too many perks, while the issue of broken promises was an ongoing irritation.

A specific detailed question on perceived satisfaction with each of the two parties in government showed that, in broad terms, neither was seen to be delivering. Each received very mixed ratings and, effectively, was favourably rated only by its own supporters. The overall impact from this October opinion poll, nine months into office, represented a serious level of rejection by the electorate and the diversity of spontaneous criticism did not augur well for the longevity of the government. Furthermore, intermittent outbreaks of internal dissension, occasioned in the main by a succession of insensitive decisions, continued to blur the government's ability to address many of the criticisms of the electorate.

NORTHERN IRELAND

In spite of this adverse backdrop, one very favourable dimension was the commitment of the Taoiseach, and of the Minister for Foreign

Affairs, Dick Spring, to the Northern Ireland peace process. The Taoiseach had made his intentions clear when first appointed and, on being re-elected in January 1993, he renewed his efforts, mainly behind the scenes. Having met and known John Major, the British Prime Minister, the two leaders developed a friendly professional relationship that, eventually, led to the signing of the Downing Street Declaration a few weeks later. Meanwhile, Dick Spring had introduced his six principles relating to peace in the North, which confirmed that there could be no change in the status of Northern Ireland unless a majority of the people there supported that change.

As a further element in the process, the government announced that, if a settlement was likely, it would hold a referendum to alter the Republic's territorial claim over the North, which would replace *Articles 2* and *3* of the Constitution with an aspiration to unity by consent. It also transpired that for some time John Hume and Gerry Adams had been meeting in secret, and were reported to be making progress in their talks.

As the year drew to a close, and against this developing positive background in Northern Ireland, the final *Irish Times*/MRBI opinion poll of 1993 was conducted on 23rd November. In addition to the usual monitoring of political issues, the questionnaire included a wide range of questions relating to the North, and the essence of the report was that the Irish electorate was ready to play its part in helping to achieve peace.

In the first instance and perhaps of greatest significant was the fact that a majority stated – for the first time – that in a referendum they would vote to replace *Articles 2* and *3* with an aspiration to unity by consent. There was also massive support for the Spring principles and a majority felt that the proposals agreed by John Hume and Gerry Adams should be made public. A similar majority also held the view that the best way to achieve peace would be to have negotiations between the two governments and the Northern Ireland parties, including Sinn Féin, but only after the IRA had ceased violence. However, although the Irish people were prepared to yield on *Articles 2* and *3* and to give every support to the process, the primary aspiration was still a united Ireland, with power sharing backed up by a dual government role, the second choice. As a people, we were prepared to change our laws to meet the demands of minorities in the interests of peace on the island of Ireland;

however, we were not prepared to accept higher taxes as part of the price. All in all, solid, but pragmatic, support.

Not surprisingly, in the light of the efforts on the Northern issue, the same opinion poll showed satisfaction ratings moving upwards and Fianna Fáil support increasing by three points from the October poll. Government ratings improved by eight points to 42 per cent, the Taoiseach by six to 53 per cent, and the Tánaiste by eight to 55 per cent. A further significant development was that Mary Harney, the new leader of the Progressive Democrats, following Des O'Malley's retirement, topped the satisfaction ratings at 59 per cent.

The signing of the Downing Street Declaration on 15th December 1993 by the two government leaders marked real progress on the road to peace, and committed both governments to taking additional formal initiatives, with the underlying principle that change would take place only with the consent and agreement of a majority of the people of Northern Ireland. It represented a very notable and praiseworthy achievement for both Albert Reynolds and Dick Spring after less than a year in government together. (The full provisions of the declaration are shown in *Chapter 14*.)

An opinion poll, early in the New Year on 31st January measured reaction to the declaration, and also to the recently published 1994 budget. Although the efforts of the two government leaders in bringing negotiations to the point of signing the declaration attracted considerable favourable comment from the media, the public at large was much less engaged. In the first instance, some 14 per cent (representing 360,000 adults) were not aware of the declaration at all and a further 59 per cent had not read any of its provisions. This meant, that a total of 73 per cent, or almost 2 million electors in the Republic, knew nothing, or virtually nothing, about its main provisions. It was, therefore, not surprising that a majority (52 per cent) felt that the provisions of the declaration should be clarified for Sinn Féin as that party was demanding, and 38 per cent considered that Albert Reynolds and John Major should do this collectively.

THE YEAR 1994

While the government may have been surprised at this lack of knowledge by a large segment of the electorate, it would also have been disappointed that the level of criticism of the budget was similar to that of the previous year. The Minister for Finance, in his budget speech, had stated that *"the budget forms part of a coherent medium-term strategy designed to give a substantial impetus to sustainable employment"*. Yet two electors in every three claimed that it would instead contribute to further job losses, a similar proportion saw it as being harmful to them, and three in every four described it as unimaginative and ordinary. While much of the criticism related to increases in the price of petrol, cigarettes and drink, considerable ambivalence was also evident, as increases in social welfare benefits and tax allowances, the abolition of the previous year's 1 per cent levy, and a reduction in PRSI attracted much favourable comment.

When the overall impact was interpreted through satisfaction ratings and party support, the net result from the swings and roundabouts was that the government and Fianna Fáil were gradually clawing back support. Furthermore, the optimism resulting from the signing of the declaration, and from some of the favourable aspects of the budget, was helping to create a more impressive picture. The Taoiseach now shared top position with Mary Harney with a satisfaction rating of 62 per cent, up nine points, while Dick Spring as Tánaiste was also up at 56 per cent. Although Fianna Fáil support was up three points to a core level of 43 per cent, neither Labour in government, nor Fine Gael in opposition had made any real headway from the previous opinion poll.

The 1994 European Parliament Elections

The next major event on the political calendar was the European parliament election, scheduled for 9th June 1994. *The Irish Times* commissioned its first poll in a European election for 30th May, nine days before polling. The European election context presents a very distinctive challenge to organisations like MRBI. Firstly, because of the orientation towards individual candidates rather than parties; secondly, since so few candidates are normally elected on the first count; and, thirdly, because electors tend to transfer on a personal rather than on a party basis. For these reasons, the most appropriate questionnaire technique is the simulated ballot paper, which lists all candidates in alphabetical sequence, identical to that in the actual election voting paper. Respondents are invited to mark their first, and subsequent, preferences, and the resulting analyses provide a measure of first preferences and also transfer patterns. One of the dangers of this technique is that, in showing figures for individual candidates, an impression of precision is indicated, when, in fact, wide statistical variations apply and, as always, the figures only refer to the day of the interview and are not predictive.

The opinion poll involved 400 in-home interviews in each of the four European constituencies – Dublin, Leinster, Munster and Connacht–Ulster – and the two main questions were:

- If the European parliament election was held today, to which of these candidates would you give your first preference vote?

- To which would you give your second, third and subsequent preferences?

While the MRBI commentary in *The Irish Times* a week before the election set out the usual caveat, which emphasised that the figures related to 30th May, each constituency was addressed in detail. The situation, in terms of possible destination of seats, is indicated in *Table 9.7*.

Constituency									
Dublin: 4 seats	**MRBI Poll**	FF	1	FG	1	Lab	1	Other	1
	Actual Result	FF	1	FG	1	Lab	1	GP	1
Leinster: 4 seats	**MRBI Poll**	FF	2	FG	1	Lab	1		
	Actual Result	FF	2	FG	1	GP	1		
Munster: 4 seats	**MRBI Poll**	FF	2	Ind	1	Other	1		
	Actual Result	FF	2	Ind	1	FG	1		
Connacht–Ulster: 3 seats	**MRBI Poll**	FF	2	FG	1				
	Actual Result	FF	2	FG	1				

Table 9.7: Comparison of results from Irish Times/MRBI *polls and the result in the 1994 European election*

The overall conclusions from the survey were that, as of 30th May:

- Fianna Fáil would obtain 7 seats   (7 seats were won)

- Fine Gael would win 3, or a possible 4 seats   (4 seats were won)

- Labour would win at least 1 and possibly   (1 seat was won)
  2 seats

- Independent likely to hold 1 seat in Munster (1 seat was held)

- The Green Party, Democratic Left and the   (2 seats were won
  Workers' Party each has a chance of seats   by the Green Party)

In the same poll, government ratings and party support levels were also measured, at which juncture satisfaction was down six points to 43 per cent. Fianna Fáil support was also down five points to a core of 38 per cent; Fine Gael was up three to 16 per cent; Labour up two to 13 per cent; and the Progressive Democrats had settled back to the earlier level of 5 per cent. Being mid-term, volatility could be expected.

However, of much greater significance were the results of two by-elections held on the same day whose outcome was to create political history.

The constituencies being contested were Dublin South-Central and Mayo West, both, up to then, held by Fianna Fáil. In the former, John O'Connell's seat was won by Eric Byrne (DL) and in Mayo West, Michael Ring (FG) beat Beverley Cooper-Flynn (FF) for the seat vacated by her father, Pádraig. (He had been appointed European Commissioner in January 1993.) When the FF/Lab government took office, it had a massive Dáil majority of 101 and the fact that it still had 99 deputies after the two by-elections was the message understood by most politicians.

However, the fact that Fianna Fáil had lost two seats, and the opposition (and potential government in waiting) had gained two appeared to have been realised by no more than a few rather interested Dáil members. The real arithmetic was now saying that the Fine Gael, Labour and Democratic Left total was a magical 84 – a majority. It is now known that the Labour leader was fully aware of the new option that the by-election opened up to him. Meanwhile the government held its breath in anticipation of the publication of the Beef Tribunal report.

THE BEEF TRIBUNAL REPORT

This report was delivered to Government Buildings on the Friday evening of the August 1994 Bank Holiday weekend. Bearing in mind the circumstances in which the tribunal was established and the conflicting evidence given by senior people who were in government at the time, the report was awaited with considerable apprehension by all involved. When the Taoiseach asked his advisors to assess the implications of the report, the consensus was that it was not unduly critical of Mr Reynolds' actions, nor did it imply any lack of integrity on his part. This led to a government announcement, or leak as some have described it, that Albert Reynolds had been vindicated by the report. This may well have been true but, since it had been decided beforehand that no comment would be made until the report had been fully studied, all hell broke loose and the Tánaiste, who was at home in Tralee, and the Labour Party in general were, not for the first time, furious.

The upshot was that the media concentrated on the internal government row over the leak rather than on the report itself, with the eventual result that in the next *Irish Times*/MRBI opinion poll just two weeks later, on 22nd August, many electors were very critical of the action of senior politicians, although most had only a limited knowledge of the contents of the report.

In the first instance, a heavy majority of electors – seven in every ten – stated that ministers who were found to have told lies to the Dáil should be either dismissed as ministers or forced to resign from the Dáil. Although almost half had insufficient knowledge to answer, three in every five who answered considered that the claims of Des O'Malley, Dick Spring and Pat Rabbitte had been upheld. With just a third undecided, three in every five of those who answered, held the view that the report did not clear Larry Goodman, Charles Haughey or Albert Reynolds. Furthermore, with three in every five undecided, 25 per cent were of the opinion that Dick Spring's version was correct, while 8 per cent favoured Albert Reynolds' view, and 9 per cent thought both could be correct. Finally, almost half considered that Albert Reynolds should not, at the time, have claimed to have been vindicated, although a third supported him on the issue. It was no surprise that the satisfaction ratings of the Taoiseach, Tánaiste and government fell 16 per cent, 12 per cent and 11 per cent, respectively, from their February level. This represented the lowest personal ratings of the two leaders for over a year. Fianna Fáil support was also down four points to 34 per cent, with Fine Gael and Labour up two and one respectively. Considering that many of the main players in the tribunal were collectively in government, the big surprise was that the administration remained intact.

One possible reason for the prolongation was the very welcome statement from the IRA, on 31st August 1994, that there would be an immediate cessation of military operations, which many interpreted as a ceasefire. Albert Reynolds had frequently hinted at such a possibility, and it was undoubtedly one of his major achievements as Taoiseach. The announcement coincided with the recall of the Dáil to debate the Beef Tribunal report, but the ceasefire overshadowed everything else, and the day was given over to debating the good news.

Fr Smyth and Albert Reynolds' Resignation

The Dáil debated the tribunal report the following day but, within a short time, the first of a series of new disagreements arose. These involved the appointment of Harry Whelehan, the then Attorney-General, to the presidency of the High Court. At the same time, questions arose about procedures in his – the Attorney General's – office in relation to the extradition to Northern Ireland of a priest, Fr Brendan Smyth, on paedophile charges. After some high drama, and many threats to leave the government, the Labour Party finally walked out on the 17th November and the next day Albert Reynolds announced his resignation as Taoiseach. *The Irish Times* commissioned an immediate opinion poll against this unprecedented and extremely volatile background.

It was conducted on 18th November, immediately following the resignations, and prior to the meeting of the Fianna Fáil party to elect a new leader. The immediate preference of two-thirds of the electorate was for a new coalition government rather than a general election – this being the choice of a majority of supporters of all parties – while Albert Reynolds was perceived by a similar majority to have been mainly responsible for the collapse of the government. A very significant three in every four electors did not agree with the appointment of Harry Whelehan as President of the High Court, while an even higher proportion was dissatisfied with the manner in which he had fulfilled his functions as Attorney-General in the case of the extradition of Fr Smyth. Finally, and very interestingly, government satisfaction ratings had increased by 11 points to 49 per cent from August, supporting the view of the public that an election was not wanted. Dick Spring's rating as Tánaiste had increased by 18 points to 62 per cent; Labour Party support had also increased; and there was no doubt that the Labour leader was in a position to enter new negotiations from a strengthened and formidable base.

Reflecting on the performance of the government, and considering its unprecedented Dáil majority and the elaborate partnership programme, the delivery was nothing short of disastrous. The record was one of recurring disputes and disagreements and, before it eventually walked out, the Labour Party must have considered the option on numerous occasions. Looking back, it was miraculous that it lasted two years.

CHAPTER 10

Continuing Coalitions 1994–2001

A NEW BEGINNING

After a brief hiatus following Albert Reynold's resignation, Bertie Ahern was unanimously elected leader of Fianna Fáil on 19th November 1994 and, to all appearances, he was on his way towards becoming Taoiseach in another FF/Lab coalition. For Dick Spring, with his party's 33 seats under his belt, and still the king maker, the vista was a choice between a renewal of the somewhat blemished FF/Lab administration or taking up John Bruton's alternative offer of a Fine Gael-led three-way coalition.

The Irish Times opinion poll, undertaken on Friday 25th November, drew the primary conclusion that the electorate was strongly supportive of the formation of a new coalition government rather than having another general election. Fianna Fáil supporters almost unanimously favoured a repeat of the FF/Lab arrangement and Labour supporters also preferred a coalition with Fianna Fáil, but Fine Gael voters, not surprisingly, opted for a three-way FG/Lab/PD coalition. Of perhaps greater significance for Dick Spring in his deliberations, was the fact that, while support for both Fianna Fáil and Fine Gael had increased over the previous week, support for the Labour Party had not. It had dropped marginally and there may have been a message there.

Although Dick Spring met with both Bertie Ahern and John Bruton, he very quickly pulled out of negotiations with the Fianna Fáil leader and opted for the rainbow coalition of Fine Gael, Labour and the Democratic Left. This was the first time in the history of the State that a new government had been formed without a general election and, although Bertie Ahern's Fianna Fáil would, almost certainly, not have delivered a voyage as hazardous as the 1992 administration, Dick Spring had experienced enough over the previous two years to decide against the wishes of both Labour and Fianna Fáil supporters.

The new government, formed after John Bruton's election as Taoiseach on 15th November 1994, reflected an interesting blend of experience and new blood, with all members contributing to what was a solid administration that served for two-and-a-half years – six months longer than its predecessor. The full cabinet is given in *Table 10.1*.

Taoiseach	John Bruton	FG
Tánaiste; Foreign Affairs	Dick Spring	Lab
Finance	Ruairi Quinn	Lab
Education	Niamh Bhreathnach	Lab
Agriculture	Ivan Yates	FG
Equality and Law Reform	Mervyn Taylor	Lab
Arts, Culture and The Gaeltacht	Michael D Higgins	Lab
Tourism and Trade	Enda Kenny	FG
Enterprise and Employment	Richard Bruton	FG
Justice	Nora Owens	FG
Social Welfare	Proinsias de Rossa	DL
Health	Michael Noonan	FG
Environment	Brendan Howlin	Lab
Transport, Energy and Communications	Michael Lowry	FG
Defence and Marine	Hugh Coveney	FG

Table 10.1: Members of the 1994 Fine Gael/Labour/Democratic Left cabinet

THE ISSUES FACING THE NEW GOVERNMENT

The new government's first budget was presented by Finance Minister Ruairi Quinn on Wednesday 8th February 1995 and the first *Irish Times*/MRBI opinion poll of the new administration was conducted five days later. John Bruton was rated very satisfactorily as Taoiseach, at 53 per cent, almost double his average as opposition leader over the previous four years. Dick Spring was also highly rated at 56 per cent. However, the most striking message from the poll was the 69 per cent rating of Bertie Ahern as leader of Fianna Fáil – ahead of all others, and considerably ahead of any other Fianna Fáil leader over the previous 12 years. This was Bertie Ahern's first measurable impact as leader and it provided a clear indication of his personal ability to attract high satisfaction ratings.

The opinion poll also contained good news for the new government. Fine Gael support remained within two points of its election performance and, while Labour might hope to reach the 19 per cent peak of 1992, its 15 per cent represented a satisfactory impact. Furthermore, the budget was given a considerably better rating among the electorate than its predecessors in 1993 and 1994. Relatively more people thought that living standards would rise as a result, while the most beneficial aspects compared to the previous years were: increased children's allowances; the widening of tax bands; reduced PRSI; and the abolition of college fees.

Finally, one-third of those polled thought that the budget would increase job opportunities, which compared favourably with one-fifth when asked a similar question in 1994.

Northern Ireland

Following his election as Taoiseach, John Bruton lost no time in turning his attention to Northern Ireland and, on 22nd February 1995, two months after taking office, he signed the "Framework Document" with the British Prime Minister John Major. This reaffirmed that self-determination must be in keeping with the principle of consent; that agreement must be pursued through exclusively democratic and peaceful means; and that any new arrangements must afford parity of esteem to both traditions. The document also set out the three interlocking strands as a basis for negotiations:

- within Northern Ireland;
- North–South institutions (the relationship between Northern Ireland and the Republic); and

- East–West structures (governing relations between Ireland and Britain).

It provided a continuation of the impetus of Albert Reynold's Downing Street Declaration of December 1993 and Garret FitzGerald's Anglo–Irish Agreement of November 1985.

The Divorce Debate

The dominant issue on the political agenda at this time was divorce, which was addressed in three in-depth surveys for the government and a series of opinion polls commissioned by *The Irish Times* (see *Chapter 11*). A 30th September 1995 poll, while primarily focusing on voting intentions in the up-coming divorce referendum, also included an assessment of government performance and the state of party support.

It was the first political monitor for seven months. John Bruton's three-party coalition had been in office for nine months and the general impact of the poll confirmed the ongoing media reports that the government had settled in well and was making a satisfactory impression. The ratings of the government, Taoiseach and Tánaiste were each up since February, while support for both Fine Gael and Labour remained solid at February levels. The message on opposition performance, however, was also very favourable. Bertie Ahern and Mary Harney were each at 62 per cent and shared top position, confirming their ability to achieve, and hold, high satisfaction ratings.

However, despite the satisfactory ratings, the government remained under pressure over the next few weeks, with every poll showing a decline in support for a 'Yes' vote in the divorce referendum scheduled for 24th November 1995. While the final result was a victory for the supporters of divorce, by the narrowest of margins (9,000 votes), the pressure on the government continued into the spring of 1996 when those opposed to divorce initiated a challenge to the result in the courts (see *Chapters 12* and *13*).

EVENTS IN 1996

As we moved into 1996, much media interest was devoted to the High Court petition by the Anti-Divorce Group, but matters in Northern

Ireland also continued to demand government attention. In February, the IRA ceasefire of August 1994 ended with the bombing of Canary Wharf on the London docks. In May, elections to the Northern Ireland Forum took place, and multi-party talks were scheduled for June.

In the next *Irish Times*/MRBI opinion poll, conducted on 4th June 1996, John Bruton's rating as Taoiseach had increased by two points, to 56 per cent; Mary Harney remained in first position on 62 per cent; with Bertie Ahern on 57 per cent; and Dick Spring 52 per cent. Fine Gael support in government had increased to 26 per cent, while Fianna Fáil remained firm on 47 per cent.

One of the reasons for the upturn in John Bruton's satisfaction rating was the perception among seven out of every ten electors that he and his government were doing all they could to find a solution to the Northern Ireland problem. However, a greater volume – four in every five – gave John Hume and the SDLP a similar accolade. John Major and the British government made a much lower impact on this criterion with just 36 per cent support. Major's impact was not inconsistent with media reports that the ending of the IRA ceasefire was related to the lack of any initiative by the British government during the 18 months over which it applied.

A September poll was undertaken before the resumption of the Dáil after the summer recess and, with the undecideds extending to 22 per cent and support for most of the parties tightening, the commentary on the findings suggested that the campaign for the next election was beginning to simmer. As of September, there were strong indicators that no party would obtain an overall majority, and that a coalition government would, again, be the most likely outcome.

The Michael Lowry Affair

The profession of politics has invariably produced the unexpected. With John Bruton's government coasting – perhaps with an eye to the forthcoming election – any complacency that existed was blown apart by the sudden resignation of Michael Lowry, Minister for Transport, Energy and Communications on 30th November 1996, following the revelation that expensive renovations to his house had been paid for by Ben Dunne. Lowry was replaced in the cabinet by Alan Dukes, and the final opinion poll of the year, on 6th December, was undertaken against this background.

Not surprisingly, the government rating was down four points to 39 per cent, its lowest level since taking office two years earlier, and John Bruton's, as Taoiseach, was also down – but by just one point. Dick Spring's rating as Tánaiste remained solid, while those for Bertie Ahern and for Mary Harney were both up. Fine Gael and Labour also dropped slightly, while Fianna Fáil remained steady at 46 per cent. Finally, and of considerably more significance, a heavy majority – three in every four electors – across all party supporters, held the view that the government had been damaged by the Lowry resignation. Reaction to the Taoiseach's handling of the situation was mixed, primarily due to the adverse reaction among Fianna Fáil and Progressive Democrat supporters. For the government, it was a political problem that marred what had been a solid performance to date.

1997: ELECTIONS AND SCANDALS

The first poll of 1997 was conducted on 28th January, against the background that a general election was on the horizon and the more immediate background of the publication of the 1997 budget. This made a favourable impact within the two main criteria; that people's standard of living would rise and that more employment would be created.

For these reasons, and in spite of the Lowry affair, the ratings of the government and Taoiseach had improved to 50 per cent and 58 per cent respectively, the highest in the Bruton administration. Fine Gael support had also increased to 27 per cent. However, Fianna Fáil, on 45 per cent, was still maintaining its heartland support, and Mary Harney's top of the scale rating of 69 per cent was very likely reflected in the Progressive Democrats' support figure of 9 per cent, considerably above its impact in the previous three general elections. The situation at the beginning of election year represented, as the MRBI report commented, *"a very wavering political environment"*. While the poll conveyed no indicators, as yet, of the likely outcome of the election, the FF/PD coalition option was preferred by 44 per cent of the population, compared with 32 per cent for the alternative FG/Lab/DL.

On 27th March, when the next poll was conducted, there was considerable anticipation that the formal announcement of the date of the general election was imminent. I wondered if the Taoiseach was allowing himself to be influenced by his recent high satisfaction ratings. This arose in the case of two of his predecessors. However, on reflection this situation was different, since the statutory date for dissolution of the Dáil (November 1997) was fast approaching and John Bruton could have exercised his option at any time once the calendar year had commenced, without incurring the displeasure of the electorate. The main messages from the March poll were further increases in Taoiseach, Tánaiste and government ratings to 63 per cent, 54 per cent and 53 per cent, respectively, and corresponding increases in Fine Gael and Labour support to 30 per cent and 11 per cent. Fianna Fáil had dropped marginally to 43 per cent, which showed that it would still be the largest party, while Progressive Democrat support remained solid at 8 per cent. Preferences on the coalition options had also narrowed by six points to 43%:37%, in favour of the FF/PD option.

The McCracken Tribunal

Following the Lowry resignation in November, rumours began to spread about payments to a much better-known politician and ex-Taoiseach – Charles Haughey. For a number of years, Haughey's lifestyle and personal wealth had been the subject of considerable media speculation, and it transpired that he and Lowry had at least one thing in common; they appeared to have shared the same benefactor, Ben Dunne.

The revelations were quickly taken up by the government and a Tribunal of Inquiry was established under Mr Justice Brian McCracken to investigate the payments to the two men. When the hearings commenced, in April 1997, it became clear from Dunne's evidence that Haughey had been the recipient of a vast amount of money, some handed to him personally, but most transmitted via a circuitous route. Prior to this, Haughey had denied, in writing, that he had received any money from Dunne.

The next MRBI opinion poll, on 5th May, measured public reaction to the two conflicting statements. The question on the issue was very explicit:

> *In the matter of the Dunnes Stores payments to politicians, Mr Ben Dunne alleges that he paid over £1 million to Mr Charles Haughey. Mr Haughey has written to the tribunal*

denying that he received any money. Whose version of the events do you believe?

Version Believed	Total	FF	FG	Lab	PD	Other	Undecided
	%	%	%	%	%	%	%
Ben Dunne	65	62	74	74	71	71	51
Charles Haughey	8	12	7	7	3	3	4
Neither	14	13	7	11	12	18	24
No opinion	13	13	12	8	14	8	21

Table 10.2: Who does the electorate believe: Ben Dunne or Charles Haughey?

The reaction of the electorate showed that, even at this early stage of the inquiry, Charles Haughey had lost considerable credibility. Only one in eight Fianna Fáil supporters believed him and, even though he was the first Fianna Fáil Taoiseach to go into coalition with the Progressive Democrats, only one in every 33 supporters of that party shared this view.

In regard to the political issues in the opinion poll, my interpretation of the results was that Bertie Ahern had already succeeded in distancing himself, and his party, from any unfavourable spin-off resulting from the Haughey disclosures. Fianna Fáil support was holding firm, as was Bertie Ahern's satisfaction rating at 59 per cent. Quite surprisingly, ratings for John Bruton as Taoiseach, Dick Spring as Tánaiste, and the government were down eight, five and four points respectively. Fine Gael support had also dropped four points. The final resting place of the floating vote was not yet apparent, but the Fianna Fáil leader had positioned himself and his party on a solid basis in preparation for the formal election campaign.

THE GENERAL ELECTION OF 1997

On 15th May, the Dáil was dissolved and the general election was fixed for 6th June. *The Irish Times* immediately commissioned the first of three campaign polls, which was undertaken on 20th May, 17 days before the election.

Not surprisingly, at the outset of the campaign, the uncommitted voters were relatively substantial, at 16 per cent, and the ratings of all party leaders had remained unchanged, indicating that many were adopting a wait-and-see approach. Furthermore, support levels for the three main parties, Fianna Fáil, Fine Gael and Labour, had also remained solid – compared to the previous poll two weeks earlier – at 43 per cent, 26 per cent and 10 per cent respectively. The MRBI commentary stated that, had the election taken place on the 20th May, Fianna Fáil would be leading the new government, and it also noted that this was the first occasion on which a Fianna Fáil leader had enjoyed a very high satisfaction rating (60 per cent) going into a campaign.

In the commentary, we noted that, in the previous three elections, Fine Gael had gained support as the campaign developed and that, at 26 per cent, support was above its comparable position in those elections. The Labour Party figure of 10 per cent indicated that it was on course to deliver on its pre-1992 average, and I concluded by saying that both the Progressive Democrats on 7 per cent and the Democratic Left on 2 per cent had the capacity to maximise their Dáil seats, as both did in 1992.

The second and penultimate opinion poll on 28th May, eight days before polling, saw virtually no change in voting intentions. The respective figures, after adjusting for the 14 per cent who remained undecided, were: Fianna Fáil 42 per cent; Fine Gael 26 per cent; Labour 11 per cent; Progressive Democrats 7 per cent; Democratic Left 2 per cent; Green Party 4 per cent; and Others 8 per cent.

The commentary referred back to the same stage in the 1992 election campaign, when it was stated that Irish politics was beginning to move towards the European norm of coalition governments. Now, five years later, the Irish electorate was being offered a choice between two coalition alternatives. It also stated that the figures did not suggest that either new coalition government would have a comfortable working majority.

The Final Poll

The final campaign survey was conducted on 6th June 1997 – polling day. In 1996, we conducted a poll for *The Irish Times* on the day of the divorce referendum, but this was the first time MRBI conducted such a poll on the day of a general election.

For legal reasons it was decided not to conduct an exit poll, as the law prohibits persons staying within 100 metres of a polling station, while people are going to vote. Instead, the more arduous and challenging task of interviewing in 1,400 homes, throughout the State, during that afternoon and evening was agreed with *The Irish Times*.

The planning stage of the survey involved selecting the statistical sample of electors, based on 200 sampling locations covering all 41 constituencies, and a total of 1,239 electors were interviewed between 2 pm and 8 pm. Because of the very demanding time factor – the report was due at *The Irish Times* at 10 pm – the questionnaire was brief. After the normal introduction, respondents were asked if they had voted and, if so, how they had voted. Those who had not yet gone to their polling station, having confirmed that they intended to, were asked how they would vote.

The data was analysed within the hour and the results, published on the morning of the 7th June in *The Irish Times*, are shown in Column A of *Table 10.3*.

Party	A Survey Totals %	B Post-Voting %	C Pre-Voting %	D Election Result %
Fianna Fáil	44	39	47	39
Fine Gael	27	28	26	28
Labour Party	8	9	7	10
Progressive Democrats	4	5	3	5
Democratic Left/ Workers' Party	3	3	3	3
Green Party	3	3	3	3
Others	11	13	11	12

Table 10.3: Comparison of results between Irish Times/MRBI *election day poll and the 1997 election result*

The overall survey figures (Column A) overstated support for Fianna Fáil by five points, and understated that for Fine Gael, Labour,

Progressive Democrats and Others, by one, two, one and one points respectively – due, primarily, to the decline in voter turnout.

Some days later when the completed questionnaires were all returned to the office, it was possible to analyse the results more fully and, to our amazement, we found very significant differences between the responses of those who had already voted before they were interviewed, and the remainder who said they intended to vote before the polling stations closed.

Among those who had already voted, most figures were virtually identical to the election results – Fianna Fáil and Fine Gael at 39 per cent and 28 per cent respectively (Column B). Those who had not yet voted, however, grossly overstated support for Fianna Fáil at 47 per cent, and the figures for all other parties – except Progressive Democrats and Democratic Left – were correspondingly understated (Column C). With the election turnout down to 65 per cent, it was apparent that a considerable number of respondents claimed that they intended to vote when they did not do so, and this was compounded by the fact that quite a number of these people claimed that they would vote for Fianna Fáil.

Declining Voter Turnout

The trend of declining voter turnout is presenting significant problems in opinion polling, and *The Irish Times* and MRBI have carried out extensive research to attempt to identify those who will not vote in an election. Direct questioning does not yield the answer, since many people either have the good intention to vote or, alternatively, are not prepared to admit that they might be less than good citizens. Indirect questioning approaches have yielded some indicators, but these can only be tested and verified in the next election.

Meanwhile, in establishing the extent to which support for the various parties was at variance with the final outcome, the election day survey of 1997 has made it possible to calculate relevant weighting factors, which now form the basis for the new MRBI adjustment procedures. This adjustment framework is factual, relevant and up to date and is structured to ensure reliability in the final published figures. In the light of declining turnout, this new methodology is the best technical option available.

The Result

The voting returns in the 1997 election delivered 77 seats to Fianna Fáil; 54 to Fine Gael; 17 to Labour; four each to Progressive Democrats and Democratic Left and ten to Others. The coalition arithmetic was FF/PD 81 and FG/Lab/DL 75; and, on 26th June after the nomination of the outgoing Taoiseach John Bruton was defeated, Bertie Ahern was elected Taoiseach on the combined votes of Fianna Fáil, Progressive Democrats, Sinn Féin and three Independents. The cabinet of the new government is given in *Table 10.4*.

Taoiseach	Bertie Ahern	FF
Tánaiste; Enterprise, Trade and Employment	Mary Harney	PD
Finance	Charlie McCreevy	FF
Foreign Affairs	Ray Burke	FF
Education	Michael Martin	FF
Agriculture and Food	Joe Walsh	FF
Defence	David Andrews	FF
Marine	Michael Woods	FF
Health and Children	Brian Cowan	FF
Environment	Noel Dempsey	FF
Public Enterprise	Mary O'Rourke	FF
Arts, Heritage and The Gaeltacht and Islands	Síle de Valera	FF
Social, Community and Family Affairs	Dermot Ahern	FF
Justice, Equality and Law Reform	John O'Donoghue	FF
Tourism, Sport and Recreation	Jim McDaid	FF

Table 10.4: Members of the 1997 Fianna Fáil/Progressive Democrat cabinet

Some saw the Fianna Fáil vote of 39 per cent as a reflection on Bertie Ahern, claiming that the party did no better than in 1992. My reading is that there was no correlation whatsoever between the two results. The 1992 downturn was contributed to mainly by the fact that a majority of the electorate – including a majority among Fianna Fáil supporters – did not want a general election at that time, and Albert Reynolds was perceived to have called it unnecessarily.

The 1997 situation was completely different, primarily because 484 candidates had been nominated – the greatest number in the history of this 166-seat Dáil, comprising 13 parties and 170 independents – and the first preference votes were divided up to a greater extent than ever before. However, after eliminations, these numbers also meant that Fianna Fáil and Fine Gael achieved a very high return of seats to first preference votes; Fianna Fáil's 39.33 per cent of votes converted to 46.4 per cent of seats, and Fine Gael's 27.95 per cent to 32.5 per cent of seats. There may have been some element of vote management as both sides have claimed, but the main contributing factor was the volume of candidates nominated.

MORE TRIBUNALS

When the new coalition government, with the support of the four Independent deputies, took office, the omens looked reasonably good. In Britain, a new Labour government, under Tony Blair, had just won a landslide victory, and the Northern Ireland peace process could now be addressed by two fresh minds. To add to the optimism, the IRA restored its ceasefire of August 1994, which had been terminated by the Canary Wharf bombing.

However, storm clouds were also appearing. For some time rumours that Ray Burke – the newly appointed Minister for Foreign Affairs – had received political donations in the late 1980s continued to make the news and, in July, Charles Haughey's appearances before the McCracken Tribunal were highly embarrassing, when he had to apologise firstly for making false statements in his affidavits and also for misleading his own legal team. For an ex-Taoiseach this was a most humiliating experience, and it was compounded when the tribunal report in August heavily criticised Haughey for receiving very substantial financial donations from prominent businessmen and the manner in which the money was diverted through overseas accounts.

The Dáil debated the McCracken report on 10th September 1997, at the end of which, the government, under severe pressure from the opposition, agreed to establish another tribunal – under Mr Justice

Moriarty – to investigate other possible sources of financial payments to both Haughey and Lowry. Earlier on the same day, Ray Burke made a personal statement to the Dáil stating that he had received a payment of £30,000 in June 1989, some of which he handed over to Fianna Fáil headquarters, while the rest was used to cover election expenses. This statement conflicted with Bertie Ahern's earlier assurances that he had investigated alleged payments to Ray Burke, and that there had not been any.

Assessing the Situation

Shortly after the Dáil debate, *The Irish Times* commissioned an extensive opinion poll, which was taken on 27th September 1997. This was the first since the new coalition government had taken office and – while the electorate was critical of Haughey, Burke and Lowry – the government, Taoiseach and Tánaiste were all seen to be performing very well. As Taoiseach, Bertie Ahern's first rating of 73 per cent was the highest ever recorded, and with Mary Harney and the government both on 62 per cent, and John Bruton and Dick Spring, in opposition, on 60 per cent and 57 per cent respectively, everyone appeared to be doing well.

While acknowledging the fact that satisfaction ratings have little or no relationship to voting behaviour, Bertie Ahern's unprecedented high rating – before he had even got into his stride – can be attributed to two factors. Firstly, his personal appeal and, secondly, his ability to distance himself from the effects of unfavourable background events. On this occasion his personal rating as Taoiseach also had a favourable impact on Fianna Fáil support, which increased by six points from the immediate pre-election poll back in June. Fine Gael and Labour were holding relatively firm; but quite inexplicably, Progressive Democrat support had dropped to three points below its election impact. Generally speaking, shortly after the formation of a new government, most of these figures would be quite irrelevant.

Of relevance, however, was the fact that 70 per cent of the electorate – including 64 per cent of Fianna Fáil supporters – were not surprised that Haughey had accepted money from Ben Dunne, and that 79 per cent – including, this time, 73 per cent of Fianna Fáil supporters – did not believe Ray Burke's Dáil statement that the £30,000 cash payment he received, was from a person he had never met and that it was a contribution towards election campaigning. Finally, 59 per cent – and

54 per cent of Fine Gael supporters – were not surprised that Michael Lowry had also accepted cash payments from Dunne. Even at that relatively early stage, thousands of electors were having reservations about the financial benefits that these politicians were organising for themselves.

THE 1997 PRESIDENTIAL CAMPAIGN

Nineteen ninety-seven was also presidential election year and, with the election due to be held on 30th October, Fianna Fáil had already taken steps to prevent a recurrence of what had arisen in 1990, when the party's nominee was defeated in a presidential election for the first time. On this occasion, the party had chosen a very formidable candidate in Mary McAleese, a 46-year-old barrister and academic who had been Professor of Criminal Law at Trinity College Dublin, and Director of the Institute of Legal Studies at Queen's University Belfast, and also Pro Vice-Chancellor. At this stage there were four nominees, all women with impressive credentials, but nominations had not yet closed. Mary Banotti, who was a grand-niece of Michael Collins and had been an MEP since 1984 (re-elected in 1989 and 1994), was the Fine Gael nominee. The other two contenders were Adi Roche, the Labour nominee, and Rosemary Scanlon (Dana), Independent – both very successful in their respective professional careers.

In this first opinion poll of the campaign, Mary McAleese was positioned in first place with 40 per cent of first preferences; Mary Banotti 27 per cent; Adi Roche 25 per cent; and Rosemary Scanlon 8 per cent. An interesting feature of the poll was the fact that party support was not very evident at that stage – some 44 per cent of Fianna Fáil supporters were not voting for McAleese; 54 per cent of Labour were not voting for Roche; and 48 per cent of Fine Gael were not voting for Banotti. However, the clear message from the poll was that Mary McAleese was favourite and held a significant lead over Mary Banotti. After the publication of the poll, Derek Nally, who was chairman of Victim Support and was a high-profile former member of An Garda Síochána, entered the contest.

MRBI conducted three subsequent opinion polls, on 11th, 22nd and 27th of October, and, in the final two polls, Mary McAleese increased her lead. The respective figures, including the first campaign poll, are given in *Table 10.5*.

Candidate	Dates of Polls				First Count Result
	27 Sept	11 Oct	22 Oct	27 Oct	
	%	%	%	%	%
M McAleese	40	39	42	46	45
M Banotti	27	29	33	30	29
A Roche	25	16	9	8	7
R Scanlon	8	8	9	10	14
D Nally	–	9	6	5	5

Table 10.5: Comparison of the actual result with Irish Times/MRBI *opinion polls leading up to the 1997 presidential campaign*

In the election, Mary McAleese, on the second count, was elected with 59 per cent of the vote, to Mary Banotti's 41 per cent. While the presidential election provided a boost to Fianna Fáil, the celebrations were short lived, as the media continued to target Ray Burke. The outcome was that, on 7th October, he resigned from both the cabinet and Dáil. This left Fianna Fáil down one seat, with an unwelcome by-election on the horizon in Dublin North. In the same Dáil session, the government was forced to establish yet another tribunal – this time to enquire into planning matters in County Dublin, not unrelated to the departed minister. The chairman of the new tribunal was Mr Justice Flood.

BY-ELECTIONS AND DEVELOPMENTS IN THE LABOUR PARTY

Shortly afterwards, Dick Spring resigned as leader of the Labour Party and was replaced by Ruairi Quinn, who set himself a formidable challenge in his first few months as Labour Party leader. He was looking to two by-elections – Dublin North and Limerick East – and his immediate requirement from MRBI was for research that would provide a reliable information base for a strategic plan in each constituency.

One of my first concerns was that we might be measuring too early, but Quinn was comfortable on this point. Back at MRBI, we looked in detail at the circumstances in which each by-election had been called, and also at the historical patterns in previous general elections. We were then ready to develop the research plan. The questionnaire first established the main issues on which the by-elections would be fought; followed by a rating of every candidate on a number of personal and political criteria; satisfaction ratings of all leaders; and, finally, the simulated ballot paper to measure first and subsequent voting intentions, which would identify transfer patterns. All figures within each constituency were analysed by geographic region and all other demographics. The two surveys were conducted over the period 9th to 11th January 1998, and the reports were presented seven days later.

It was gratifying to see the extent to which the Labour Party accepted that the research was setting out a course of action from a benchmark position and was not, as most politicians appear to assume today, predicting the result per se. In fact, the research indicated that two different strategies were necessary because Sean Ryan, in Dublin North, was positioned ahead on all criteria, and was also attracting more transfers than any other candidate. However, in Limerick East, although it was the late Jim Kemmy's Labour seat, the challenge to Jan O'Sullivan (Lab) was formidable. The research confirmed that both Mary Jackman (FG) and the new Fianna Fáil nominee, Sandra Marsh, would be very strong competitors. It positioned Jackman marginally ahead of O'Sullivan and Marsh on most criteria and indicated that further work needed to be done by the Labour Party on first preferences and on transfers before polling day.

When the by-election in Dublin North took place, Sean Ryan (Lab) topped the poll with 33 per cent of the first preference vote; followed by Michael Kennedy (FF) on 31 per cent; and Philip Jenkinson (FG) in third place on 10 per cent. The Labour candidate led all the way to the 14th count when he was elected, having exceeded the quota, and was at that stage over 3,000 votes ahead of the Fianna Fáil candidate.

Limerick East was much closer with a first count cliff-hanger: O'Sullivan (Lab) 25 per cent; Jackman (FG) 24 per cent; and Marsh (FF) also 24 per cent. The elimination of the six lowest candidates made little difference, but when the next candidate John Ryan (DL) was

171

eliminated, over 2,000 of his 3,500 votes transferred to O'Sullivan. This was very much as the research had indicated, and the Labour candidate then proceeded to pick up further transfers from Tim O'Malley (PD) and, finally, from Mary Jackman, after which she was elected on the fifth count. It was an excellent result for Ruairi Quinn and the Labour Party. The part played by the local media in Limerick was also crucial to the outcome there.

THE BELFAST AGREEMENT

After considerable difficulties and tedious and contentious discussions, the signing of the Belfast Agreement on Good Friday 10th April 1998 was the pinnacle, up to that date, of Bertie Ahern's political career. Both he, Tony Blair and all the party leaders who signed, brought new hope to what was an unremitting political dilemma. Its potential to create a new sense of optimism meant it was always possible that, when the time came, the Taoiseach of the day would benefit both personally and politically from any progress towards peace in Northern Ireland and, indeed, this certainly materialised.

In an *Irish Times*/MRBI poll of 14th April – five days after the signing – Bertie Ahern's personal rating and that of his government surpassed all previous figures. His impact as Taoiseach, at 84 per cent, was above the previous all-time high and included a 95 per cent level of satisfaction among Fianna Fáil supporters and an average of 80 per cent among those of all other parties. The government rating was 73 per cent and Fianna Fáil support was also up to 57 per cent.

Of immediate relevance in the poll was the fact that, following the agreement, three out of every five electors stated that they would vote yes if a referendum was held to amend *Articles* 2 and 3 of the Constitution. One in five were against and a similar number were undecided. The net figures, adjusting for the undecideds, were: 'Yes' 76 per cent; 'No' 24 per cent. However, of more relevance, was the fact that half of those against, and also half of the undecideds, were Fianna Fáil supporters – the government still had some communicating to do. Finally, electors were reasonably optimistic about the chances of the agreement bringing lasting peace to the North. Three in five felt the chances were reasonably strong or better. It appeared many of the remaining two in five were adopting a wait-and-see attitude and felt there was still some distance to go.

The government's selling of the agreement was successful, and, when the referendum in the Republic on *Articles 2* and *3*, was held on 22nd June 1998, it was carried by an overwhelming majority: 94 per cent for and 6 per cent against.

THE TURN OF THE CENTURY

On the home front, the remainder of 1998 saw the government having to contend with numerous recurring problems. The tribunals were ongoing and revelations relating to different Fianna Fáil and ex-Fianna Fáil members continued to hit the headlines. Further payments to Ray Burke from business interests were disclosed and the terms of reference of the Flood Tribunal were extended to cover this development. The final political bombshell before the next opinion poll was the tax assessment served on Charles Haughey following the Dunne payments, and its subsequent reduction to zero. The final opinion poll of the year was undertaken on 6th October 1998 and it showed all government-related ratings changed marginally, but little or no change in support levels for the opposition parties.

Since taking up office 16 months earlier, the government had enjoyed a political honeymoon and the various upheavals that surfaced did not create any serious levels of dissatisfaction among the electorate. This, however, was soon to change. The new year saw an increase in both the intensity and frequency of revelations – virtually all of which were Fianna Fáil-oriented – and, after waiting and watching for many months, the electorate was now beginning to sit up and take notice. In fact, during 1999 and 2000, the government appeared to be on the brink of falling apart and was seriously threatened on a number of occasions. It was kept together solely, it would appear, by the collective determination of the Taoiseach and Tánaiste, although each, in turn, had precipitated a crisis on at least one occasion.

Irish Times/MRBI Polls

The first opinion poll of 1999, taken on 24th February, saw a substantial downturn in two areas, a marginal drop in two others and, generally, bad news for the government. Its rating had dropped 16 points to 52 per cent over the previous four months; that for the Taoiseach by 11 to 70 per cent; and Fianna Fáil support was also down by eight points to 48 per cent. Fine Gael, Labour and the Progressive Democrats were all up.

In a more specific context, a majority of three electors in every five felt that the type of unacceptable behaviour, which had emerged at the various tribunals, was common to most politicians rather than being limited to just a few. This viewpoint was held by 60 per cent of Fianna Fáil supporters and, indeed, by majorities of supporters of all parties. A much greater majority – four in every five electors – also held the view that the behaviour that emerged at the tribunals still existed and was not a thing of the past. There was no doubt that the revelations from the tribunals were beginning to influence reaction in the public mind. The general unsatisfactory impact brought into focus the media reports that the Taoiseach was being urged by some cabinet members to call an election on the basis of the earlier high ratings, with the objective of achieving the long-sought single-party government. The Taoiseach desisted.

During the spring of 1999, the outlook for the government continued to be considerably less than bright. In January the media reported that businessman Tom Gilmartin had given £50,000 to Pádraig Flynn in 1989, which Bertie Ahern was reported to have known about, resulted in a Dáil censure for the commissioner. Around the same time, what became known as the Sheehy Affair also surfaced, when a young man was released from jail before completion of his sentence, and the ensuing investigation led to the resignations of both a Supreme Court and a High Court judge. When the Taoiseach made a statement to the Dáil that he also had made representations on the young man's behalf, the tension within government rose.

The next opinion poll, taken on 10th May, showed a further deterioration on all criteria. The Taoiseach's rating was down a further 12 points to 58 per cent, representing a massive 26-point drop from his post-Good Friday level. Mary Harney's rating was also down, but marginally; while Fianna Fáil support had dropped two points to 46 per cent. The government's rating of 51 per cent was its lowest since the general election. However, the most unfavourable fallout was that four in every five electors did not believe that the public had been fully informed on what had happened in the Sheehy Affair. In spite of this, a majority (55 per cent) felt that the government would survive until at least the end of the year.

Further revelations from the Moriarty Tribunal continued to occupy the media headlines – the writing-off of a large slice of Charles Haughey's £1 million overdraft with AIB; his expenditure on shirts; and Bertie Ahern's appearance before the Moriarty Tribunal – where he confirmed that it was normal practice for him to pre-sign blank cheques drawn on the party leader's account – provided strong indications that the perceived shelf-life of the government might be overstated.

However, a reasonable performance in the European and local elections brought a temporary respite to both the government and Fianna Fáil, and a June opinion poll saw an increase in ratings for the government, the Taoiseach and the party. The improvements were, however, temporary.

The End of the Millennium

The final *Irish Times*/MRBI opinion poll of 1999 – and of the millennium – was taken on 3rd November, six days after Dr Mary Upton had won another by-election for the Labour Party. She won the seat in Dublin South-Central left vacant by the death of her brother, Dr Pat Upton. While the year-end poll showed a further and highly significant downturn to 46 per cent in government satisfaction ratings, the remarkable ability of Bertie Ahern, as Taoiseach, to distance himself from adversity was, again, clearly evident, in that, simultaneously, his personal rating had increased again to 69 per cent.

The Taoiseach's high rating is all the more remarkable when the reasons for the government downturn are assessed. These were a combination of tribunal revelations; dishonesty in politics; ongoing problems in the health service, exacerbated by a nurses' strike; pay rises for politicians; and high taxation. Looking at the demographic groups, it is evident that all were satisfied with Ahern's performance as Taoiseach, but in no group – except Fianna Fáil supporters – were a majority satisfied with the government. Sixty-six per cent of those aged under 24 were satisfied with Ahern as Taoiseach; the corresponding figure for the government was 44 per cent. Seventy-one per cent of the 25–34 age group were satisfied with Ahern, compared with 45 per cent for the government. In Dublin, the relative figures were 66 per cent and 44 per cent and among working-class electors, 69 per cent and 43 per cent.

These analyses identify the existence of a personal phenomenon that makes Bertie Ahern a formidable politician. While the Fianna Fáil support level was 47 per cent net, having allowed for the undecideds, MRBI, for the first time, applied the new adjustment, derived from the 1997 election day survey, and the final adjusted figure was 41 per cent.

Party	A Core	B Net	C Adjusted
	%	%	%
Fianna Fáil	38	47	41
Fine Gael	18	23	25
Labour Party	11	14	17
Progressive Democrats	3	4	4
Sinn Féin	3	4	4
Green Party	2	2	3
Others	5	6	6
Undecided	20	–	–

Table 10.6: 1999 year-end party support – Irish Times/MRBI poll
(November 1999)

At the end of the millennium, the MRBI contention was that, if an election had been held on 3rd November 1999, the actual result would have been close to the figures shown in Column C in *Table 10.6*.

THE STATE OF PLAY IN 2000

The first opinion poll of the year 2000, on 18th January, saw an improvement in government ratings. However, notwithstanding the improved ratings, Charlie McCreevy's December budget – specifically the individualisation concept – received a negative response, with 52 per cent dissatisfied generally and 20 per cent specifically so. Other criticisms related to the fact that there were insufficient provisions for the lower paid; too much for the better off; unfair taxation and the usual criticism of the increase in cigarette prices.

Further polls were conducted in April, June and September 2000, against a background of more sleaze revelations. Frank Dunlop, the former Fianna Fáil government press secretary, told the Flood Tribunal that he had dispensed cash to numerous TDs and county councillors, in relation to planning matters. Denis Foley, a member of the Public Accounts Committee that sat in judgment on the financial institutions of the State, was discovered not to be depending on these same institutions, but had instead placed his money in an Ansbacher off-shore account. The government nominated former Justice Hugh O'Flaherty as a vice-president of the European Investment Bank, even though it had suggested his impeachment only a year earlier. Not surprisingly, at the year-end, both the government satisfaction rating and Bertie Ahern's personal rating, were down to their lowest levels since the formation of the government in 1997. Mary Harney's rating had also dropped significantly – from the low-sixties in the early years of the coalition to 42 per cent at the end of 2000.

However, 2001 saw support for the government return, most likely due to a notably favourable reaction to Charlie McCreevy's December budget. Seven in every ten electors held the view that it was good for the country, while the expectation of a rise, rather than a fall, in living standards was supported in a ratio of three to one. This reaction was in direct contrast to the reservations expressed by the European Commission, which claimed that EU guidelines had been breached. However, considering that the opinion poll was conducted during the week following the committal of Liam Lawlor – a Fianna Fáil TD in the Dublin West constituency – to prison for one week by the High Court for failing to provide the Flood Tribunal with full details of his financial affairs, the government emerged surprisingly well.

In a number of specific instances in the poll, the public had serious messages for all politicians and showed that many were becoming increasingly unhappy. A considerable majority – three in every five – were satisfied with the manner in which the Flood Tribunal and the High Court had dealt with Liam Lawlor in sending him to prison. The electorate was less happy with the way the government handled the case, and almost nine in every ten electors felt that Liam Lawlor should have resigned his Dáil seat. It remains to be seen whether this reaction will influence voting behaviour in the next election but, irrespective of this, a final timely point was that two-thirds of the electorate felt that one of the main reasons why people do not vote today is that they have lost respect for politicians. With the countdown to the next election already underway, the omens for an improvement in turnout look bleak.

2001 AND BEYOND

Despite the revelations and the problems besetting the government, the opposition parties throughout 1999 and 2000 failed to make any worthwhile gains. Shortly after the publication of the January opinion poll, on 31st January, the Fine Gael parliamentary party passed a vote of no confidence in John Bruton's leadership. Just over a week later, Michael Noonan was elected as the new party leader. Noonan has been a TD in the Limerick East constituency since 1981 and has held ministerial office in four departments: Energy, Industry and Commerce, Justice, and Health.

He got off to a difficult start. His planned Ard-Fheis for March had to be curtailed because of the threat posed by the outbreak of foot and mouth disease in the UK, and this was followed by questions in the media and, subsequently, at the Moriarty Tribunal, about a $50,000 donation channelled to Fine Gael – the source of which is, as yet, unclear.

The next (and latest, at the time of writing) poll on 15th May, showed an upturn of four points in support for Fine Gael, but no increase in Noonan's personal rating over that achieved by John Bruton.

The government, Tánaiste and, particularly, the Taoiseach, continued to receive high satisfaction ratings, and Fianna Fáil support held firm. The adjusted figures for all parties show that, had an election been held on 15th May 2001, the situation would have been: Fianna Fáil 42 per cent; Fine Gael 24 per cent; Labour 13 per cent; Sinn Féin 6 per cent; Progressive Democrats 4 per cent; Green Party 3 per cent; and Others 8 per cent.

With a general election due, most parties have started the warm-up process. One of the recent polls included a question on coalition preferences – and the results make for some interesting reading. Four different combinations tie at 14 per cent. The first three – FF/Lab,

FF/PD and FG/Lab – are not surprising choices. However, the fourth – an alliance of FF/FG – could be termed a surprise. Like everything in life, times change, but for a FF/FG coalition option to emerge to the same extent as the other three, indicates that changes are being considered and are within the bounds of possibility. Of some significance is the fact that support for the concept is higher than average among Fianna Fáil and Fine Gael supporters.

In the late autumn of 2000, TG4 contacted MRBI with an innovative proposal that we conduct a series of opinion polls in a number of pre-selected constituencies in a political environment in which the next general election was at least a year away. The concept was attractive since the simulated ballot paper technique was envisaged and this would highlight the impact, at present, of the sitting TDs, and the TG4 coverage would almost certainly be taken up by RTÉ and the national newspapers. My only concern was that some commentators – external to TG4 – might continue to make the illogical assumption that the figures were predicting the outcome of the next general election in each of the constituencies. To date, six polls have been completed – the last one, taken in Tipperary South in June 2001, was published three days before polling day in the by-election there.

The poll, being quite close to an actual by-election, did identify that Senator Tom Hayes of Fine Gael was the front runner, and his eventual election did not surprise me. However, by a strange irony, this poll also led to a Dáil motion to ban both the taking and publication of opinion polls within seven days of an election, which, if Joe Duffy's *Liveline* programme is to be taken as another monitor of public opinion, did not please the electorate.

CHAPTER 11

Divorce: The People Decide Again (1995)

The divorce referendum of 1995, taken during the life of the rainbow coalition government under John Bruton, was a period of unprecedented activity on the opinion-polling front. Over the course of the nine months leading up to the referendum in November, MRBI conducted ten research projects – seven for *The Irish Times* and three for the government. The seven *Irish Times* projects were conventional opinion polls in the *Irish Times*/MRBI poll series, each of which measured voting intentions on the divorce issue.

Date	Client	Yes %	No %
13th February	*The Irish Times*	62.7	37.3
7th–11th March	Minister for Equity and Law Reform	62.6	37.4
20th–22nd May	*The Irish Times*	71.8	28.2
26th–27th July	*The Irish Times*	71.5	28.5
29th–30th September	*The Irish Times*	67.0	33.0
20th–21st October	Minister for Equity and Law Reform	65.9	34.1
3rd–4th November	*The Irish Times*	59.7	40.3
13th November	Minister for Equity and Law Reform	52.8	47.2
18th November	*The Irish Times*	51.7	48.3
24th November	*The Irish Times*	51.6	48.4
24th November	**Actual result of the referendum**	**50.3**	**49.7**

Table 11.1: MRBI schedule of polls in the 1995 divorce referendum campaign

The three government projects were specifically structured to provide a basis for government decision-taking during the campaign and were, consequently, much more extensive in terms of information coverage, though they also included voting intentions. Their contribution, therefore, was much more strategic than is the case with conventional opinion polls, and their application was much more akin to the normal usage of market research in the commercial sector. The full MRBI schedule is given in *Table 11.1*.

EARLY 1995

At the time of the first *Irish Times* opinion poll conducted, on 13th February 1995, most people understood that the referendum would be held later in the year, but the actual date had not yet been made public. Minds were still generally unfocused and the two to one ratio supporting the 'Yes' vote was generally consistent with other opinion polls conducted over the previous five years. That February poll also showed that a relatively large volume of electors – slightly more than half – felt the government had not done enough to enable people to make up their minds, with one in four unaware of the relevant family law legislation that had been introduced since 1986.

Although no precise information was available as to when the referendum would be held, and also in spite of the 25 points differential in voting intentions, the final comments in *The Irish Times* drew attention to the downturn in support for the 'Yes' vote in the latter stage of the 1986 campaign, and concluded by saying that "*the final months, and specifically the final weeks, will be especially crucial*".

A few weeks later, on being approached by the Office of the Minister for Equality and Law Reform, Mervyn Taylor, MRBI had two meetings with the minister and other people from the department to discuss the issues in the upcoming campaign. Following the submission of a research proposal, clearance was given to proceed with a survey. In keeping with the ethics of market research, all details of the meetings and of the surveys were confidential and were treated as such throughout the year 1995. However, since the High Court hearing of January and February 1996 – when I spent three days in the witness box – the details of all MRBI projects on the referendum have been placed in the public arena.

The Early Surveys: Government and *The Irish Times*

This first survey for the government was conducted from 7th to 11th March 1995 and showed, *inter alia*, that referendum voting intentions had not changed over the four weeks since 13th February. The public appeared to be waiting and, of course, we already knew from the February opinion poll that many were not aware of the relevant family law legislation. The MRBI report to the minister, however, provided a more comprehensive and timely framework for the planning of what was a hard-fought and competitive campaign. The report embodied a detailed commentary, conclusions, suggested courses of action and supporting statistical tables. It addressed the following requirements:

- Reaction to, and preferences between, a number of legal options that were being considered by the government.

- Spontaneous (unprompted) perception of the issues about which people were most concerned.

- A rating-scale measure of the extent to which each of a number of relevant factors would make people more likely to vote to remove the constitutional ban.

- A measure of awareness of the grounds for a judicial separation (legislated for since 1989).

- Preferences (again using rating-scale techniques) between each of a number of possible optional conditions to be written into the constitutional amendment.

All information was analysed by demographics, by current party voting intentions and by voting intentions in the referendum.

By any criterion, this was a very detailed project and the final MRBI comment in the report prepared for the government was that:

> *The impact and,* ipso facto, *success of the campaign, should be professionally monitored in research terms, on a reasonably regular basis. A measure of voting intentions per se [as was done in 1986] would be technically inadequate since informational deficits must be clearly identified, to enable remedial action to be taken within the ongoing campaign.*

On 3rd May, the minister, Mervyn Taylor, announced that it was the government's intention to include the detailed conditions for divorce in the proposed amendment and in the next *Irish Times* poll, conducted just three weeks later on 22nd May, the 'Yes' vote had increased by nine points to 72 per cent. The 'No' vote had, correspondingly, dropped nine points to 28 per cent, the differential was now 44 points. The survey also showed that a majority of those who intended to vote yes wished to have the conditions written into the Constitution; that a time-span of three years between breakdown and remarriage was the preferred option; and, finally, one-third maintained that the government had not done enough to help people make up their minds.

The next comparable poll was conducted two months later on 27th July, and showed that the 'Yes' vote had remained solid, while a majority (55 per cent) also continued to hold the view that the conditions should be written into the Constitution and the preferred interval between breakdown and remarriage was still three years.

On 14th September, the actual wording of the proposed amendment was published by the minister, who also announced that the referendum would be held on Friday 24th November. It soon became evident that campaigning from both sides would now be much more focused. Over the previous five months, MRBI had conducted four projects, including the March survey for the government, and the growing intensity of the campaign was evident from the fact that a further six projects were undertaken over the final two-and-a-half months.

The Fifth Survey

On September 29th and 30th, two weeks after the minister's announcement, the next MRBI poll for *The Irish Times* was taken. On this occasion, in addition to the primary question on voting intentions, respondents were also asked the reasons why they intended voting yes or no. With the date now fixed, it was assumed that many would be more focused than before. As stated in *The Irish Times* at the time, the minister had now put his cards on the table, and the electorate were fully aware of what was on offer.

The slight reduction in the 'Yes' vote by five points to 67 per cent, while not dramatic, nevertheless represented the first downturn in support in the campaign to date. This trend continued relentlessly until 18th November, one week before the referendum. However, it stabilised, very noticeably, during that final week, the relevance of which we will return to later. While the reasons given by those who intended voting yes did not at the time appear to be very enlightening, in retrospect the main reasons were particularly so. Some 43 per cent of all electors (or 71 per cent of those who were voting yes which equates with over 1 million people) stated that they intended to do so, *"to enable people to have a choice to remarry"*. This spontaneous comment was made four weeks before the government's press campaign had commenced on 29th October.

It strongly suggests that, when the campaign came on stream, it was very much in line with the thinking of the electorate. This time dimension is crucial, since the main thrust of the case in the subsequent High Court petition in January of 1996, was that the government print campaign was influential in securing victory for the 'Yes' vote. (The issue is addressed in detail in *Chapters 12* and *13*.)

In the concluding comments in the March survey for the government, I suggested that progress should be professionally monitored on a reasonably regular basis as the campaign developed. The series of *Irish Times*/MRBI opinion polls since February had, of course, been doing this but, ideally, the government required a more detailed monitor, in line with its strategic objectives. A further relevant point is that *The Irish Times,* material was in the public arena, and available to all interested parties on both sides of the argument. This was how the general background looked when the department made contact with me again to discuss and plan a further survey.

The Sixth Survey

This second poll for the minister was conducted on 20th and 21st October – just over four weeks before the referendum – and was structured to meet the following objectives:

- to measure and monitor ongoing voting intentions in the referendum; and
- to ascertain the reasons for current intentions and for movements in attitudes.

In addressing these objectives, the questionnaire sought responses covering the voter's:

- awareness of referendum date;
- current voting intentions;
- reasons supporting 'Yes', 'No' and 'Undecided' voting intentions;
- perception of likely outcome;
- recall of credible arguments, by those in favour of divorce;
- recall of arguments by those in favour, which lacked credibility;
- recall of credible arguments by those against divorce; and
- recall of arguments by those against, which lacked credibility.

Also covered were whether or not:

- the voter's mind was definitely made up, or if could be persuaded to change; and
- the voter was satisfied with government handling of the case for a 'Yes' vote.

All aspects were again analysed by full demographics and by party support.

This was the second survey since the minister announced the date of the referendum five weeks earlier, and the primary finding was that support for the 'Yes' vote was down one point to 66 per cent, with the 'No' vote, correspondingly, up one to 34 per cent – the differential was now 32 points, with just over a month remaining.

In this October poll, some 30 per cent – or approximately 750,000 electors – now intended to vote yes, in order *"to give people the choice to remarry"*, which compared with 43 per cent three weeks earlier. Furthermore, a further 15 per cent (375,000) were also doing so *"to give people a fresh start to get on with their lives"*. Again, the most interesting aspect about those attitudes is that they were expressed by so many people over a week before the government print campaign commenced.

The Seventh Survey

Less than two weeks later, on 4th November 1995, the next *Irish Times* opinion poll gave the first real indication of the likelihood of a close contest. The figures were now 60%:40% in favour, a swing of six further points away from the 'Yes' vote. At the same stage in the 1986 campaign, the position was 50%:50%. The interpretative commentary drew attention to the fact that the crucial undecided element – which had increased to 12 per cent since the previous poll – was confused, and required more information and enlightenment. It was also pointed out that both attitudes and intentions were changing rapidly, and the survey findings set out the following scenarios, with three weeks to go:

- *If the positions remain as they are, or if the 'Yes' vote increases, the amendment will be carried.*

- *If the current swing to 'No' continues at the same rate, the amendment will be carried with a very marginal majority.*

- *A swing of ten points will leave the result wide open.*

- *A swing of greater than ten points (13 per cent in the same period in 1986) and the amendment will be defeated.*

The Third Government Survey

The government commissioned a further monitor, conducted on 13th November, 11 days before polling. The government's worst fears were confirmed, as the new figures showed a further deterioration in the 'Yes' vote by seven points to 53 per cent. This represented a daily average drop of 0.7 per cent over the previous ten days and compared unfavourably with the daily average fallout of 0.4 per cent in the two weeks prior to the previous poll on 4th November. The rate of downturn had accelerated and, from the government's viewpoint, the immediate objective was to arrest the downward swing over the remaining ten days.

The point was strongly made in the report that, should the present rate of swing continue, the amendment would be defeated and, in setting out a course of remedial action for the final countdown, commented:

> *The remaining days should see the most impressive and credible speakers taking to the airwaves on the government side with the sole objective of halting the slide and holding the current position. This can best be achieved by drawing attention in a more emphatic manner than heretofore, to the fact that many people should have the choice to remarry, and should be given the opportunity for a fresh start.*

The Ninth Survey

What turned out to be the penultimate poll of the campaign for *The Irish Times* was conducted on Saturday 18th November, five days before the referendum, against a political background of high tension and drama. This was contributed to partially by the continuing downturn in the 'Yes' vote but, primarily, because of the *McKenna* Supreme Court hearing of the previous day, Friday 17th. The court held that the use of public funds by the government to finance its print campaign in favour of a 'Yes' vote was unconstitutional and was an interference with the democratic process. The government immediately withdrew all print advertising.

When the eagerly awaited poll results were published, the situation was that the rate of decline in the 'Yes' vote had been arrested – the downturn over the previous five days was one point, i.e. a daily average drop of 0.2 per cent, with the 'Yes' vote now positioned on 52 per cent – in precise terms 51.7 per cent. With the 'No' vote on 48.3 per cent and six days to go, MRBI's comment was that *"the coming days would be momentous and crucial"*. The gap of 44 points back in May had been reduced to minute proportions and was now within the statistical variation that applies to sample surveys. It was not possible to estimate with any degree of precision what the outcome would be. The average daily downturn over the previous five days was 0.2 per cent and, if this continued at the same rate, the outcome would be immeasurably close.

The Final Poll

Some weeks previously, *The Irish Times* asked MRBI to consider the possibility of conducting an exit poll outside polling stations on referendum day. Because of provisions in the 1992 Electoral Act, this was not possible, so we considered other options, which resulted in our conducting an in-home survey of 1,250 electors during the afternoon and evening of referendum day Friday 24th November.

The first stage of the interviewing procedure was to determine if the respondent had yet voted and, if so, whether they had voted yes to remove the ban, or no to keep it. Those who had not yet voted were asked if they were definitely going to vote or if there was a possibility that they might not do so. The interview was continued only for those who definitely intended to vote and these, in turn, were asked what their intention was. Interviewing commenced in the early afternoon and finished at 8 pm. The results were then telephoned or faxed to the office by the interviewers, after which all records were checked, tabulated, analysed and a written commentary prepared for delivery to *The Irish Times* by 10.15 pm.

The relevant sample base – those who had voted, or stated that they intended voting – was 1,074 out of the original 1,250 respondents, and was broadly in line with the 1,000 sample size used in all opinion polls for *The Irish Times*. When I first looked at the figures, I could hardly believe what I was seeing. In precise terms, the 'Yes' vote of 51.6 per cent, and the 'No' of 48.4 per cent were virtually identical to those of the previous Saturday. This indicated that the vote had held solid for the final week, and the downturn had been halted. The performance of a number of senior cabinet members on the news and on other current affairs programmes had been crucial and, while the downturn was halted, there were some negative messages in the research (see *Table 11.1* on *page 181* and *Figure 11.1*.

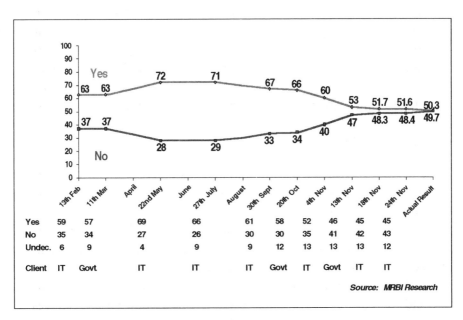

Figure 11.1: Results of the MRBI polls in the 1995 divorce referendum campaign

Although a marginal majority favoured the 'Yes' vote, this was within the statistical variation applying to sample surveys. It was the classic market researcher's nightmare scenario. Having looked at all the figures again, I started to write, in the full knowledge that the words would appear in *The Irish Times* well before the count had commenced. My report to *The Irish Times*, printed on the morning of Saturday 25th November 1995, read:

Survey Indicates that Capital voted 'Yes' and Regions 'No'
Dublin to Decide Poll Outcome

The first indication from this referendum day survey is that the margin between the two sides will be closer than in any previous referendum in the history of the State.

There is strong evidence that the amendment has been carried comfortably in Dublin, but has been defeated in Leinster, Munster and Connacht–Ulster, and it is not clear that the margin in Dublin will be sufficient to carry the day, in favour of a 'Yes' vote.

Over the past eight months, the Irish Times/MRBI *opinion polls have shown a steady erosion of support for the 'Yes' vote. When the campaign proper got underway in early October, the average swing was 3 per cent per week. By mid-November, this had eased to approximately 1 per cent. It was further reduced in the final stages of the campaign, and the current position is that the margin is within the statistical variation of the sample. The outcome remains a cliff-hanger.*

Before the formal count began, I was intrigued but not surprised to hear a number of politicians making the point that the outcome would be a *"cliff-hanger"* and that the referendum would be *"carried in Dublin"*; all giving the impression that the views were their own. The final result when the count was completed was: 'Yes' 50.3 per cent; 'No' 49.7 per cent.

The outcome, as MRBI had indicated, was the closest referendum result in the history of the State; the 'Yes' vote was carried comfortably in Dublin, and was defeated in the other provinces. The margin in favour was 9,114 or 0.6 per cent; and the detailed figures are given in *Table 11.2*.

Region	Voted Yes		Voted No	
	Number	%	Number	%
Dublin	305,592	63.6	175,234	36.4
Rest of Leinster	185,993	49.4	190,352	50.6
Munster	208,545	43.9	266,682	56.1
Connacht	80,045	40.6	117,343	59.4
Ulster (part)	38,667	39.1	60,117	60.9
Total	818,842	50.3	809,728	49.7
Electorate:	2,628,834			
Total Valid Poll:	1,628,570			
Turnout:	62%			

Table 11.2: Result of the 1995 divorce referendum

CHAPTER 12

Divorce: The Courts Decide – Part I (1996)

With a margin of victory of 0.6 per cent on such a crucial issue, it was not surprising that a challenge was mounted to the outcome of the divorce referendum. The petitioner was Des Hanafin, chairman of the Anti-Divorce Group, and his case was summarised by the judge, Mr Justice Murphy, as follows:

> *The government of Ireland sought to influence the outcome of the referendum by the expenditure of a sum of approximately £500,000 of public funds in mounting an advertisement campaign to advocate support for the proposals contained in the referendum.*
>
> *It was constitutionally impermissible for the government to advocate a particular outcome for the referendum or to spend public funds in supporting such advocacy.*
>
> *The activities of the government aforesaid constituted an obstruction of, interference with or irregularity in the conduct of the referendum.*
>
> *The nature and extent of the advertising campaign mounted by the government materially affected the outcome of the referendum.*

The case was heard in the High Court before three judges, with heavy hitting legal teams on both sides, in January 1996.

The judges	Mr Justice Murphy (Court President)
	Mr Justice Barr
	Mr Justice Lynch
For the petitioner	Mr Garrett Cooney SC
	Mr Peter Kelly SC
	Mr Shane Murphy SC
Instructed by	Collins Crowley and Company
For the minister, the Attorney-General and the government	Mr Dermot Gleeson SC AG
	Mr Peter Shanley SC
	Mr Paul Gallagher SC
	Mr David Barniville BL
Instructed by	Mr Louis J Dockery (Chief State Solicitor)
For the returning officer	Mr James O'Reilly SC
	Mr Diarmaid McGuinness BL
Instructed by	Mr Richard Walker (Chief State Solicitor's Office)
For the Director of Public Prosecutions, a notice party	Mr Maurice Gaffney SC
	Ms Adrienne Egan BL
Instructed by	Mr Edward Kent (Chief State Solicitor's Office)

Table 12.1: The players

BACKGROUND TO THE CASE

To set the scene, it is necessary to revert to the immediate post-referendum position, just two months earlier.

In November 1995, two events had provided the stimulus to the Anti-Divorce Group, under Hanafin, to mount a High Court challenge. The first was the *McKenna* Supreme Court judgment directing that the use of public funds by the government to finance its print advertising campaign was unconstitutional, following which the government immediately discontinued the campaign.

The second factor was the closeness of the outcome – a victory for the 'Yes' vote by a margin of 9,114 in a total valid poll of 1.6 million. This meant that, had 5,000 people voted no instead of yes, the amendment would have been defeated. The differential, as foreshadowed in the *Irish Times*/MRBI referendum day opinion poll, was the closest in the history of the State.

On 2nd December 1995, just a week or so after the referendum, Mr Gordon Heald, the managing director of Opinion Research Business London, visited Dublin and, having inspected the documentation relating to the government print campaign, signed an affidavit in the interests of the petitioner stating that, in his opinion, the print campaign had influenced the outcome by a margin of between 3 and 5 percentage points in favour of the 'Yes' vote. The implication was that, but for the newspaper advertising, the amendment would have been defeated. On 6th December, the High Court granted leave to Hanafin to present the petition, and the hearing was fixed for early in the new year.

In early January 1996, Áine O'Donoghue and I attended a meeting in Government Buildings with the late Peter Shanley SC, and a number of other people from the offices of the minister, Mervyn Taylor, and of the Chief State Solicitor. The agenda consisted of a detailed review of the three survey projects that MRBI had conducted for the government, following which I prepared a review document for the Attorney-General's office. This was comprehensive and covered the methodology and findings of the MRBI research and also identified nine factors, each of which had the potential to influence electors in their voting behaviour. It also stated that there may have been other unidentified factors. The identified ones were:

- anti-divorce spokespersons on televison, radio and in the press;
- anti-divorce advertising in print media;
- anti-divorce posters;
- the Catholic Church;
- government/pro-divorce spokespersons on television, radio and in the press;
- government advertising in print media;
- political party posters;
- Fianna Fáil policy statements; and
- MRBI published reports.

The document went on to conclude that:

> *In our professional experience it was not possible, in retrospect, in the absence of relevant tracking and recall research to estimate, with any degree of confidence, the individual influence of each of the nine factors mentioned. It was also likely that the impact of certain factors could have been offset by a subsequent factor and that those most evident in the final days of the campaign were likely to have been the most effective. During this period, the government print campaign was no longer in operation.*

Although I did not realise it at the time, this observation was to be of considerable relevance when given as evidence four weeks later in the High Court.

Having had the experience some years earlier of appearing as an expert witness, I fully realised the relevance of being as knowledgeable as possible about the matter at issue. I was comfortable that the primary objective of all three MRBI surveys was to provide information as a basis for the total campaign strategy to the government, and I realised that the MRBI involvement was similar to our involvement in the commercial sector, where research findings make a contribution to executive decisions. The print campaign per se was never mentioned in any of the MRBI briefings and we had no professional contact with the advertising agency, QMP, at any stage – before, during or after the campaign – as advertising was handled by them independently of MRBI.

On 12th January I received a subpoena from Collins Crowley and Company, solicitors for the petitioner, Des Hanafin, requiring me to attend High Court No. 6 at 11 am on Tuesday 16th January 1996 to give evidence on behalf of the petitioner. I subsequently received a telephone call informing me that I would not be required until 11 am on Tuesday 23rd and also asking me to attend a consultation at 9 am on the same day. I called my solicitor for advice and asked him to explain the legal and personal implications. He told me that I was legally obliged to attend at High Court No. 6 at 11 am on 23rd, but that there was no legal obligation to attend the earlier meeting at 9 am.

My position, as I understood it, was unusual since I was already under notice from the Chief State Solicitor's Office to appear as a witness for the government and, although the sensitivity and complexity of the situation was explained to me by my own legal advisor, I did not fully understand the legal niceties. However, in the light of the advice I decided not to attend the 9 am consultation.

There are two overall memories I have of the case. The first was the highly impressive impact of all three judges, each of whom displayed characteristics of understanding and impartiality, and all showed a remarkable capacity to absorb subtle technical detail with which they could not have been previously familiar. Their interjections were always strikingly relevant and perfectly timed and, on more than one occasion, I felt much more comfortable than I thought I would.

My other main memory relates to the extent to which the UK witnesses appeared to me not to have had sufficient knowledge of some of the more fundamental nuances of the campaign. None appeared to me to have done much homework on the ground in Dublin. Their lack of knowledge of the detail and personalities of the campaign surprised many and was remarkably injudicious, in my view, bearing in mind that they would be facing detailed cross-examination by Dermot Gleeson, Peter Shanley or Paul Gallagher.

THE EVIDENCE OF MR JACK JONES

I was the first witness and commenced giving evidence in answer to questions from Mr Garrett Cooney SC, who was appearing for the petitioner Des Hanafin. The first part of my examination by Mr Cooney was directed towards establishing my acceptability as an expert witness for the petitioner. Over some 50 or 60 questions, the setting up and development of the company was covered in detail, and he then led on to the technical aspects of market research. He covered my professional experience, lectureships, seminars and the competitive impact of MRBI in the marketplace.

I had occasion to refer, at one point, to research that MRBI had conducted for the government during the first divorce campaign of April 1986. Immediately after I did so, Peter Shanley objected on the grounds that I was now giving opinion poll results. He made the point that, as indicated to the court at the outset, the government's legal team would be objecting to opinion poll results, at the appropriate time, on the basis of the guarantee from the State to electors of the secrecy of the ballot; and, secondly, that such evidence was hearsay. This gave rise to a legal debate between Court President Justice Murphy and Mr Shanley, with justices Barr and Lynch also involved.

While Mr Cooney outlined case law examples to support his examination, Mr Shanley replied that no submission had yet addressed the critical point that, to allow survey evidence on voting intentions of the people, would be to encroach upon the secrecy of the ballot. The debate continued and the issue took up the entire afternoon until the court rose at 4 pm and adjourned until the following morning at 11 am.

Allowing the Use of MRBI Polls

On resumption, Mr Justice Murphy reviewed the factual evidence to date, set out the objections and then proceded to quote from, and comment on, the law cases that were quoted in the arguments the previous day. Summing up, he said that the court fully accepted the principle of the secrecy of the ballot, but did not see that it would be jeopardised in any way by the admission of the proposed evidence, and that there was no question of any voter being required by the court or anyone else to reveal his actions in relation to the vote cast by him or her in the referendum. He concluded by saying the court, therefore, was satisfied to admit the disputed evidence.

I was put back on the stand and Mr Cooney moved at once to the first MRBI survey for the government in March, and the circumstances surrounding its commissioning. I was taken in considerable detail through the technical procedures – the research and questionnaire plan; the individual questions; the statistical procedures; the interviewing process; the handling of the field documents in the office; the transfer of the data to computer; the analyses; the commentary and the presentation of the survey report.

Mr Cooney moved on to questions of a more strategic nature. (The questions are paraphrased below and some are abbreviated.)

Cooney: What part was this [March] MRBI poll to play in the removal of the constitutional ban on divorce?

Jones: As of March, I have no idea what part it played.

Cooney: Was it intended to play a part?

Jones:	Yes, of course. The government was MRBI's client, and when we present survey information we do so in the interests of the client. That is normal market research practice. We knew that the government objective was to have the referendum carried.
Cooney:	Was this poll to assist that objective?
Jones:	It was conducted in March and, at that time, it would have contributed at an early stage of the campaign plan. When I say *"campaign"* I mean in the broadest possible sense.

In the survey commentary, the final point was that *"information deficits must be clearly identified, to enable remedial action to be taken within the ongoing campaign"*, so the questioning continued.

Cooney:	What do you mean by *"informational deficits"*?
Jones:	Where people are getting the wrong impression or where there is a misunderstanding.
Cooney:	Wrong impressions or misunderstandings from whose standards?
Jones:	From the government's.
Cooney:	Which would be pro-divorce?
Jones:	Misunderstandings are from every viewpoint. People were not aware of all the facets of the legislation of the Judicial Separation Act.
Cooney:	What do you mean by *"remedial action"*?
Jones:	To correct a wrong impression by further promotion or education, and to make people aware of the correct conditions. If a lot of people were not aware of these, it would be a much bigger problem for the government.
Cooney:	What do you mean by *"problem for the government"*?
Jones:	A problem in having its objective met, which was to get the divorce referendum passed. There is no secret about the intentions of the government in terms of the result it wanted.

Cooney:	Is there any secret about the purpose of the advice that you were giving to the government in this report?
Jones:	No, the brief made it clear that the government was going to hold a referendum and that the plan was to have a positive result, a 'Yes' vote. This was understood from the beginning.

Mr Cooney asked a number of further questions, such as whether or not the survey conclusions accurately reflected the processed data. He then moved on to MRBI's presentation of its reports and the identity of the people attending each of the presentations. Since the third meeting was attended by members of the cabinet, the question of cabinet confidentiality arose, leading to further legal argument.

Mr Cooney next turned to the October survey, and asked what I meant by the term *"corrective action"* in my letter to Richard Humphries of the minister's office. I gave the same answer as I did when asked about remedial action earlier in the evidence. The methodology was again clarified and I was asked to authenticate the fact that the survey was conducted within the technical standards of the profession. It was now becoming quite repetitive.

In a number of respects, the October survey was different to March, which probably explains why Mr Cooney continued to read extracts from the report and then ask a question. However, one of the objectives of the October survey was *"to identify current attitudes as a basis for remedial action"*, and Mr Cooney asked me again what I had in mind when I wrote that. I replied by giving an example of people getting a wrong message or misunderstanding the conditions for divorce. Mr Cooney continued reading from the report and asking questions and, after a few further exchanges, he returned to the issue of remedial action sparking a lively debate. On re-reading the transcript, I now note a level of impatience and lack of clarity creeping into my answers.

Cooney:	What do you mean by *"campaign remedial action"*?
Jones:	In the referendum campaign.
Cooney:	And remedial action?
Jones:	This has been asked at least three times already.

Attorney-General: This *has* been asked about three times already, perhaps six times.

Court President: I think you were correct the first time. Maybe it was not associated with the word *"campaign"*.

Cooney: It was not, my Lord. I think Mr Gleeson knows as well as I do that this witness is his witness, he refused to attend a consultation.

Jones: I did not refuse to attend. I was advised not to attend.

Attorney-General: He is not my witness. He is Mr Cooney's witness.

Court President: I think Mr Cooney, to be perfectly fair, he has been a very helpful witness, as far as I can discern. He may not have given the answers in the manner which you expect, but I do not detect any note of hostility.

Mr Justice Lynch: Mr Cooney, you mentioned that he refused to attend the consultation. I think that if you were not in the case and, if the matter proceeded as Mr Jones says, and if the solicitor asked you should he attend the consultation, I venture to think you would have said – no, do not attend a consultation with anybody; but on subpoena, answer fully and honestly.

Cooney: What I would have said, my Lord, is that his entitlement was not to attend any consultation.

Mr Justice Lynch: No, he would not be asking just for his entitlement, he would be asking your advice, and I venture to say you would have so advised him.

Cooney: In the context of what you were saying: *"One of the objectives of the survey was to identify current thinking and attitudes as a basis for remedial action."*

Jones: This is right.

Cooney: What remedial action did you have in mind?

Jones: I had none whatsoever. It is not my job to take

action on behalf of the government. I am a
researcher, the demarcation line ends when I give
the information.

Cooney: Clearly, Mr Jones, you could not take action?

Jones: You asked me that.

Cooney: I am asking you were you advising?

Jones: No, you asked me would I take action?

Cooney: I am asking you now, what did you mean by
"remedial action"?

Jones: The same as I meant when I answered you four
times already.

Cooney: Can you identify one such action that might be
taken?

Jones: No, I can't.

Cooney: Let me finish. Please describe any specific act or
action which the government might take as a
remedy for current trends.

Jones: I have no idea; it is not the researcher's job to either
take action or suggest action.

Mr Justice Barr: I gather, Mr Jones, that what you can do is to point
out that the survey indicates remedial action in
certain respects... Para. 2.3 of the report states how
remedial action can best be achieved and you set
out two matters that may be effective. You spell
them out clearly there... Is that not a very specific
recommendation of remedial action? Do you agree
with that?

Jones: Yes, I agree with that.

Mr Justice Barr: I thought you said earlier that it was not part of
your function to suggest remedial action.

Jones: If I see an area I may well suggest it, but it is not a
direct responsibility of the researcher. If I feel it
might help, I may well decide to suggest it. The
demarcation line is taking the action. That is what I
mean.

Mr Cooney then moved on to the third and final survey for the government conducted on 13th November 1995, four days before the *McKenna* Supreme Court judgment. In most respects, the questions were very similar to those relating to the October project, and I am sure I answered *"yes, that is correct"* at least 20 times at this stage. However, I understand the requirement of proving every issue in open court, and the answers to a number of Mr Cooney's later questions were amongst those that, in my opinion, had a very strong influence on the outcome of the case. The following outline illustrates the point.

Having read a three-paragraph passage from the report commentary, which had concluded with the text *"and full advantage should be taken in imparting these messages via the most effective media"*, I was asked:

Cooney:	That *"media"* included newspapers, of course?
Jones:	No, the most effective media would not be newspapers. If I could refer you back to Para. 2.3.1, *"the most impressive and credible speakers"*, I said.
Cooney:	Yes, okay.
Jones:	That means electronic media...
Cooney:	During 1995, Mr Jones, MRBI was also conducting polls for *The Irish Times*. Is that not right?
Jones:	That is correct, yes.
Cooney:	Could you tell the court what are the significant differences between the polls you conducted for *The Irish Times* and those conducted for the government, from the point of view of the reports?
Jones:	In the first instance, they were conducted for two different purposes. I think I made that point yesterday.
Cooney:	Could you tell us what the purposes are?
Jones:	We know that the purpose of the government research was to provide information for decision-taking. For *The Irish Times*, the purpose was to monitor political opinions – this has been ongoing for 15 years.

Cooney:	Were the surveys for *The Irish Times* accompanied by a report?
Jones:	The reports for *The Irish Times* consisted of a brief foreword, a technical appendix setting out the timings and methodology, and an interpretative commentary. However, *The Irish Times* commentary is different. When we work for a client we present the report from the client's viewpoint and in the client's interest. In *The Irish Times*, I stand back and draw conclusions from both viewpoints.
Cooney:	Did your report to *The Irish Times* contain phrases like *"remedial action"* and *"corrective action"*?
Jones:	No, no. It was for an entirely different purpose. I have already made that point. The findings are for editorial interest.
Cooney:	Please look at this chart. Is that chart prepared by you? [*Figure 12.1* as illustrated.]

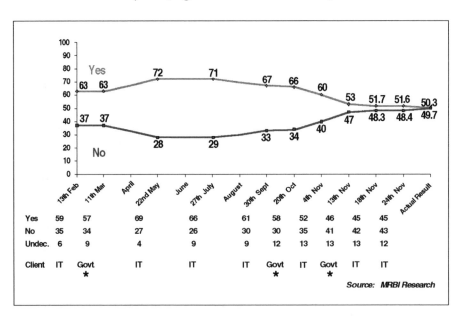

Figure 12.1: Comparison of results between the 1995 divorce referendum and MRBI polls taken during the campaign

Jones:	It is yes, prepared by MRBI...
Cooney:	The surveys that are referred to in the chart, include those for *The Irish Times* and those for the government. Is that correct?
Jones:	Yes, the government surveys are marked with an asterisk.
Cooney:	We can see that support for the amendment starts at 63 per cent in February, rises to 72 per cent in May and then declines to 71 per cent, 67 per cent, 66 per cent, and then from October a steep decline?
Jones:	Yes, a steep decline from October onwards.
Cooney:	Down to 13th November. Is that not right?
Jones:	That is correct, yes.
Cooney:	It seems to level out then from 13th November onwards. Is that not right?
Jones:	There was a drop of 1 per cent between 13th and 18th November.
Cooney:	Then a flattening out for its support as well – I think?
Jones:	In the last week it flattened out. Only in the last week.
Cooney:	The flattening out occurred in the last week. Is that not right?
Jones:	Yes, in the last week from 18th until the 24th, the 'Yes' vote stabilised.

This concluded my direct evidence by Mr Cooney, but, significantly, the last point relating to the stabilisation of the 'Yes' vote surfaced again in my cross-examination by Mr Shanley, which commenced immediately. Mr Shanley first took me through the series of questions relating to the reasons given for voting yes and no, and then asked (paraphrased).

Shanley:	In that final survey, am I right in thinking that not one single person indicated to the interviewer

that they intended voting in any particular way having regard to a government print advertising campaign?

Jones: No respondent who stated that they were voting yes, said that they were doing so because of the government's asking them to do so; that is correct.

Shanley: As a result of that did you come to any conclusion as to the effectiveness of the government print campaign that had been conducted up to 13th November?

Jones: One might have expected some level of response in that regard. While I say that no one recalled that specific reason for voting yes, it is not a measure of advertising effectiveness, but it does indicate that on that criterion, it did not have an effect.

Shanley: Can I ask you as a professional researcher, whether you or anyone else would be able to measure the effectiveness of such a campaign?

Jones: No, in my opinion there were at least nine other factors or variables which had the capability to influence electors to vote one way or another. Many of these in my opinion, had much greater potential to influence electors than the government print campaign that you mentioned... when the government print campaign was taken off on 18th November, for the first time in the entire campaign, the 'Yes' vote stabilised. That indicates to me that, if it had been as effective as people are claiming, it should have dropped further, but this did not happen. I think it could have been counter-productive.

Shanley: What do you mean by that?

Jones: From previous MRBI research, and in the March survey, there was evidence that 80 per cent were not prepared to trust the government to provide legislation in what was a moral issue.

Shanley: You say there were a number of influences being

	brought to bear on the 'Yes' and, indeed, the 'No' vote?
Jones:	Yes, there were about nine by my observations.
Shanley:	Allowing the government's print campaign as an influence, is it your opinion in relation to that influence, among all those other influences, that it was essentially ineffective as an influence?
Jones:	Yes, for the reason I have just given.
Shanley:	And, secondly, because it was so minute as an influence it was immeasurable?
Jones:	No, not because it was so minute, I have no idea what the influence was. It was immeasurable because there was an amalgam of many other influences out there. I will name them if the court would wish.
Shanley:	Perhaps just a few, Mr Jones?
Jones:	Primarily at that stage, the television and radio campaign in the last week by government speakers.
Shanley:	This is the point when the government's advertising campaign had been halted by the Supreme Court… You were recommending credible speakers of substance.
Jones:	Yes, credible speakers. At the meeting on 15th, I specifically mentioned using the airwaves.

Having mentioned a number of media programmes covering the referendum, Mr Shanley continued.

Shanley:	I do not want to go into what was debated, but did the context accord with the advice you had given in the November survey report?
Jones:	Yes. There was another reason, too. The *McKenna* judgment was handed down a day after I made this recommendation for credible speakers to get out and speak on the airwaves. The judgment, in my opinion, also motivated ministers to get out and speak.

After I commented on the performance of a number of speakers on television and radio in the final week, Mr Cooney interjected to say that what I was now saying was pure speculation about matters on which I had no expertise. While he accepted that I was an expert in polling and interpretation, I was now giving evidence that anyone could hear in pubs all over Ireland. Mr Justice Murphy said that he was inclined to agree with Mr Cooney, adding that the evidence would be admissible but that the weight to be attached to it would be a matter for the court to determine.

Although my personal viewpoint on the matter was that I could reasonably be seen as competent to assess the manner in which my recommendations were being implemented, I decided not to make any comment.

Mr Shanley's final question in cross-examination led to the recording of another crucial piece of evidence.

Shanley: Mr Jones, your professional experience has been set out by Mr Cooney at the outset, and I want to ask you a question based on those long years of professional expertise in this area: whether you consider it possible, in the absence of any tracking or recall research, to estimate with any degree of confidence, the individual influence or effect of the government's print advertising campaign in relation to this referendum?

Jones: Because of the factors that I am aware of, which have had the potential to influence the situation, particularly the most potent ones in the last week, I do not consider it possible to provide even a theoretical estimate of the effect of that campaign. The kernel of the whole situation is what happened on 24th November. The effect of the government campaign up to the 18th is irrelevant. My viewpoint is that, whatever residual support was there on the 18th, if there was any at all, it had evaporated by the 24th, and I will tell you why. If the influence of the Catholic Church had evaporated by 14 points in one week (based on the final and referendum day opinion polls), it is

> reasonable to assume that whatever residual influence the government's advertising campaign had on the 18th, it had well evaporated by the 24th.

The first question in the re-examination by Mr Cooney the following morning, was asked against the background that no one had stated that they had voted yes because of the government advertising campaign. He asked if it was correct that the majority had done so because of *"the right to remarry"*; *"the right to make a fresh start"*; and *"the right to make a choice"*. I agreed that this was so. Mr Cooney then referred to the government advertisements which I had seen, and which he displayed, and asked:

Cooney: Can you see any connection between these advertisements, which you have seen, and the predominant answers that people gave in answer to the question in the survey?

Jones: The answers that people gave do correspond to the advertisements, but I would like to refer you back to the October survey, when we asked the same question.

In preparing my answer, I had a number of reports in front of me and, instead of referring to the October government survey as I intended, I inadvertently looked at the September *Irish Times*/MRBI report. When I realised I had quoted a wrong figure, I said, *"Sorry, I am looking at the wrong report. I will re-phrase what I said."*

Mr Cooney then interjected to say that I would avoid confusion if I would *"simply confine my answers to the question I was asked"*. However, I knew where I was going and the Attorney-General appeared to recognise where we were going because he intervened to say that *"the witness may answer whatever way he likes"*. I then continued with my answer as I had originally intended.

Jones: I will now expand on the answer as necessary. I emphasise that on 20th October, 30 per cent stated that they were voting yes because people should have *"the choice to remarry"* and should have *"the right to choose"*. This 30 per cent were not influenced in their answers by the print

	campaign because it had not commenced at that stage.
Cooney:	What was the percentage in the November opinion poll?
Jones:	Relative to the 30 per cent, the November poll figure was 24 per cent.

In other words, the volume who claimed to be voting yes to give people the right to choose and remarry, was higher before the print campaign started. It was a crucial piece of evidence to surface, particularly at a relatively late stage.

The final question was, if MRBI had conducted any research relating to divorce, subsequent to the referendum on 24th November. The answer was that MRBI had not, and that concluded my three days in the witness box.

CHAPTER 13

Divorce: The Courts Decide – Part II (1996)

As the case taken by Mr Hanafin was underpinned by an affidavit sworn by Gordon Heald, which stated that the print campaign had influenced the 'Yes' vote to the extent of 3 to 5 percentage points, it was not surprising that the court then expected the petitioner and his counsel to substantiate these claims.

Three expert witnesses from the UK and a further two from Ireland appeared next for the petitioner. In the case of one, Mr Cal O'Herlihy, it was decided that his expertise was not relevant to the case.

EXPERTS FROM THE UK

Evidence of Mr Phil Harris

Mr Phil Harris, a lecturer in marketing at Manchester University was the next witness. His experience was in political marketing and he had stood as a candidate for the Liberal Party in Britain in the 1992 election and in the European election of 1994. The thrust of Mr Cooney's examination was primarily to highlight Mr Harris' view that the government's advertising campaign was highly professional and to isolate the impact of the government's campaign from that of the pro-divorce pressure groups. His position was that the government advertising would have added 2–3 per cent to the 'Yes' vote.

The examination centred on the variety of influences affecting the entire campaign and the ability of Mr Harris to differentiate between the elements, and so isolate the effect of the government press campaign. The elements investigated by Mr Shanley touched on the witness' awareness of the involvement of the Knights of Columbanus; the Church of Ireland and its publication, *The Church of Ireland Gazette*; the impact of the Catholic Church; and of the Green Party. It addressed the television coverage; the party political broadcasts; the activities of the groups opposed to divorce; and, finally, the part played by the local newspapers, where *The Kerryman* featured prominently. The questioning highlighted the intensity of the campaign and the challenge to the petitioner to isolate the government press advertising.

Before Harris stood down, Mr Cooney, for the petitioner, sought to have him reinforce his contention that it was possible to isolate and measure the impact of the government advertising.

Evidence of Mr Gordon Heald

The next UK witness was Mr Gordon Heald, Managing Director of Opinion Research Business in London. He graduated from London and Cambridge universities and is a very experienced market researcher. Mr Heald was a crucial witness since it was he who had sworn the affidavit back in November 1995, which set the wheels in motion for the High Court hearing, and his primary function would have been to affirm the affidavit. However, the first task of Mr Peter Kelly SC for Hanafin was to establish Mr Heald's professional expertise and credibility, and this was done in the normal way, by taking the witness through his qualifications, career and experience.

When his examination came to the stage of discussing the three MRBI surveys for the government, Mr Heald's initial comments were very favourable. He said they were very professionally carried out, were very accurate and that MRBI should be commended on that. However, he then proceeded, in my view, to misread the surveys and the context in which they were conducted.

To set the scene, it is necessary to elaborate on the types of research projects that apply in the area of quantitative political measurements, as they have evolved over the past 20 years. There are three distinct categories:

1. Political Opinion Polls: without commentary

Opinion polls that provide basic figures, with a limited factual commentary usually written by a staff journalist and normally commissioned by newspapers for publication.

2. Political Opinion Polls: with formal commentary

The main example of this in Ireland is the *Irish Times*/MRBI series, where the results are presented, along with an interpretative commentary. This commentary has normally been written by myself, as chairman of MRBI. In these instances, the commentary is objective and factual, since the purpose of the research is to provide a service for *Irish Times* readers. Another example would be the regular opinion polls conducted by Gallup UK for the *Daily Telegraph*, with the professional commentary written by Dr Anthony King. The prime purpose of this category is also publication.

3. Political Surveys: with detailed analysis and professional interpretative commentary

Conducted as a basis for executive decision-taking. These are technically similar to research in the commercial sector; their contribution is invariably strategic and consequently are confidential to the commissioning client.

The fact that the three MRBI surveys for the government during the referendum campaign were in this third category was clearly apparent in all three reports. They were all described as surveys, with the research objectives clearly set out, and the term 'opinion poll' was never mentioned in either the title, methodology, commentary or recommendations of any of the three reports. In all three instances the primary objective was to provide information as a basis for executive action. The analysis of the results was followed by an interpretative commentary, conclusions and suggested courses of action geared specifically to the client.

Mr Heald's responses to Mr Kelly's questions on the MRBI reports showed the extent to which he misread and misinterpreted the description and function of these surveys.

Kelly: You have had a look, I think, at the polls that were carried out by Mr Jones: the three MRBI polls, the first in March 1995, is that not so?

Heald:	Yes.
Kelly:	Do you have any comment to make on that poll?
Heald:	I think the first comment I would like to make is that they were very professionally carried out and were very accurate. I think Mr Jones should be commended on that. When I first swore my affidavit, I was told there were opinion polls done by Mr Jones' organisation and I thought they would be straight opinion polls on divorce and people's attitudes and everything else.
Kelly:	These are the ones which were in the newspapers?
Heald:	That is right, but after Mr Jones revealed the nature of the questionnaire and the results, I was really quite surprised at *"the nature of the polling"*. This was a very sophisticated exercise, not a normal market research sort of exercise. It was quite clearly very carefully thought-out. It was a kind of planning strategy for the government – this is not what you normally find in ordinary opinion polls. But the government was paying for it and this is what they wanted to know.

Mr Heald then continued to comment in quite a critical manner, e.g. *"one has to be very careful in writing reports for the government since it is civil service money and you have to be totally objective in the way you present it"*. He then went on to criticise my recommendation when I wrote that the implementation of the findings *"must be supported by an emphatic, intelligent, effective, educational and professional campaign"*. He further said that he did not disagree with any of the results; he found them *"interesting"*, but the whole tone *"was clearly designed to influence the government and to help them devise a campaign"*.

I was not surprised when Mr Shanley interjected at this point to question Mr Heald's motives in questioning the nature of the MRBI research, since in doing so *"he was criticising a fellow witness for the petitioner"*.

However, in further response to Mr Kelly's direct examination, Mr Heald said that the advertising campaign was very effective and professional and that, in his opinion, it influenced the outcome. He also made the point that because it was government rather than political party advertising it carried more influence, since the government "*is held in very high esteem*". I had earlier made the point in my evidence that MRBI research in Ireland showed that government advertising on moral issues does not carry the same influence as is the case when advertising conventional topics.

Mr Heald then produced two graphics, which were designed to show the impact of the government press campaign. I, being in the public gallery at the time, did not actually see these but I recall his explanation to the court.

The first related to the MRBI monitoring of the 'Yes' and 'No' vote as the campaign moved towards referendum day, and indicated that, had the 'Yes' and 'No' votes not remained static during the final week, the 'No' vote would have won. While I don't disagree with this viewpoint, it can be visualised from *Figure 12.1* (see *page 204*), I disagree strongly with his theoretical estimate of 55%:45%. It would more likely have been of the order of 51%:49%, in favour of the 'No' vote.

The second graph showed the percentage of the electorate exposed to government advertising on one axis, and the dates of the campaign from 30th September to 24th November on the other. Mr Heald's conclusion was that, during the first week of the press campaign, the whole electorate had an opportunity to see at least one of the advertisements; at the end of the second week, approximately three; and, after the fourth week, eight. He made the point that the numbers were based on newspaper circulation but, if one takes the readership figures as a multiple (i.e. more than one person can read a copy of a newspaper), the result would be of the order of 24 opportunities for the electorate to see the advertising. Mr Heald stated that the exercise was an attempt to quantify the situation.

He concluded his presentation and interpretation of his graphs with the comment that he thought the government's advertising was timed to stop the vote going wrong and was successful in this because of its weight and its professional targeting.

Mr Kelly then moved to the crucial question:

Kelly: Can you put a figure, by way of quantification, on the effect that the advertising had, in your opinion?

| *Heald*: | When I first signed the affidavit, but not knowing of Jack Jones' poll, I said 3 per cent to 5 per cent. However, because the ads have been much more carefully devised, it may have been even higher, but my relative conservativeness in December was 3 per cent to 5 per cent. |

This concluded Mr Kelly's direct examination of Mr Heald and, before briefly illustrating the nature of the cross-examination by Mr Shanley, it is relevant to point out that I totally disagree with Mr Heald's opinion that the government press campaign succeeded in stopping the 'Yes' vote disintegrating. My evidence made it clear that, during the entire period of the press campaign, the 'Yes' vote was dropping at times quite dramatically and it was only after the campaign was withdrawn, following the *McKenna* judgment, that the 'Yes' vote stabilised and remained stable for the final week up to the 24th. The press campaign was replaced by the very effective television and radio appearances of the Taoiseach John Bruton and of government ministers Michael Noonan and Mervyn Taylor. These appearances were impressive and, in my opinion, were effective in holding the 'Yes' vote over the final seven days – when the press campaign had been withdrawn.

Although I formed the view that, in general terms, Mr Heald handled Mr Shanley's cross-examination very well, particularly the questions relating to technical issues, he got off to a tough start.

Shanley:	Can you tell me when the campaign started, Mr Heald?
Heald:	Do you mean the press campaign?
Shanley:	No, I do not. I mean the divorce referendum campaign.
Heald:	I cannot.
Shanley:	Can you tell me when it ended?
Heald:	I know the government stopped advertising the last week. I presume television went on right to the end.
Shanley:	That is not what I asked. Do you know when the divorce campaign ended?
Heald:	What do you mean by "*campaign*"?
Shanley:	You do not understand what I mean by "*campaign*"?

Heald:	Do you mean the formal campaign or the informal campaign?
Shanley:	I mean the entire effort that was directed for and against the proposed amendment to the Constitution.
Heald:	The answer is that I do not know, but I would suspect on the day of the referendum itself.
Shanley:	When was that?
Heald:	The 28th November.
Shanley:	You will be glad to know it was the 24th.
Heald:	My mistake, sorry!
Shanley:	You do not know when the campaign began. Is that fair to say? I do not want to be unfair to you.
Heald:	Yes.
Shanley:	Would I be correct in saying, when you were asked to swear an affidavit in December, that you knew then when the campaign had begun and when it ended. Is that correct?
Heald:	I just looked at the weight of the advertising when I swore my affidavit in December.
Shanley:	That is not, of course, the question I asked, in fairness to you.
Heald:	With respect, a campaign can run on television for a long time. If debate continues, it could run for years before the referendum.
Shanley:	I am really trying to get at the state of your knowledge on 2nd December 1995 when you swore on oath what you thought the effect of a government advertising campaign was.
Heald:	I made an assumption that it was a normal, efficient advertising campaign when I swore the affidavit.

The cross-examination then moved on to the documentation that Mr Heald had seen when he swore the affidavit and he was put considerably on the defensive, particularly when he said that he "*would have seen five or six ads at the time and thought he saw all of them, as far as he knew".*

Although it was apparent from his answers that Mr Heald was a very experienced practitioner, particularly when dealing with advertising coverage, cost and impact, I was surprised to observe that he did not appear to be aware of many of the relevant informational aspects of the divorce issue. Peter Shanley posed a range of searching questions to determine the extent of Mr Heald's knowledge of the television coverage of the campaign; the party political broadcasts; and, most significantly, the advertising campaigns of the 'No' side.

Shanley:	I had better establish the state of your knowledge of the 'No' campaign. There were two groups campaigning for a 'No' vote, two major groups. Did you know their names?
Heald:	I was told their names, but I have forgotten them.
Shanley:	There was the 'No Divorce Campaign', and the 'Anti-Divorce Campaign', and a number of small political parties as well. Is that not so?
Heald:	I looked at their ads, yes.
Shanley:	I think you will concede that in assessing the impact of the 'Yes' campaign, the 'No' advertising campaign is a relevant factor in that assessment?
Heald:	It could be a factor, depending on the level of spend by the 'No' campaign.
Shanley:	You do not know anything about the level of spend of the 'No' campaign, is that not where we started from?
Heald:	No. I did make enquiries and I found it difficult to ascertain what was spent on the 'No' campaign. I suspect that was because it was not all together.
Shanley:	You see, what mystifies me, Mr Heald, is you come over here as an expert, which you undoubtedly are, and you have an exhibit in a sworn affidavit that purports to put together all the different types of 'Yes' advertisements, and you cannot do that for the 'No' advertisements.

Heald: I looked at the 'No' advertisements, as I have already said, and I asked what level of spend they had, and I was given the answer *"we do not know"*. It is probably about a third of the government spend from what they could ascertain.

Mr Justice Lynch: You produce here a diagram which gives the total column inches of the 'Yes' ads.

Heald: That is right.

Mr Justice Lynch: What is the problem about producing a diagram giving the total column inches of the 'No' advertisements?

Heald: I did ask the size of the 'No' campaign and, when I came to Dublin last week, it was not all pulled together.

Although Mr Heald defended himself well on his lack of knowledge of some of the informational nuances of the campaign, I formed the impression that his professional impact on the court was damaged to some extent. This came sharply into focus when he did not know that the petitioner – on whose behalf he was appearing – was chairman of the Anti-Divorce Campaign. However, in my opinon, his most significant omission was that, having presented a detailed analysis of the 'Yes' vote, he had not undertaken a comparable or even a less sophisticated exercise on the 'No' side.

IRISH EXPERTS

The Irish experts who appeared were Mr Anthony Coughlan, a senior lecturer in Social Policy at Trinity College Dublin, and Dr Cathal Brugha, a lecturer in the Faculty of Commerce at University College Dublin. Dr Brugha was called at very short notice (two days) to replace Mr O'Herlihy whose expertise was deemed not to be relevant to the case.

The Evidence of Anthony Coughlan

The first to be questioned by Mr Cooney was Mr Coughlan. Having initially established Mr Coughlan's professional credentials, including his interest in, and writings on, social policy aspects of the Irish Constitution, and his further interest in national referenda and the manner in which some of these have been presented to the electorate, Mr Cooney moved on to the main issue, the referendum on divorce. Mr Coughlan was particularly critical of what he saw as the government attempting to influence the outcome of a number of referenda commencing with the Single European Act. He then moved on to comment on the decision of the government to spend £500,000 on a press campaign in the referendum under discussion. He was a very enthusiastic witness, very committed to the task of monitoring the progress of the campaigns, but the primary issue for the court was to establish his expertise to draw inferences and conclusions from his observations. The matter was contested by the Attorney-General but, after consideration, Mr Justice Murphy announced that the court accepted that Mr Coughlan had asserted expertise in the area; that he should be permitted to give an expert opinion; and that his opinion would be subject to cross-examination.

Having referred the witness to the basis for his opinion, including his readings and the observations, which he had earlier referred to, Mr Cooney continued:

Cooney:	You have already given evidence that the government campaign did have an effect on the result of the referendum when the referendum was carried by something just less than 5,000 votes. (Interjection)
O'Reilly:	My Lord, it is a fact that the majority was just over 9,000.
Cooney:	All right, the majority was 9,000 or 0.57 of 1 per cent. What is your view of the effect of the relationship between the government campaign and that figure?
Coughlan:	I am of the view, because of the volume of the government advertising campaign and because of its nature as emanating from the government, that

it had a significant effect on the result in modifying the 'Yes' vote. Such a slender majority, half the difference is what matters. So it is 5,000 or 4,800 that is what is significant.

Cooney: I put it to you another way, Mr Coughlan. Had the effort behind the campaign not been in the campaign, what, in your view, would the result of the referendum have been?

Coughlan: In my opinion and conviction and firm belief, I am quite convinced, on the basis of my knowledge and political background, I am quite firmly convinced that the 'No' vote would have won this referendum.

Mr Justice Murphy: By roughly how many votes?

Coughlan: I have no idea, my Lord, but significantly.

Mr Justice Murphy: Tens or hundreds of thousands?

Coughlan: Quite possibly hundreds of thousands. Certainly many tens of thousands. It is the sheer volume of the matter and the effect on the decline in the 'Yes' vote which I gather is demonstrable.

On conclusion of the direct evidence of Mr Coughlan, the witness was subjected to a very lengthy and detailed cross-examination by the Attorney-General Mr Gleeson. The flavour of the cross-examination is evident in the following exchange, which was again geared to the measurement of the advertising campaigns on both the 'Yes' and 'No' sides:

Gleeson: How do you go about estimating the effect of an advertising campaign?

Coughlan: The first step would be to give a judgement whether it would have an effect or not.

Gleeson: That is the first thing you would do, is it?

Coughlan: On the basis of my knowledge, experience and common sense, advertising is meant to have an effect. In the last three or four referenda, in my opinion, it inevitably did have an effect, and would

	have an effect. The issue came up in several debates one way or another.
Gleeson:	Mr Coughlan. You say you are an expert. I am interested in the technique. What is the technique? If I hand you a set of advertisements, and ask you what is the effect of that advertising, what is the technique?
Coughlan:	Well, one can estimate. One can look at the volume and on the assumption that advertising generally has an effect, the greater the volume, the greater the effect. That is at the most rudimentary level.
Gleeson:	It sounds very rudimentary. Is there anyone in this courtroom that you think that that would not have crossed their minds?
Coughlan:	It is very fundamental, but short of doing special studies...
Gleeson:	Your technique, which is not, I have to confess, clear to me, by which you estimate the efficacy of advertising. Do you measure its volume, for instance?
Coughlan:	I have not done a practical volume exercise. I am not a practitioner in that sense.
Gleeson:	In what sense?
Coughlan:	I am not like Mr Jones, formally employed as a consultant in the campaign. I am a political scientist and a politically interested citizen.
Gleeson:	When you were preparing to give your opinion to the court, can you just describe the methodology? You looked at the advertisements, read them, presumably counted them?
Coughlan:	I had done this long before I was asked to become a witness.
Gleeson:	I know that, Mr Coughlan. I want to know your method. You have all these advertisements, tell us your technique, tell us what happens next.

Coughlan: The question was how I came to an estimate. What is relevant, if I may, is how I get an estimate of the effect.

Mr Justice Murphy: What is relevant is the answer to the question. What technique did you adopt?

Coughlan: I read the material. I made an estimate of the general volume of the material. I did not do an inch-by-inch measurement.

Mr Justice Murphy: What is next?

Coughlan: I also looked at all the other material. I was well aware of the various issues and the interaction of all the forces on both sides. I came to the judgement that the volume on the government side was such that it was overwhelmingly preponderant and therefore significant.

Gleeson: What was your technique?

Coughlan: My technique was reading the material, following the events and making myself aware of the details of the referendum process, and coming to a judgement on that basis.

Gleeson: With respect, Mr Coughlan. I do not mean this disrespectfully, the public houses in this city and in Cork are full of people who did just that; who followed the campaign and had views on everything. What do you present to this court as the expertise, the extra value we are getting because you are an expert. What was the technique? What routine did you use?

Coughlan: I was able to look at this material and assess it, on the basis of the fact that I have a political science background, that I am knowledgeable and have read quite widely the referenda literature. The man in the pub cannot bring that background. One then can make a judgement on the basis of that.

Gleeson: I have this picture of you in your study. You are not in a public house like all the other people?

Coughlan:	I sometimes go to public houses.
Gleeson:	Very good. You are in your study. You tell me that the first thing you did was estimate the general volume of the material, what was the result of your estimate? Is it written down? Did you put it on a sheet of paper?
Mr Justice Murphy:	Mr Coughlan. I think the question you are asked needs an answer, yes or no. Did you write it down?
Coughlan:	In the form of press statements...
Mr Justice Murphy:	No, no, no – on a sheet of paper; in a jotter, did you write it down with a pen, ink or pencil?
Coughlan:	Not as such in that form.
Gleeson:	Well, in what form did you do it? Was it invisible ink you used?
Coughlan:	I came to a judgement. I made an estimate.
Gleeson:	When you said, about five minutes ago, that you made a general estimate of the volume of the material, that did not involve any writing, did it involve any counting?
Coughlan:	It certainly involved counting.
Gleeson:	What was the figure you ended up with when you had done the counting?
Coughlan:	Well broadly or basically...
Gleeson:	No, no the figure, Mr Coughlan?
Coughlan:	I did not put in a figure, except that the volume of government advertising was considerably greater than the volume on the other side.
Gleeson:	You told us you did some counting. Is that true or not? Do you want to change your answer?
Coughlan:	I assessed volume.
Gleeson:	No, no. Did you do some counting?
Coughlan:	Yes.
Gleeson:	Tell us what you counted.

Coughlan:	I counted the number of ads in the newspapers; on both sides, their size and frequency.
Gleeson:	Where is that information?
Coughlan:	In my head.
Gleeson:	Tell us the answers for the 'No' side. How many ads did they have?
Coughlan:	They had significantly less.
Gleeson:	No, no, the number? You counted them.
Coughlan:	No, sorry. I did not say I did the exercise of counting the ads on both sides. I did not do that.
Gleeson:	Mr Coughlan. I believe the record will show that this is what you did say.

The issue of counting and note taking continued for a considerable time in detailed and searching fashion into the early afternoon of Friday 26th January, when Mr Coughlan was briefly re-examined by Mr Cooney before leaving the witness box.

The Evidence of Dr Cathal Brugha

The sixth and final witness for the petitioner was Dr Cathal Brugha. He presented an interesting proposition, the basis of which was a comparison between the downturn in the respective 'Yes' votes in the two divorce referenda of 1986 and 1995. At the outset of each campaign – approximately seven weeks prior to referendum day – the differential in the two 'Yes' votes was 6 per cent. On 29th April 1986 it was 61 per cent, and on 30th September 1995 it was 67 per cent.

From 29th April to 26th June 1986, support for the amendment dropped (see *Chapter 6*) and the final 'Yes' figure was 36.5 per cent. Dr Brugha's theory was that there was no reason why the 6 per cent differential should not have continued to apply at the result stages of the two referenda, if, as he said, there had been no major factors to influence the 1995 outcome. If there was no such influence in 1995, the expected result could have been 36.5 per cent plus 6 per cent, i.e. 42.5 per cent. The actual result of the 'Yes' vote was 50.3 per cent, and his argument was that the difference – approximately 7.5 per cent

– was probably due to the formal involvement of the government (see *Figure 13.1*).

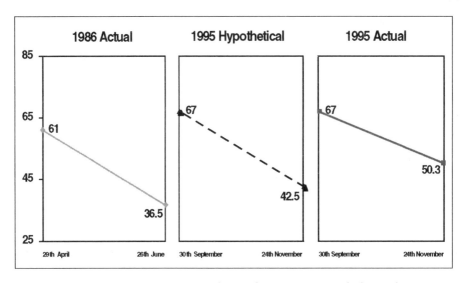

Figure 13.1: Proposition to the High Court: Dr Cathal Brugha. The 'Yes' vote

Dr Brugha also addressed what he saw as the changed circumstances that arose during the period between the two referenda. He said these applied primarily in the economic and social areas, and included action by political parties and other interests, by pro and anti-divorce groups, and considerable television coverage, all of which he said would have cancelled each other out. The one significant factor that stood out, he claimed, was the government involvement as a government.

He also drew attention to the increase from 9 per cent to 13 per cent among the undecided in the space of a month leading up to the referendum and felt that this suggested an increase in the level of uncertainty among the non-committed. This uncertainty, which indicated high volatility, represented a likelihood that people's opinions could be changed by various issues as they arose. He pointed to the effect of Archbishop Connell's letter, which caused an immediate downturn in the 'Yes' vote but which recovered within a week. This he said further reflected the nature of electorate volatility at the time. He again made the point that the official government campaign had the potential to influence those who were uncertain and drew attention to the government's strategy of accusing the other side of telling lies. The government advertising was, in his opinion, a very significant factor.

In answer to a question on the timing of the government advertising, Dr Brugha said that approximately half of the November advertising budget went on the country newspapers, i.e. the local weeklies. About one-third was spent between 5th and 11th using one advertisement when the downturn was approximately 0.4 per cent per day. During the period 12th to 18th, two ads were used including the one "*You have been lied to*". At that time the drop was 0.7 per cent per day, and the following week it was down to 0.2 per cent per day. That, in Dr Brugha's opinion, was significant. Finally, in answer to Mr Kelly, for the petitioner, he concluded:

Brugha: If we had not had this unusual impact from the government, one could have had a referendum result, which could have been anything up to a 7.5 per cent loss by the 'Yes' vote. I think because there are uncertainties in a lot of issues, one needs to be careful about making such judgements. If I was to be conservative, I would split the difference and say in the order of 4 per cent, rather than 7.5 per cent. Therefore, the figure that Mr Heald I think indicated of 3 per cent to 5 per cent, I would tend to accept, although he is coming from a very different viewpoint. Four per cent is probably a reasonable estimate. Obviously these things are impossible to say with exactness.

In his cross-examination by Mr Paul Gallagher, Cathal Brugha, not unlike most of the previous witnesses, was put on the defensive at the very first question.

Gallagher: Dr Brugha, could you tell me the wording of the divorce referendum amendment?

Brugha: That is a good one. I do not remember the wording.

Gallagher: Could you tell me what the wording of the 1986 referendum was?

227

Brugha:	I do not remember the exact wording.
Gallagher:	Did you study them yesterday, their comparative wordings between the 1986 and the 1995 referenda?
Brugha:	No, I did not study the wordings.
Gallagher:	Can you tell the court what are the essential differences between the wordings of the two referenda?
Brugha:	No.
Gallagher:	Do you think, as an expert, that the difference in wording between the two referenda might account for the difference in the result?
Brugha:	I think it is possible.
Gallagher:	Given that you think it is possible, could you explain to the court why you were prepared to give evidence as to the different factors between the 1986 and the 1995 campaigns without having regard to the difference in wording?
Brugha:	I would have voted in both myself, so I would have seen them at the time. If there was something of particular relevance that seemed to stand out, I would have recalled it.
Gallagher:	You now accept, if I understood your last answer, that it is possible that the difference in wording may have accounted for the different result?
Brugha:	It is possible, but not likely.

Other issues were explored, but the involvement of government as government was highlighted as significant and, in further probing, Dr Brugha felt this influence might account for 7.5 per cent of the differential *vis-à-vis* 1986 with a myriad of factors – changes in the electorate, changes in the preferences of the newly eligible voters, changes due to legislation – accounting for the opening differential of 6 per cent. Not surprisingly, Dr Brugha's conclusion, that a figure of 4 per cent would be a realistic estimate of the effect of the government advertising campaign, was called into question.

Gallagher: Could you explain how you arrived at the 4 per cent as being the difference attributable to government involvement qua government?

Brugha: Essentially, what I was trying to project was that, if there had not been significant outside involvement which was different to 1986, then we could have projected that the 6 per cent differential would have remained. But given some of the other factors that you have mentioned, I think that 7.5 per cent might be a bit extreme, and I said I would like to be conservative and say something of the order of 4 per cent.

Gallagher: I do not understand why you are prepared to put 4 per cent on the government involvement qua government, and 3.5 per cent on all the other influences when you have not weighted them in any specific manner?

Brugha: I prefer to take it on a global basis rather than to weight each of them individually. I think if you do the latter you lose a lot of judgement. You are talking about a judgement call between 0 per cent and 7.5 per cent. I think it would also be extreme to say it had no effect. Using common sense and simple evaluations as I have done, I would say somewhere close to the middle.

Gallagher: Is the 4 per cent, then, a judgement call by you?

Brugha: Yes.

Gallagher: A judgement call based not on the difference of the wording between the two referenda, not knowing anything, in any detail, about the legislation background, and the difference in the legislative background between 1986 and 1995. Is that correct?

Brugha: Yes, that is right.

When Dr Brugha's cross-examination by Mr Gallagher concluded, his re-examination by Mr Kelly brought an interesting exchange with the court, relative to my evidence:

229

Kelly: What would your view be of expert opinion, which might be proffered, to the effect that the government advertising accounted for a differential of less than 0.57 per cent?

Mr Justice Murphy: We have had evidence already given that it had no effect at all.

Kelly: I am just asking this witness for his view on the suggestion of less than 0.57 per cent, and then I was going to move on to ask about the evidence that suggested there was no effect.

Brugha: I think it would be extraordinary. I do not think that could be tenable at all. If this was not effective, I think the whole advertising industry would collapse.

Mr Justice Murphy: That is what I find very interesting.

Kelly: What is your view on the opinion that it made no difference at all?

Brugha: I think that is speculative and hopeful on the part of those who are hoping that the small majority of 50.3 per cent would not be overturned. I think it is speculative and wishful thinking.

Mr Justice Murphy: Did you hear Mr Jones give his evidence?

Brugha: No, I did not.

Mr Justice Murphy: It was his view that the government sponsored, supplied and paid-for press campaign had no effect at all.

Brugha: I am afraid that I cannot understand that view because I think this was highly well researched and very cleverly done. The key issues were identified, and open-ended questions were used to do this. They hit the nail directly on the head twice.

Mr Justice Murphy: And through it, the 'Yes' vote was falling. Notwithstanding this campaign it was falling. It ceased, or it certainly was not falling, when the government campaign was not there. That, I think, is the point that Mr Jones latches onto.

Brugha: That it was not falling when the government campaign was not there? That it stabilised?

Mr Justice Murphy: Yes.

Brugha: I think the government campaign had its effect by then. The campaign was there while it [the drop in the 'Yes' vote] was at 0.4 per cent per day, then 0.7 per cent per day and then it stabilised at 0.2 per cent per day, which was manageable in terms of winning. I think it had an effect. I cannot see how it could not have. I think it is the coincidence of the event of the government campaign.

Mr Justice Murphy: I think Mr Jones was saying that the coincidence was the stabilisation of the vote and the non-campaign in the last week to which he draws attention?

Brugha: I think that the changes had taken place by then, as a consequence of the campaign.

Mr Justice Murphy: And the last week did not alter it?

Brugha: It was very small.

Mr Justice Murphy drew attention to the difference in opinion between Dr Brugha and myself and raised again Brugha's view that individual events, such as Archbishop Connell's pastoral letter, could have an immediate, if short-lived, effect – the implication being that the effect of the advertising campaign could have been similarly short lived.

THE SUMMING-UP

Following completion of the evidence on behalf of the petitioner, the Attorney-General, Mr Dermot Gleeson, for the government, applied for the petition to be dismissed. He said:

The funding irregularity did not vitiate the freedom and integrity of the referendum vote, the onus was on the petitioner to show that the evidence displaced the referendum result. The evidence of the plaintiff witnesses fell noticeably short of doing this, and the matter should not continue further. No evidence, forged any link between the funding irregularity and the casting of votes on 24th November.

...The law was that a government was entitled to make its views known on referenda, and there was no contention raised that any advertisements were misleading or deceptive. They could not have been objected to if placed in the name of the political parties that formed the government. There was no causal relationship between the funding of the advertisements and the freedom of the vote, and no amount of passionate assertion by the witnesses was capable of surmounting this logical background.

Witnesses had conceded that, in order to disentangle one factor, one needed to weigh others. The two UK witnesses, Mr Phil Harris and Mr Gordon Heald, clearly knew bits about the rest of the campaign, but had startling gaps in their knowledge, while Mr Anthony Coughlan of Trinity College said that he could measure the advertising campaign but nothing else, and his evidence was weightless. Mr Cathal Brugha of UCD compared the 1986 referendum with that of 1995, but there was no theoretic justification to say that was the legitimate way of doing it. He also acknowledged the range of factors that could have affected the voter.

Mr Gleeson concluded by saying that, without the basis laid by myself, the other witnesses could not have given evidence at all.

Mr Peter Kelly, replying, said:

The government's wrongdoing was established, and the question remained: did the wrongdoing have a material effect on the outcome? The McKenna judgment has made it clear that people were entitled to reach a decision free from unauthorised interference by any of the organs of the State, and the government campaign was an unauthorised inter- ference. It had the stamp and approval of the government and should never have been there. All witnesses gave expert testimony, and the Attorney-General had taken the court through a checklist of what the witnesses did not know. However, nowhere did it emerge that the experts resiled from the opinion they had expressed. The opinion evidence had not been displaced in cross-examination, and the onus now shifted to the State to controvert what was said. There was no doubt that it was a very professional and vigorous campaign, and it defied both common sense and the experts to say there was no evidence. There was no justification for having the case dismissed at this juncture.

The court then adjourned for a week until Wednesday 7th February.

THE JUDGMENT OF MR JUSTICE MURPHY

Before moving on to the judgment of the court, it is worth recalling that the petitioner's claim was that the result of the referendum was affected materially, by an obstruction and/or interference with the conduct of the referendum, and/or by an irregularity in the conduct of the referendum. Specifically, the claim related to the publicly funded government press advertising campaign, which was conducted for a period of approximately four weeks up to the 17th November, at which stage, seven days before the referendum, it was discontinued.

In delivering the judgment, Court President Mr Justice Murphy set out the details of the petition and then moved on to the relevant articles of the Constitution and acts of the Oireachtas that govern the conduct of referenda. He described the historical and procedural aspects of the referendum of 24th November, the arguments put forward by the petitioner and the response presented by the Attorney-General on behalf of the government.

Mr Justice Murphy went on to say that, while the Supreme Court had decided that public funds may not be used to promote the acceptance or rejection of a proposed amendment to the Constitution, he did not accept that the decision of the Supreme Court prohibited the government from lending its authority to a particular viewpoint. He was satisfied, for the purposes of his judgment:

To approach the petition on the basis that what the government had done, both in relation to the provision of finances, and the use of their authority as government, was constitutionally impermissible... The petitioner's claim failed fairly and squarely on the grounds that the constitutional

233

wrong perpetrated by the government... does not translate into an electoral wrongdoing within the meaning of the 1994 Act... The manifestation of the constitutional abuse in the form of a highly organised advertising campaign, whether or not an influential factor in the outcome, was not an interference, obstruction, hindrance or irregularity in the conduct of the referendum. The fact that the costs of a campaign were defrayed out of monies that were obtained unlawfully, unconstitutionally or even illegally could not alter the nature of the campaign from a permissible communica-tion of information to an impermissible interference with the free will of the electorate.

Rather than rule on the preliminary objections and the defence raised by the Attorney-General and the minister, the court heard the evidence produced by the petitioner in support of his contention... There were obvious difficulties for the petitioner in adducing evidence, which might show the effect of the activities carried out by or on behalf of the government in relation to the referendum... Voters cannot be compelled to disclose how they voted.

Accordingly, the only means available to the petitioner was to attempt to establish, by means of a series of opinion polls conducted by MRBI Ltd in March, October and November 1995, what the voting intentions of the Irish people were at different times, and to present expert evidence as to what factors influenced the intentions so ascertained. This evidence was admitted by a ruling of the court and Mr Jack Jones, chairman and former managing director of MRBI, gave evidence as to the circumstances in which the research was undertaken and the conclusions which were drawn.

Mr Justice Murphy then went on to say that this research had been undertaken at the request and expense of the government and, clearly, the government placed very considerable reliance thereon, in the design and modification of its advertising strategy. He continued:

While it was clearly demonstrated that Mr Jones was mistaken in saying that his company did not advise on the strategy... [I have] formed a very favourable impression of the integrity of the witness and his expertise in identifying the factors that influenced public opinion during the course of the campaign, and quantifying to some extent the influence of these factors.

Mr Justice Murphy then said that he would return to my evidence later, and moved on to the other witnesses. He described Mr Anthony Coughlan as an interested and careful observer of the Irish political scene, but he did not think that he possessed the professional expertise in the interpretation of opinion polls, and the factors that influence public opinion. He said that:

Mr Coughlan – whose personal integrity and dedication was not questioned – in cross-examination was unable to identify any technique by which the volume of advertising could be related to the number of votes ultimately cast in favour of the referendum proposal.

Referring to the witness, Mr Phil Harris of Manchester University, Mr Justice Murphy commented that neither this witness, nor Mr Gordon Heald, had the opportunity of monitoring the referendum campaign in any detail; nor the political, religious or social events that might have had an impact on the result. He noted that Mr Harris expressed the opinion that the advertisements would have brought a positive difference of 2 per cent to 3 per cent to the 'Yes' campaign.

Turning to Gordon Heald, the Court President quoted the witness' affidavit, and subsequent evidence that the government advertising campaign had resulted in a swing of at least 3–5 per cent, and he continued that both he and Mr Harris:

...seemed unable to go beyond the point of drawing a conclusion, based virtually exclusively on the impression made on them by the government advertising campaign, and a general, but somewhat imperfect, knowledge of the dates and extent to which these advertisements were published. Whilst both also freely acknowledged that other factors were capable of impacting on the outcome, they did not attempt to make any calculation as to what that impact might be.

Mr Justice Murphy then drew attention to the fact that Gordon Heald dismissed as *"white noise in the background"*, factors that he conceded could have had some impact, but which he did not attempt to evaluate, and as *"he had founded his opinion on the effectiveness of the press advertisements, he must and did concede that the nature and extent of the 'No' press campaign was necessarily material"*. While Mr Heald made enquiries as to the 'No' press campaign, he obtained no material in that crucial area, even though he recognised that agencies were available that could provide an analysis of press advertising, but it was extraordinary that this was not made available, and he *"felt it possible to express a view, and a very precise view, on the effectiveness of one press campaign, without a careful analysis of the campaign... advocating the alternative view"*.

Again, while both Mr Heald and Mr Harris recognised the significance of television as a medium of communication and advocacy, neither made any attempt to calculate its effect on the referendum. *"This was all the more surprising,"* the judge continued, *"when it was recognised that the first witness, Mr Jack Jones, had given emphatic evidence that the television campaign in the last week preceding the referendum, was of decisive importance."*

Mr Justice Murphy then turned to the evidence of Dr Cathal Brugha, whom he described as a highly qualified academic in disciplines, which would lend authority to any view he expressed on the interpretation of figures or statistics in electoral matters. The justice also noted that Dr Brugha was invited to give evidence at very short notice which created particular problems for him, but that he did have the advantage of a long interest in Irish politics and, unlike the experts from the UK, he was fully familiar with the background to the referendum.

The justice then addressed Dr Brugha's technical submission with considerable precision and exactness and commented that the opinion had the merit that the witness explained the basis on which he reached the figure of up to 7.8 per cent, *"even if questions might arise as to the validity of the approach and, more particularly, to the discount which he was prepared to allow against it"*. Mr Justice Murphy then noted the various extraneous factors mentioned by Dr Brugha relative to the referendum that formed the basis of the discount figure, but added that the witness *"gave no explanation or justification for the discount"*. Dr Brugha had *"fairly said that it was a professional judgement and it was the best that could be done in the circumstances. Unfortunately,"* Mr Justice Murphy concluded, *"this left the figure wholly at large"*.

Mr Justice Murphy then returned to my evidence and said that I had claimed to identify at least nine factors or variables that had the capacity and capability of influencing electors to vote one way or the other, and that I also expressed the opinion that many of these had a greater potential to influence electors than the government print campaign. He continued that I produced a chart showing a continual slide in the 'Yes' vote and an upturn in the 'No' vote, from May 1995 right up to 18th November. In other words, the 'Yes' vote was dropping throughout the government print campaign. That campaign ceased on 18th November and Mr Justice Murphy then quoted verbatim from my evidence:

> 'That indicates to me that, if it was as effective as people are claiming, the 'Yes' vote should have dropped further after 18th, but it did not. This happened for a number of reasons, one of which is that the campaign could have been counter-productive.'
>
> It was Mr Jones' evidence that the campaign was won by the government in the last week primarily as a result of the television and radio appearances led by government speakers.
>
> I consider that the final week of the campaign was crucial, and I consider that the effect of the government campaign up to 17th November was irrelevant. It is what effect it had on referendum day 24th that was the real issue. I think that whatever residual support was there on 18th, if there was any at all, had evaporated by the 24th.

Mr Justice Murphy then concluded by saying that:

> ...the undisputed figures showing the stabilisation in the 'Yes' and 'No' votes respectively, after the 17th November when the government print campaign ceased and was replaced by radio and television appearances offer dramatic support for what would otherwise have been an improbable conclusion".

He concluded by saying that, having heard all the witnesses give their evidence and be cross-examined thereon, he was *"unconvinced that the campaign materially affected the result of the referendum"*. Accordingly, he would dismiss the petition, and make the orders as requested by *section 57* of the 1994 Act.

Both Mr Justice Lynch and Mr Justice Barr agreed with this order. On appeal to the Supreme Court, the High Court decision was upheld.

MY WITNESS BOX EXPERIENCE

Although I spent three days in the witness box being examined, cross-examined and re-examined, my memories of the event are pleasant and satisfying and, whilst there were a few tough exchanges, at no stage did I feel under stress or pressure. From my viewpoint, the most fulfilling aspect of the time in court was the crucial and influential role played by MRBI and, specifically, the fact that the research conclusions given in evidence, were significant factors on which the court based its decision. Although my direct examination related primarily to the research conducted for the government, the opinion polls for *The Irish Times,* and, specifically, those on 18th and 24th that identified the stabilisation of the 'Yes' and 'No' votes, were also highly influential in the court decision. This is evident from the verbatim quotations of Mr Justice Murphy in his summing-up.

Until Mr Justice Murphy commented that I was mistaken in saying that MRBI did not advise on strategy, I was unaware that I had given that impression to the court. I remember early in my examination answering yes, when Mr Cooney asked me, *"In that sentence, were you offering advice to the government?"* The impression apparently arose when I misunderstood a later question from Mr Cooney when he asked, *"What remedial action did you have in mind?"* I said none whatsoever, and added that it was not my job to take action on behalf of the government.

The essence of all three MRBI reports for the government were advisory and all contained numerous recommendations culminating with the final crucial suggestion that senior spokespersons, including ministers, should use the airwaves during the final week of the campaign to secure the 'Yes' vote. The government won the war but the market research profession, and specifically MRBI, certainly won a battle.

CHAPTER 14

Northern Ireland

BACKGROUND

When, in May 1982, MRBI was first asked to undertake political research in Northern Ireland, many significant events had already taken place during the previous ten years or so. The SDLP had been established in August 1970; the Bloody Sunday shootings of January 1972 still remained a dark cloud in the memories of many; direct rule from Westminster had been introduced in March 1972; and a referendum to remain within the United Kingdom had been passed in March 1973. May saw the Northern Ireland Assembly Act enacted in Westminster and, in June, the assembly election took place. In July, the Northern Ireland Constitution Act provided for an executive in lieu of parliament and, in December 1973, the Sunningdale Agreement established a power-sharing executive. However, when the Ulster Workers' Council, which was set up to oppose Sunningdale, called a loyalist strike in early May 1974, the executive fell within a month.

The late 1970s saw activity extend below the border and, in July 1976, British Ambassador Sir Christopher Ewart-Biggs and civil servant Judith Cooke were killed in an explosion in Sandyford, south County Dublin. On 27th August 1979, Earl Mountbatten and two teenagers were killed by an explosion on his boat in County Sligo. On the same day, 18 British soldiers also lost their lives in an explosion at Warrenpoint in County Down.

In March 1981, IRA prisoners in Long Kesh, seeking special category status, began a hunger strike and by October, when the strike was called off, ten had died. These included Bobby Sands, who had won a by-election in April and was elected MP for Fermanagh–Tyrone, and Kieran Doherty, who had also been elected TD for Cavan–Monaghan in the 1981 general election.

SURVEY ON THE PRIOR PROPOSALS

On 5th April 1982, James Prior, the Northern Ireland Secretary, introduced proposals at Westminster that provided for the election of a new consultative assembly, to which, in certain circumstances, executive power would be devolved.

Jim Downey, then deputy editor of *The Irish Times*, set out the brief for a research project in Northern Ireland, the objective of which was to measure reaction to Prior's proposals. This was the first occasion on which the company had been commissioned to work in the political arena in the North and, of perhaps greater significance, it was also the first MRBI project for *The Irish Times*.

Methodology of the Survey

The statistical sample of 1,000 electors was fully representative of the Northern Ireland electorate. We decided on in-home interviewing, on the basis that, although more expensive, it was considerably more reliable than either street or telephone interviewing. The questionnaire covered the following topics:

- Whether or not in favour of a new elected assembly for Northern Ireland.

- The likelihood of voting in the event of an election to the new assembly.

- Current party voting intentions, if an assembly election was held on the day.

- Second preference voting intentions, should proportional representation be used in an election.

- Whether or not a new assembly should elect an executive to conduct the internal affairs of Northern Ireland.

- Whether or not an executive should have control over education; housing; security; law and order; and economic policy.

- If in favour, or not, of power sharing on such an executive.

- How the rights of the minority should be protected, among those who would not favour power sharing.

- Whether or not there should be North–South co-operation on tourism and energy policy.

- Whether or not the Anglo–Irish talks should be extended to talks between elected representatives in Northern Ireland and Dublin.

- Whether or not the Anglo–Irish talks should continue at civil service and at ministerial levels.

- Extent to which each of a number of alternatives would be preferred to an elected assembly.

- Reaction to the concept of a united Ireland sometime in the future.

The survey was conducted over the period 10th–14th May 1982, and the results provided MRBI with the first direct evidence of the problems facing the nationalist community at the time. It also highlighted the difficulties facing nationalist leaders, with whom we were later to develop very strong relationships.

Results

Although two in every three electors (the majority of whom were within the unionist community) favoured the concept of a new elected assembly and the election of an executive to run Northern Ireland's affairs, there was noticeably less support for power sharing in such an executive. Not surprisingly, this latter concept was very strongly supported by the minority nationalist community. When those who were against power sharing (almost exclusively unionist) were asked how the rights of the minority community should be protected, a third of them claimed that *"they [the nationalists] were doing all right"* or were *"already protected"*, while a further third had no idea how the minority could be protected. These signals were ominous at the time, and clearly identified the depth of feeling of those diehard elements, who continue to resist change.

Further evidence of a reluctance to share power was apparent when preferences for suggested alternatives to an elected assembly were measured. The main preferences – exclusively unionist – were integration with Great Britain or a continuation of Direct Rule, mentioned by 60 per cent. This was followed by 14 per cent who favoured federation with the Republic (exclusively nationalist), with 9 per cent favouring an independent Northern Ireland. The remaining 17 per cent, which was equally divided between unionists and nationalists, favoured none of the four suggested options. The final question measured reaction to a united Ireland and provided no surprises with a two to one majority against. The assembly was established in the autumn of 1982, but was boycotted by the SDLP representatives.

THE 1983 GENERAL ELECTION

The Westminster election of 9th June 1983 was the first general election in Northern Ireland in which MRBI was involved in opinion polling. Our client was the Belfast newpaper *Irish News* and interviewing took place just nine days before the election with the sample of 1,000 electors distributed representatively across all 17 constituencies in the North. The report made the point that the extreme manifestations of rivalry, not just between, but, more significantly, within the two main communities had created numerous imponderables.

The questionnaire took account of the fact that the political environment was completely different to that in which we had been operating in the Republic. In addition to the main questions on current voting intentions, respondents were also asked which parties, if any, they would definitely not vote for, and all were also asked to state the reasons for their choice of party, and also for not voting for particular parties. Preferred candidates were identified, as was perception of the main issues in the election. The foreword to the report drew attention to the fact that the share of seats obtained by each party would not necessarily be directly related to its corresponding share of votes, and also illustrated the wide variation in the ratio of seats to votes that materialised in the previous election of 1979.

Having adjusted for the one in five who were undecided, the survey figures on voting intentions, relative to the actual election results, are given in *Table 14.1*.

Party	MRBI	Election
	%	%
UUP	35	34
DUP	21	20
SDLP	16	18
Sinn Féin	8	13
Alliance	13	8
Others	7	7

Table 14.1: Voting intentions as stated in the Irish News/MRBI *survey of June 1983*

While the figures for the top three parties were very close to the actual election results, the now well-identified understatement of support for Sinn Féin and overstatement for the Alliance Party became apparent to us for the first time. The report stated that, while the outcome of 11 constituencies was fairly predictable, the result in six was uncertain, in that in three instances UUP and DUP candidates were very closely in contention. In one, the UUP and SDLP were sharing the lead; in another, UUP, SDLP and Sinn Féin; while in the final one, a four-way battle was taking place. In overall terms, the survey showed that the UUP was leading in seven constituencies; the DUP in two; SDLP in one; an Independent in one; and in the remainder the outcome was uncertain.

Survey in December 1983

Some six months later, in December 1983, the scene was examined again. On this occasion MRBI was approached by BBC Northern Ireland to measure reaction to the Northern Ireland Assembly, which, at that stage, was just over a year old. Again, the sample was fully representative of the electorate throughout the province, and the questionnaire addressed the following issues:

Northern Ireland Assembly
• Had it brought devolved government closer or not?

- Did it give hope of an agreement, which would lead to the devolution of power from Westminster?

- Preference or not for survival of the assembly.

- Reaction to the SDLP boycott of the assembly.

- Whether or not the Secretary of State should start negotiations with the other main constitutional parties, if the SDLP boycott continued.

- Reaction to the assembly walkout by the UUP following the Darkley Church murders on 20th November.

- Preference among a number of options should the assembly collapse or be wound up?

New Ireland Forum

- Opinion as to whether or not it could make a contribution towards solving the problem in Northern Ireland.

- Reaction to the 'New Ireland' proposal that was being considered by the forum.

General

- Current party support levels.

Reaction to the assembly was very much in keeping with the political divide, which could have been expected since the SDLP and Sinn Féin had not participated from the outset. It was not perceived to have brought devolved government any closer, a viewpoint shared by supporters of all parties, nor was it seen to offer hope of agreement that would lead to devolution or transfer of power from Westminster. All parties were unanimous on this point, but the nationalist parties were very clearly associated with negative reaction.

The slight majority that would like the assembly to survive, comprised primarily UUP, DUP and Alliance voters. Reaction to the SDLP boycott was interesting in that, while UUP, DUP and Alliance disagreed with it, support was forthcoming from Sinn Féin, although SDLP voters themselves were divided on the issue. Overall comment on the concept of the Secretary of State commencing negotiations with the other parties in the absence of the SDLP was also mixed, with unionist parties and the Alliance Party in favour, and the two nationalist parties against.

The results from those interviewed, when asked to state their preferred option – from a prompted list of eight – should the assembly collapse, are given in *Table 14.2*.

Option	%	Mainly Supported By
Restore power to Stormont	33	UUP and DUP
Direct rule from Westminster	17	UUP, DUP and Alliance
United Ireland, under new agreement	15	SDLP and Sinn Féin
Integrate Northern Ireland into the UK	14	Alliance, UUP and DUP
Federal Ireland outside the UK	7	SDLP
British and Irish government agreement on Northern Ireland	6	SDLP
Marxist 32-county Republic	3	Sinn Féin
United Ireland under Republic of Ireland	3	Sinn Féin
None/Undecided	2	

Table 14.2: Preferred options should the Northern Ireland Assembly collapse

THE NEW IRELAND FORUM

Perception of whether or not the New Ireland Forum (which, at the time of the survey, was being held in Dublin and had been sitting since the previous May) would make a contribution towards solving the problems of Northern Ireland, was divided very much along the conventional two-way split.

The survey indicated some ambivalence within the nationalist community, with a considerable majority (four in every five) of SDLP supporters considering that the forum could help. However, the fact that one in five did not agree, was in conflict with the formal SDLP acceptance of the forum. Conversely, a marginal majority of Sinn Féin supporters held the view that the forum could be of help, but this, in turn, was also in conflict with that party's formal rejection of it. That it was not seen as helpful by supporters of the two main unionist parties was consistent with the stated position of the respective leaders of the UUP and DUP.

Options	Total	UUP	DUP	Alliance	SDLP	SF	Other	Und.
	%	%	%	%	%	%	%	%
Forum can help	32	6	6	50	79	54	34	42
Forum cannot help	62	89	89	48	19	39	48	44
Undecided	6	5	5	2	2	7	8	14

Table 14.3: Reaction to the New Ireland Forum – BBC/MRBI survey

Reaction to the "New Ireland Forum Report"

In early May 1984, the "New Ireland Forum Report" was published, having taken submissions over the previous year and, a week or so later, *The Irish Times* commissioned research in both jurisdictions on public reaction to the report.

Reaction to its perceived usefulness in the Republic was rather more mixed than might have been expected, with just a marginal majority rating it as useful. Almost a third were negatively disposed, with a surprising 16 per cent having no opinion or being entirely unaware of it. In Northern Ireland, reaction on the same criterion of its usefulness was much less enthusiastic, with a heavy minority (46 per cent) seeing it as not useful, and just one in four favourably disposed. The more detailed analyses showed that, even among SDLP and Sinn Féin supporters, a considerable number (one in four) did not see it being likely to make a useful contribution to progress.

The report had outlined three possible options to move matters forward: a unitary state, federation or a joint authority. In the Republic, two-thirds were in favour of the unitary state option, while, in the North, a similar volume were directly opposed to it. Joint authority was rejected in both jurisdictions. In terms of absolute preferences, the figure of 50 per cent for a unitary state, among the southern electorate, indicated that the united Ireland concept was no longer an over-whelming demand.

In Northern Ireland, a massive three in every five electors rejected all three forum options. This increased to nine in every ten among unionists, while nationalists were divided in their preferences. Sinn Féin supporters strongly preferred the unitary state concept, while SDLP voters supported all three options.

A. Perceived Usefulness	Republic of Ireland		Northern Ireland	
	%		%	
Very useful	16		8	
Fairly useful	37	53	18	26
Not really useful	14		17	
Not at all useful	17	31	29	46
No opinion	12		16	
Unaware of it	4		12	

B. Reaction to Proposed Solutions	Unitary State	Feder-ation	Joint Authority	Unitary State	Feder-ation	Joint Authority
		%			%	
In favour: very much	40	18	7	12	8	6
In favour: somewhat	26	37	20	11	21	14
Against: somewhat	16	19	26	9	10	15
Against: very much	8	13	34	54	46	50
No opinion	10	13	13	14	15	15

C. Overall Preference	%	%
Unitary State	50	14
Federation	22	13
Joint Authority	15	14
None of these	13	59

Source: Irish Times/*MRBI*

Figure 14.4: Reaction to the alternatives proposed in the "New Ireland Forum Report"

THE ANGLO–IRISH AGREEMENT

The "New Ireland Forum Report" was a prelude to discussions between British Prime Minister Margaret Thatcher and Taoiseach Garret FitzGerald. The three options – a unitary state, federation or joint authority – were the focus of the *"out, out, out"* dismissal by Margaret Thatcher at her press conference following the Chequers meeting with FitzGerald in November 1984. However, relations improved and the two signed the Anglo–Irish Agreement a year later, on 15th November 1985, at Hillsboro, County Down.

The agreement was politically therapeutic in that it set down markers for the future, in the form of bilateral commitments by the two sovereign governments. It had three main provisions:

- That both governments affirmed that change in the status of Northern Ireland could only come about through the consent of a majority of the people of Northern Ireland. It was also recognised that, should there be a clear wish for a united Ireland by a majority in the future, both the British and Irish governments would introduce legislation to that effect.

- That an intergovernmental conference be established to handle political, security and legal matters and to promote cross-border co-operation. The conference would have a secretariat at Maryfield near Belfast, and would be manned by British and Irish civil servants.

- The concept of establishing an Anglo–Irish parliamentary body was left to the two governments.

The fact that the agreement provided for the involvement of the Irish government in Northern Irish affairs caused shock waves in the unionist community and, in January 1986, 15 unionist MPs simultaneously resigned from the Westminster parliament in protest. While the ensuing by-elections saw the unionist parties lose one of their 15 seats to the SDLP, the outcome of the episode provided a gratifying experience for a number of people in MRBI, including myself.

By-Election Surveys

After the resignations were announced, and the by-elections fixed for later in January, Shane Molloy and the late Sean Murray contacted us with an urgent request to consider the possibility of conducting an immediate research project in the Newry–Armagh constituency on behalf of Seamus Mallon of the SDLP. At that stage, Mallon had not yet made the breakthrough to Westminster. Jim Nicholson of the UUP held the seat and John Hume had been the sole standard-bearer for the SDLP from the province.

The research was completed and, while Seamus emerged relatively well in the findings, the crucial message was that many young nationalists, potential SDLP supporters, had absolutely no interest whatsoever in politics and saw voting as a futile exercise. The main conclusion was that, if the nationalist vote could be motivated to turn out, Seamus Mallon would have a fighting chance of winning. The rest is history. He won the seat for the first time in 1986 and has held it successfully ever since.

In April 1987, prior to the Westminster election of that year, I received a phone call from Eddie McGrady from his office in Downpatrick, as a result of which Áine and I met him. The situation in the South Down constituency was very similar to Newry–Armagh – the SDLP had not yet made the breakthrough and the seat had been held for some time by Enoch Powell, who had moved over from the UK some time earlier to run as a unionist candidate. Powell was a very high-profile figure in the British establishment and had previously been a Conservative minister.

McGrady had an outstanding knowledge of the constituency and of the precise location of the nationalist and unionist pockets. It was apparent that a different strategy was necessary in his constituency and that a carefully constructed plan would be required if McGrady was to secure victory.

The first step was to divide the constituency into four geographical areas, the main criterion being the general political orientation. In addition to the conventional questions on current voting intentions and associated reasons and the identification of the local and national issues, the questionnaire was also structured to enable respondents to identify the relevant personal and political characteristics of each of the two main candidates; and their perceived attributes and deficiencies. The research plan worked wonderfully and, not only was Eddie McGrady armed with a very detailed campaign strategy for each region of the constituency, but he implemented it to the letter.

Being aware of his own and his opponent's deficiencies meant that he could aim to eliminate his own, and concentrate on those of his main opponent. Similar to the Seamus Mallon situation in Newry–Armagh the previous year, the outcome made history when, after a nail-biting count, McGrady emerged victorious by 800 votes. For those of us who worked on the project, it was one of the most satisfying that we had ever undertaken, and my regret at not being able to attend the celebrations in Downpatrick was offset by a very enjoyable reunion with McGrady at the MRBI 25th anniversary reception in Dublin, in the summer of 1987. Since then, McGrady has considerably strengthened his position as the poll-topper in South Down, and has held the seat.

In that Westminster election, the SDLP, for the first time, won three seats – John Hume (Foyle), Seamus Mallon (Newry–Armagh) and of course Eddie McGrady (South Down). The remaining seats were: nine to the UUP; three to the DUP; one to Sinn Féin; and one to another unionist.

GROWING VIOLENCE

While the inter-government dialogue that followed the signing of the Anglo–Irish Agreement continued, the succeeding years saw a serious resumption of violence on both sides. In May 1987, eight members of the IRA were killed in an ambush in Loughgall, County Armagh, and, in November, 11 people were killed in an explosion at a Remembrance Day ceremony in Enniskillen. In March 1988, three members of the IRA died in an SAS killing in Gibraltar, and a further three people were killed at their funerals. Later in August, eight British soldiers died in an explosion at Ballygawley, County Tyrone, and the following year, in September 1989, ten British army bandsmen were killed in an explosion at their headquarters in Deal in the UK.

The next two years brought two highly significant events, which had remarkable implications. In October 1989, the Guildford Four, who had been in prison in Britain since October 1975, were released. In March 1991, the Birmingham Six, who, in 1974, had been convicted of bombings that had killed 18 people, also had their convictions quashed and were released.

The violence, however, continued and, in January 1992, eight work-men lost their lives in an explosion at Teebane, County Tyrone, and, in the following months, five men were shot dead in a betting shop in Belfast, reportedly by the UDA. Shortly after this, four IRA men were killed following an attack on Cookstown RUC station.

In October, an IRA bomb exploded prematurely in the Shankill Road in Belfast and killed ten people, including the bomber, and a week later loyalist gunmen shot seven people dead in a public house in Greysteel in County Derry. In June 1994, six were killed in another public house in County Down while they were watching the Republic of Ireland playing in a World Cup soccer match.

For some time, background moves had been taking place to end these deplorable incidents from both sides, and finally in August 1994, the IRA declared a ceasefire that was followed, in October, by a similar declaration from loyalist paramilitaries.

THE DOWNING STREET DECLARATION

Following the November 1992 general election in the Republic, Albert Reynolds was re-elected Taoiseach of a FF/Lab coalition government, having earlier taken over that position following the resignation of Charles Haughey. Mr Reynolds embraced the mantle of Taoiseach with considerable enthusiasm, particularly in relation to Northern Ireland and, building on his relationship with British Prime Minister John Major, they co-signed the Downing Street Declaration on 15th December 1993. This represented a reaffirmation of the Anglo–Irish Agreement of 1985, and reflected the progress in mutual understanding that had developed between the two governments. It had five main provisions:

- The British government affirmed that it was for the people of Ireland alone to exercise their right of self-determination, and stated that it had no selfish, strategic or economic interest in Northern Ireland.

- The Irish government accepted that Irish self-determination must be achieved and exercised with the consent and agreement of a majority of the people in Northern Ireland.

- The Irish government pledged that, in the case of a balanced constitutional accommodation, it would put forward and support changes to the Irish Constitution, which would reflect the principle of consent.

- Both governments confirmed that democratically mandated

251

parties, who demonstrated a commitment to exclusively peaceful methods, would be free to participate fully in the democratic process.

● The Irish government announced that it would establish a Forum for Peace and Reconciliation.

THE 1995 FRAMEWORK DOCUMENT

When the FF/Lab coalition government fell in November 1994, it was replaced without an election by a new coalition comprising Fine Gael, Labour and the Democratic Left, under a new Taoiseach John Bruton, the Fine Gael leader. Within a few months, in February 1995, John Bruton and British Prime Minister John Major had signed a new Framework Document on Northern Ireland. This built on the two previous agreements and committed both governments to a continuation of the peace process. Its main provisions were that:

● the principle of self-determination must be in keeping with the principle of consent;

● agreement must be pursued and achieved through exclusively democratic and peaceful methods; and

● any new political arrangements must afford parity of esteem to both traditions.

The document went on to set out three levels as a basis for negotiation.

● **Within Northern Ireland**
Locally elected representatives would exercise shared administrative and legislative control over agreed matters.

● **North–South Institutions**
These would be consultative, harmonising and executive, and a parliamentary forum, drawing members from a Northern Assembly and the Dáil, would be established.

● **East–West Structures**
These would involve a new agreement between the two governments reflecting the *"totality of relationships between the two islands"*, supported by a permanent secretariat.

The document concluded with both governments agreeing that the matters raised should be examined in negotiations between demo-cratically mandated parties committed to peaceful means, and that the outcome to these negotiations should be submitted for ratification through referenda, North and South.

The document, particularly the new North–South dimension, did not go down well with the unionist community, but both governments stood by its provisions, and its publication represented a further move forward in the overall peace process.

In November 1995, US President Bill Clinton and his wife, Hillary, visited Dublin and Belfast, and his party included former US Senator George Mitchell, who was soon to play a very influential role. However, a number of political hiccups were still to come before further progress became apparent.

The Public Gives its Opinion Across the Three Jurisdictions

In February 1996, the situation changed dramatically when the 17-month IRA ceasefire was hideously terminated, by the bombing of Canary Wharf on the London Docks.

Without delay, the people of the three jurisdictions were given an opportunity of expressing their reaction, with the commissioning of an extensive opinion poll in the Republic, Northern Ireland and the UK. The *Irish Times*/MRBI survey was conducted on 22nd and 23rd February, and provided very clear and unambiguous indications of the courses of action that the vast majority saw as being fundamentally necessary.

The overall messages were that people were now very seriously concerned at the deterioration in the peace process, and demanded that individual agendas by all parties should be tapered down, and should be immediately replaced by compromise on the part of all. In short, the public were demanding peace, without reservations and, although this was seen as a collective responsibility, there were also very clear messages for each of the main players.

In the first instance, and very significantly, the people in the Republic no longer saw a united Ireland as the only solution to the problem. Attitudes had changed, and the united Ireland aspiration now had equal acceptance to Northern Ireland being linked to both the UK and the

Republic. This represented an unmistakable marker, and while many may have seen it as a concession, it set the pattern for a number of modifications that the public were suggesting to those who shared the responsibility for the restoration of peace in the province.

One of the most significant suggestions related to the perceived preconditions for Sinn Féin participation in all-party talks. There was heavy all-round support for a resumption of the IRA ceasefire, and also for the decommissioning of IRA weapons, either prior to or during talks. Both the IRA and the British government were, in all jurisdictions, seen to have been the most blameworthy for the breakdown, and for the former, a resumption of the ceasefire was seen to be an immediate priority. While this was the main message from the public to the IRA, the message to the British government was a strong request to set an early date for the resumption of all-party talks.

The changed priorities in favour of a resumption of peace at all costs, was reflected in the extent to which electors across the island of Ireland and in the UK saw the border as no longer being important.

It was also significant that the preferred solution among UK electors was for the UK to shed its responsibility for Northern Ireland, and for the latter to become an independent state; however, a marginal majority within Northern Ireland wished it to remain part of the UK. Finally, John Hume's proposal for a referendum in the Republic and in Northern Ireland (on an end to violence and a start to all-party talks) received majority support in the UK and the Republic and heavy, but not majority, support within Northern Ireland itself.

These conclusions provided a motivation and focus to the main players to maintain the impetus, and to continue to work towards the overall objective of a peaceful solution. While the survey was conducted during the immediate disappointment following the ending of the IRA ceasefire, the more positive memories of the Anglo–Irish Agreement, the Downing Street Declaration and the Framework Document still remained. These three benchmark events had been negotiated by three successive Taoisigh and this wide-ranging survey can also be seen to have made its own modest contribution to the peace process.

	Jurisdiction		
	NI	RoI	UK
	%	%	%
A. Current perception: peace process			
Finished	26	18	10
Stalled	56	56	35
Continuing	14	23	46
No opinion	4	3	9
B. Blameworthiness			
The IRA	72	51	74
British government	40	73	45
Ulster unionists	16	34	32
Irish government	13	19	34
Others	3	1	5
No opinion	3	5	13
C. Resumption of peace process – how?			
IRA resume ceasefire	62	32	38
British government all-party talks	27	46	26
Unionists – agree to talks	5	12	4
Irish government own peace plan	2	7	17
No opinion	4	6	15
D. Preconditions for Sinn Féin involvement			
IRA resume ceasefire	35	36	32
IRA decommission before talks	31	10	28
IRA decommission as talks progress	15	24	27
No preconditions	18	26	11
No opinion	1	4	2

*Table 14.5: Northern Ireland: Irish Times/MRBI survey situation
February 1996 (post-cessation of the IRA ceasefire)*

	Jurisdiction		
	NI	RoI	UK
	%	%	%
E. Ceasefire breakdown: perception of Gerry Adams' knowledge			
Knew and said nothing	55	29	50
Knew nothing about it	37	56	26
No opinion	8	15	24
F. Preferred solution: overall			
NI remain part of UK	55	11	17
NI linked to UK and RoI	23	29	18
NI part of United Ireland	12	30	14
NI independent	6	22	32
No opinion	4	8	19
G. John Hume proposal for all-Ireland referendum			
Important to restore peace	44	64	53
Make little difference	41	26	29
Unhelpful	11	5	6
No opinion	4	5	12
H. The border: perception of importance			
It matters and people should be prepared to fight for it	17	7	6
It matters but is not worth risking lives for it	42	47	37
Border does not matter anymore	38	42	44
No opinion	3	4	13

Source: Irish Times/MRBI

Table 14.5 (continued): Northern Ireland: Irish Times/MRBI survey situation February 1996 (post-cessation of the IRA ceasefire)

THE MITCHELL PRINCIPLES AND
THE ONGOING PEACE PROCESS

A few weeks prior to the Canary Wharf bombing in February 1996, a three-man committee led by Senator George Mitchell had published a report on the decommissioning of arms and explosives, which had been requested by the British and Irish governments, in an attempt to progress this contentious issue. The other two members of the committee were former Finnish Prime Minister Harri Holkeri, and Canadian General John de Chastelain. The report contained what have since been referred to as the 'Six Mitchell Principles of Democracy' to which parties, to proposed multi-party talks, were required to give their full commitment. The principles were:

- to use democratic and exclusively peaceful means to resolve political issues;
- the total disarmament of paramilitary weapons;
- to agree that disarmament must be independently verifiable;
- to renounce the use of force by themselves or by other organisations;
- to accept the outcome of negotiations and to use only democratic methods to alter the outcome; and
- to call an end to 'punishment' killings and beatings.

The report recommended that decommissioning of illegally held paramilitary weapons should take place during multi-party talks, as a tangible confidence-building measure and that elections should also be held as a further measure.

While the February *Irish Times*/MRBI opinion poll did not measure reaction to the Mitchell Report, per se, it drew attention to it, and asked respondents if they believed that Senator Mitchell's intervention would help at this stage. Reaction in each jurisdiction, in terms of three suggested statements, is given in *Table 14.6*.

Senator Mitchell's intervention would	NI %	RoI %	UK %
Play an important part in helping to restore peace	28	57	27
Make little difference either way	52	29	42
Would be unhelpful, and would make the situation worse	15	5	12
No opinion	5	9	19

Source: Irish Times/*MRBI*

Table 14.6: Reaction to Senator George Mitchell's intervention in Northern Ireland

The concept of an intervention by Senator Mitchell at this stage made a relatively low impact and, at best, could be described as mixed. In the Republic, a very modest majority were favourably disposed and a somewhat surprising one in three felt it would make little difference or would be unhelpful. This latter view was supported by majorities in Northern Ireland (67 per cent) and the UK (54 per cent).

The Mitchell report on decommissioning and the associated recommendations were taken on board by the British Prime Minister John Major when he stated, in a House of Commons speech in January 1996, that he accepted the Senator's suggestion that an election would be an appropriate confidence-building measure. In March, the British government published a paper that provided for elections to a Northern Ireland Forum to be held on 30th May, and for multi-party talks to commence on 10th June. The successful 110 members elected to the forum were distributed over the ten parties: UUP 30; DUP 24; SDLP 21; Sinn Féin 17; Alliance 7; UKUP 3; PUP 2; UDP 2; NIWC 2; and Labour 2.

Multi-Party Talks: 1996

The talks were declared open by the Taoiseach John Bruton and the British Prime Minister John Major on 10th June 1996, and the delegates were drawn from those elected to the forum. Due to the termination of the ceasefire in February, Sinn Féin was refused entry and, with Senator Mitchell in the chair, the talks involved representatives from the other nine parties in the forum. The representation was: UUP 3; DUP 3; SDLP 3; Alliance 3; UKUP 3; PUP 2; UDP 2; NIWC 2; and Labour 2.

The talks were based on the provisions of the Framework Document agreed between Taoiseach John Bruton and British Prime Minister John Major in February 1995, which also set out the three levels or strands – within Northern Ireland, North–South institutions and East-West structures.

To say that the talks got off to a slow start would be a gross understatement. From the outset, unionists were unhappy with the choice of Senator Mitchell as chairman, and procedural wrangling was the order of the day. On 29th July, Rules of Procedure were agreed and the talks were adjourned for the summer recess. When they resumed on 9th September, progress continued to be slow with the question of decommissioning the main focus.

The Christmas adjournment on 18th December brought a comment from the chairman on the slow progress and, when talks resumed on 13th January 1997, he called on all participants to renew their efforts towards making progress. At this stage, John Hume and Gerry Adams had met behind the scenes, following which – as Deaglán de Bréadún illustrates in his book *The Far Side of Revenge* – the SDLP leader sent a list of questions to the British government stating that *"if suitable answers were received, it would lead to an IRA ceasefire"*. This, however, was not responded to directly – de Bréadún, in fact, refers to the British reply as *"minimalist and unenthusiastic"*. It was obvious that little real progress would be made until and unless the IRA ceasefire was restored, and the situation appeared to deteriorate further when, on 12th February, a British soldier on duty in County Armagh was shot dead. At that time, the next Westminster election was mooted, and to some it appeared that the IRA was sending a message to the next British government.

New Players

On 5th March 1997, the talks were adjourned for the Westminster elections, which were held in May. The UUP won ten seats, the SDLP three, Sinn Féin two, DUP two and Other Unionists one. Following the Labour Party victory, Tony Blair was elected Prime Minister and Mo Mowlam was appointed as the new Secretary of State for Northern Ireland. The talks resumed on 3rd June and, on the 26th June, following a general election in the Republic, Fianna Fáil formed a new coalition government with the Progressive Democrats, supported by four independent deputies. Bertie Ahern, who had taken over from Albert Reynolds as leader of Fianna Fáil in November 1994, was appointed Taoiseach, and took up the baton for what appeared to be the last lap of the process on which three of his predecessors had made their respective personal imprints.

The landslide Labour victory in Britain seemed to give the political situation a new impetus and, in June 1997, Prime Minister Tony Blair announced that the 15th September would signal the beginning of substantial talks. The British government also asked the IRA to call another ceasefire, and Mo Mowlam's more informal approach, particularly with the people themselves, was in direct contrast to that of some of her predecessors. Meanwhile, on 14th July, the two newly elected governments published a joint document on decommissioning, which had been initiated a few months earlier by their predecessors, John Bruton and John Major.

On 19th July 1997, the IRA announced a new ceasefire, which, according to de Bréadún:

>...*badly wrong-footed the unionists, putting them in a position where if they now rejected the Anglo–Irish joint document on decommissioning and walked out of the talks, they would be seen as unreasonable in the eyes of the world... Sinn Féin strategists were among the first to sense that there had been not just a change in government, but a fundamental alteration in the whole political landscape, and read the situation better than some unionists.*

While the personal influence of the three previous Taoisigh – Garret FitzGerald, Albert Reynolds and John Bruton – in furthering the peace process, was on the public record, Bertie Ahern's arrival as Taoiseach brought what many saw as a new dimension to the situation. He was young, in comparative terms, having been appointed Taoiseach at 46 years of age, and had developed a personal expertise as a negotiator over the five years when he was Minister for Labour from 1987–1992. He took on the new responsibility with considerable enthusiasm and commitment, and was determined to see the process finalised. However, this could not have been achieved without concomitant contributions from Tony Blair, John Hume, David Trimble, Gerry Adams, George Mitchell and a host of others, including the people in both jurisdictions – North and South – who gave the necessary backing and support when required to do so in the ballot box.

THE BELFAST (GOOD FRIDAY) AGREEMENT

Back on the ground, a month or so after confirmation of the resumption of the IRA ceasefire, the new Secretary of State announced that Sinn Féin would be admitted to talks when they re-opened on 15th September 1997 and, on 30th September, it was announced that substantive negotiations covering all three strands of the talks would begin on 6th October.

The new level of talks which were chaired by George Mitchell were held at Stormont Castle and, after many hiccups, blocking mechanisms, concessions and compromises throughout the autumn of 1997 and early spring of 1998, the agreed deadline of 9th April was looming dangerously close. By all accounts, the final days leading up to the deadline were dramatic, tedious and fatiguing for all concerned and for Bertie Ahern it was particularly distressing as his mother died early on Monday 6th April in Dublin.

Agreement was finally reached on the late afternoon of Good Friday, 10th April 1998, and was signed by Taoiseach Bertie Ahern, Prime Minister Tony Blair and representatives of the Alliance Party, the Labour Party, the Northern Ireland Women's Coalition, the Progressive Unionist Party, the Social Democratic and Labour Party, Sinn Féin, the Ulster Democratic Party and the Ulster Unionist Party.

It was agreed that the Irish government would hold a referendum in the Republic on amending *Articles 2 and 3* of the Irish Constitution, while a referendum on the agreement would be held in the North. The British government would repeal the 1920 Government of Ireland Act (this provided for Home Rule for the 26 counties of Southern Ireland, and made the six northern counties of Antrim, Armagh, Derry, Down, Fermanagh and Tyrone a separate state within the United Kingdom); a new assembly would be established in Northern Ireland; a new North–South Ministerial Council would be set up; a British–Irish Council and a British–Irish Inter-governmental Conference would also be established. (The details of the agreement are set out in the Appendix to this chapter.)

Reaction to the Agreement

A few days after the signing, *The Irish Times* made contact and commissioned another opinion poll in the three jurisdictions to measure immediate reaction. Perhaps not surprisingly, people in the Republic and in the North, appeared to be considerably more involved than were those in Britain, the latter seeing themselves as more remote from the action. Majorities in the two involved areas gave the agreement a strong chance of bringing lasting peace. In Britain, however, more than a third sat on the fence on this question, and rather more had negative thoughts on the chances of success. Of considerable significance was that more than four in five of committed electors in the North stated that they would vote in favour of the agreement, while three in every four in the Republic made the crucially similar commitment to vote in favour of changing *Articles 2* and *3* of the Irish Constitution (see *Table 14.7*).

This was consistent with the *Irish Times*/MRBI poll findings of two years earlier which, for the first time, saw a majority no longer perceiving a united Ireland as the preferred solution, a Northern Ireland linked to both Ireland and the UK being equally acceptable. Finally, the post-agreement poll also saw a majority of electors in the Republic saying that the constitutional claim to Northern Ireland could be set aside in the interests of peace.

The broad conclusions in the MRBI commentary a week after the signing were that:

> As of now, each referendum would be carried substantially, while marginal majorities in each jurisdiction also see the agreement as having a reasonable chance of bringing lasting peace.

A month later, on 12th May 1998, MRBI conducted a further opinion poll in the Republic and Northern Ireland, again on behalf of *The Irish Times*, the objective being to measure voting intentions in the two referenda which were due to be held ten days later on 22nd May. In both areas, the direct question – "How do you intend to vote in the referendum on the Northern Ireland Agreement?" – was used, although the planned ballot paper for the actual referendum in the Republic was phrased "Do you approve of the proposal to amend the Constitution contained in the Nineteenth Amendment of the Constitution Bill 1998?"

	Jurisdiction		
	NI	RoI	UK
	%	%	%
A. Chances of lasting peace, following the agreement			
Strong chance	57	52	17
Maybe/maybe not	25	31	36
Poor chance	17	15	41
No opinion	1	2	6
B. Current voting intentions in referendum			
In favour	61 (75)	73 (84)	81 (95)
Against	20 (25)	14 (16)	4 (5)
No opinion	19	13	15
C. Opinions on constitutional claim to NI (RoI only)			
Is justified	20		
Justified but could be given up for peace	51		
Major obstacle to peace	16		
No opinion	13		

Source: Irish Times/*MRBI*

Table 14.7: Reaction to the Belfast Agreement (14th April 1998)

The referendum in the Republic allowed for the required changes in *Articles 2* and *3*, with the new *Article 2* defining the nation in terms of its people rather than its territory, and *Article 3* enshrining the principle of consent, and expressing the wish of the majority for a united Ireland.

The commentary in *The Irish Times* indicated that the referendum would be carried very comfortably in the Republic and quite comfortably in the North. The MRBI figures in both jurisdictions were remarkably close to the actual results. In the Republic, the 94 per cent survey figure in favour was identical to the eventual outcome, while in the North the 70 per cent survey figure in favour compared with the actual referendum figure of 71 per cent.

	Republic of Ireland		Northern Ireland	
	Survey	Referendum	Survey	Referendum
	%	%	%	%
A. Overall				
In favour	94	94	70	71
Against	6	6	30	29

B. By party support (NI)

	Total	UUP	DUP	SDLP	SF	Alliance	Other
	%	%	%	%	%	%	%
In favour	70	73	2	100	97	100	43
Against	30	27	98	–	3	–	57

Source: Irish Times/*MRBI*

Table 14.8: Voting intentions in the referenda on the Belfast Agreement (May 1998)

No supporters of either the SDLP or Alliance, and a minute minority of Sinn Féin supporters, were against the agreement, and in essence only unionist supporters were negatively disposed.

Many people deserve credit for contributing to the signing of the Belfast Agreement, and while those who were present on the day – following many long and difficult sessions – come immediately to mind, it would not have been possible if the electorate of the Republic had not voted to amend *Articles 2 and 3* of the Irish Constitution. This was effected against a background in which their inclusion had been seen as politically sacrosanct over a period of 61 years since the Constitution was introduced on 1st July 1937.

Decommissioning

There remained just one blip. An article in the agreement stated that:

> *Participants will use their influence to achieve decommissioning of all illegally held arms in the possession of paramilitary groups within two years of the May referendum in the context of an overall settlement.*

In the euphoria of the day, this type of arms-length commitment was very probably seen as both appropriate and adequate – but three years after the referendum, decommissioning remains a serious unresolved problem, although all *"participants"* undoubtedly hold the view that they have been *"using their influence"* in this regard.

Decommissioning had been on the agenda long before April 1998 – during John Major's term as Prime Minister – and many electors in both jurisdictions can be excused if they now feel cynical about the lack of progress on the issue.

THE NORTHERN IRELAND ASSEMBLY

The assembly elections, which were provided for in Strand One of the agreement, were scheduled to take place on 25th June 1998 – just ten weeks after the agreement had been signed. On 1st and 15th June, MRBI conducted two campaign opinion polls for *The Irish Times*, the primary objectives of which were to measure party voting intentions and to identify the perceived issues facing the assembly.

The proposed voting system PR STV (proportional representation – single transferable vote) was similar to that used in the Republic and each of 18 constituencies would return six members to the 108-seat assembly. The MRBI experience was that it would be unwise to attempt to forecast the number of seats that each party was likely to win, and the commentary was, therefore, confined to the likely first preference vote for each party. We were also aware of the nature of likely over and understatement for the SDLP, UUP, DUP and Sinn Féin. As *Table 14.9* shows, these anticipated variations materialised; although in the later poll on 15th June, the figures were considerably closer to the actual election results than was the case in the earlier project.

The two surveys identified decommissioning and peace as the two primary issues about which electors were concerned, and, since they were perceived as being complementary to each other, the fact that decommissioning had not yet taken place represented a continuing threat to peace.

A. First preference voting intentions and result	MRBI (1) 1st June	MRBI (2) 15th June	Election Result
	%	%	%
SDLP	27	26	22
UUP	33	27	21
DUP	13	16	18
Alliance	8	10	7
Sinn Féin	10	9	18
UK Unionists	3	3	4
PUP	1	3	3
Labour	1	2	*
Women's coalition	2	1	2
Other	2	3	5

* Less than 0.5 per cent

B. Most important assembly issues		
Decommissioning	28	19
Peace	28	45
Release of prisoners	14	14
Economic development	9	6
Power-sharing executive	9	1
Reform of RUC	8	7
Communication between parties	6	10
Unemployment	6	6
Other issues	32	58
None/Don't know	12	8

Source: Irish Times/MRBI

Table 14.9: Voting intentions and issues in the assembly election (June 1998)

The assembly elections took place on 25th June and, although the SDLP obtained the highest first preference vote, the UUP had a greater conversion to seats ratio, and topped the poll in terms of seats won.

The UUP won 26 per cent of seats from 21 per cent of first preference votes, a ratio of 100:124. In second place on this criterion was the DUP, with 19 per cent of seats from 18 per cent of votes, a ratio of 100:106. SDLP, UKUP and the Women's Coalition all achieved a par return, while Sinn Féin, Alliance and the PUP obtained a lower than par ratio.

The new Northern Ireland Assembly met on 1st July 1998, and writing about that first meeting, de Bréadún states that:

> ...the standard of oratory was high, compared to what I was used to from years of reporting Southern politics, and it was interesting how few speakers relied on notes, much less prepared scripts. Trimble and Mallon were among those who spoke impromptu and from the heart.

Lord Alderdice, the leader of the Alliance Party, was nominated by Mo Mowlam as the new assembly speaker, and the UUP leader David Trimble was elected first minister, with Seamus Mallon of the SDLP elected to the post of deputy first minister.

However, less than two weeks after the first meeting of the assembly, on 13th July, three young Catholic brothers, all aged under ten, were burned to death in a petrol bomb attack on their home in Ballymoney, County Antrim, and a month later, on 15th August, one of the most notorious atrocities associated with Northern Ireland was perpetrated, when 29 people were killed and over 300 injured in a bomb explosion in Omagh. This brought an immediate expression of outrage across Britain and Ireland and was followed by a political hiatus to allow time for funerals and mourning. These outrages placed further pressure on the two governments to deal with a situation that had all the hallmarks of dissident paramilitaries at work. However, a week later the Real IRA group announced that it was suspending all military operations – this was generally accepted as a ceasefire.

At this stage, a little over four months after the agreement was signed, both governments had already implemented some of their commitments on the constitutional provisions: the assembly elections had taken place and the first meeting of its 108 members on 1st July 1998 had elected the first minister and the deputy first minister. However, a lot remained to be done. The appointment of the executive committee and the allocation of the ministerial posts within Strand One were awaiting implementation, as was the completion of – Strands Two and Three – the setting up of the inter-governmental conference along with the provisions under rights, safeguards, equality of opportunity, security, policing, justice and prisoners. Finally, there was the increasingly intractable issue of decommissioning.

Although there were no immediate time commitments associated with any of the constitutional or Strand One provisions in the agreement, a number of these, such as the repeal of the 1920 Government of Ireland Act (by the British government) and the referendum on *Articles* 2 and 3 of the Constitution (by the Irish government), were implemented without delay.

However, Strand Two specified that a North–South Ministerial Council would be established within one year, which carried a further implied commitment that the 12-person executive committee drawn from assembly members would also be in place within the same period, and those who had observed the twists and turns and procrastinations of the pre-agreement talks would not have been surprised when the pattern was repeated as soon as the post-agreement talks commenced.

The Way Forward and Further Research

While real progress on most aspects of the agreement was very slow, and while all sides – except perhaps the leaders of the two governments – contributed to the lack of progress, there remained a noticeable sense of achievement and relief. Word games continued to be the order of the day, but everyone remained on board and General de Chastelain and Chris Patten were moving on their respective responsibilities for decommissioning and policing. In October, Mo Mowlam was replaced as Secretary of State by Peter Mandelson and, although the new appointee brought a very contrasting approach to the situation, the talks continued at their frustratingly slow pace throughout the winter and into the spring of 1999.

Finally, after what turned out to be one of the most constructive meetings between representatives of the two governments in early July 1999 – 15 months after the signing of the agreement – a document called "The Way Forward" was published. Its main provisions were that, *mirabile dictu*, the all-party executive would be set up on 18th July, and that the decommissioning process was to begin within days of the formation of the executive; actual decommissioning was to start within 30 days, and was to be completed by May 2000. This confirmed the completion date already set out in the Belfast Agreement. The two governments also announced that, should the all-party executive not be established on 18th July, or should the decommissioning process not have commenced within days of the executive formation, the institutions already established would be suspended as a fail-safe measure. At the same time, Tony Blair announced that if any of the parties did not abide by the rules of the agreement, they would be excluded from the executive; the existing institutions would be suspended and the other parties could then decide whether to continue without them or not. Bertie Ahern said that it would be helpful if the Provisional IRA were to make a statement indicating its support for the proposals put forward by the two governments.

Within a week, *The Irish Times* commissioned a further opinion poll covering both jurisdictions, the objective of which was to measure reaction to the main provisions and implications of "The Way Forward" document and to the statements of both government leaders. When the survey commenced, the UUP had not formally responded to the governments' proposals and had requested clarification on the nature of the fail-safe mechanism, nor had the IRA indicated whether or not it supported the initiatives.

The primary findings of the survey (see *Table 14.10*) were that heavy majorities in both jurisdictions supported the formation of the executive, and also the fact that decommissioning should proceed as planned, with the initiatives being typically more enthusiastically received in the South. Given the slow pace of progress both prior and subsequent to the agreement, it was not surprising that only one in four, both North and South, were confident that decommissioning would be completed by the May 2000 deadline and a slightly larger minority – one in three – felt that the de Chastelain commission could eventually bring about total decommissioning. How right the majority were!

Reaction was very mixed as to whether or not the fail-safe legislation guarantee was sufficient for all parties to set up the executive. Bertie Ahern's request to the IRA to make a statement in support of the proposals was much more enthusiastically received – four in every five were in favour – compared to Tony Blair's comment that the executive should continue to operate without parties that did not abide by the rules of the agreement.

Neither electorate could be described as being confident that the agreement would be fully implemented by May 2000. In the Republic only one in ten was very confident and a further four in ten were confident with reservations. The remainder – almost half – were negatively disposed in this regard. In the North, people were considerably less optimistic. A marginal majority (53 per cent) were not confident and, among the 44 per cent who expressed some level of confidence, only a third of them were very confident that it would be implemented within the timeframe. This was a very bipolar outlook in the North and, overall, the confidence levels could only be seen as very mixed.

Broadly speaking, there were high levels of satisfaction with the two governments on their handling of the negotiations with electors in the Republic again considerably more enthusiastic – more than four in every five in the South were satisfied; with lower levels – three in every five – in the North. When asked how they would vote now if the agreement referendum was being held, the figures represented a slight downturn from the actual result. Overall, the survey at the time indicated that both governments could take comfort from the fact that majorities were satisfied with the manner in which they had handled the negotiations with the Irish government faring better generally.

The agreement included a clause that ministerial posts in the 12-member executive would be allocated in proportion to party strength, and that the executive committee would be headed by a first minister and deputy first minister. David Trimble (UUP) and Seamus Mallon (SDLP), respectively, had already been elected to these positions a year earlier at the first meeting of the assembly, and the party strength criterion meant that the ten remaining ministerial posts would be on the basis: UUP 3; SDLP 3; Sinn Féin 2; and DUP 2. The ministers eventually appointed were:

UUP	Reg Empey; Sam Foster; Michael McGimpsey
SDLP	Mark Durkan; Sean Farren; Brid Rodgers
Sinn Féin	Bairbre de Brun; Martin McGuinness
DUP	Peter Robinson; Nigel Dodds

The process had moved a stage further; the formal devolution of power followed and became a *fait accompli* from midnight on 1st December 1999.

	RoI	NI
	%	%
A. All-party executive – general reaction		
Should be formed	84	65
Should not be formed	3	25
Undecided	13	10
B. Should decommissioning proceed as planned?		
Should proceed as planned	85	75
Should not be formed	8	28
Undecided	7	7
C. Opinions as to whether or not decommissioning will be complete by May 2000		
Yes: will be complete	27	26
No: will not be complete	55	54
Undecided	18	20
D. Opinions as to whether or not de Chastelain commission can bring total decommissioning		
Yes	37	36
No	33	44
Undecided	30	20
E. Is the fail-safe legislation sufficient for all parties to set up the executive?		
Yes	43	46
No	25	37
Undecided	32	17
F. Should the executive continue without any parties that do not abide by the rules (Blair statement)?		
Yes: should continue without them	55	65
No: should not continue	34	26
Undecided	11	9

Table 14.10: Reaction to "The Way Forward" document and leaders' statements – Irish Times/MRBI poll (July 1999)

	RoI	NI
	%	%

G. Should the IRA make a statement indicating support for the proposals (Ahern statement)?

Yes	82	76
No	9	15
Undecided	9	9

H. Confidence in agreement being fully implemented by May 2000

Very confident	9	15
Fairly confident	42	29
Not particularly confident	35	26
No confidence	10	27
Undecided	4	3

I. Satisfaction with Irish government's handling of the negotiations on the Belfast Agreement

Satisfied	86	63
Dissatisfied	9	27
Undecided	5	10

J. Satisfaction with British government's handling of the negotiations on the Belfast agreement

Satisfied	81	57
Dissatisfied	12	34
Undecided	7	9

K. Current voting intentions if a referendum on the agreement was held today

Would vote 'Yes'	85 (95)	58 (68)
Would vote 'No'	4 (5)	27 (32)
Undecided	11	15

Source: Irish Times/MRBI

Table 14.10 (continued): Reaction to "The Way Forward" document and leaders' statements – Irish Times/MRBI poll (July 1999)

APPENDIX

THE BELFAST AGREEMENT

- Signed on Good Friday, 10th April 1998, by Taoiseach Bertie Ahern, Prime Minister Tony Blair and by representatives of the Alliance Party; the NI Labour Party; the NI Women's Coalition; the PUP; the SDLP; Sinn Féin; the UDP and the UUP.

Constitutional Issues

- The British government will repeal, through legislation, the 1920 Government of Ireland Act.

- The Secretary of State for Northern Ireland may order a poll on the status of Northern Ireland, on the question of remaining within the UK or unification with the Republic. Such polls must be held at least seven years apart.

- The Irish government will submit *Articles* 2 and 3 of *Bunreacht na hÉireann* for amendment by referendum.

Strand One

- A Northern Ireland Assembly will be established with 108 seats; six members will be returned by proportional representation from the 18 Westminster constituencies.

- The Assembly will elect a 12-member executive committee of ministers. The committee will be headed by a first minister and a deputy first minister, and ministerial posts will be allocated in proportion to party strength.

Strand Two

- A North–South Ministerial Council will be established within one year, consisting of ministers from the Dáil and the assembly. Its remit will be to consider matters of mutual interest through consultation, co-operation and action. The council will be accountable to the assembly and the Oireachtas.

Strand Three

- A British–Irish Council, supported by a permanent secretariat will be established, drawing members from the assembly, the Dáil, the House of Commons, the Isle of Man, the Channel Islands and the new assemblies in Scotland and Wales.

British–Irish Inter-Governmental Conference

- A new British–Irish Agreement will establish a new conference to replace that set up by the Anglo–Irish Agreement in 1985.

Rights, Safeguards and Equality of Opportunity

- The European Convention on Human Rights will be incorporated into Northern Ireland law.
- A Human Rights Commission and a statutory Equality Commission will be established in Northern Ireland.
- The Irish government will establish a Human Rights Commission. A joint North–South committee of these commissions, will also be established.
- The British government will take resolute action to promote the Irish language.

Decommissioning

- Participants will use their influence to achieve decommissioning of all illegally held arms in the possession of paramilitary groups within two years of the May referendum, in the context of an overall settlement.

Security, Policing, Justice and Prisoners

- The British government will seek to normalise security in Northern Ireland through reducing the numbers and role of security forces, removing security installations and ending emergency powers.

- The Irish government will initiate a review of the Offences Against the State Acts, with a view to reforming and dispensing with certain provisions.

- An independent commission will make recommendations on the future of policing in Northern Ireland by May 1999.

- A review of criminal justice will be undertaken by the British government.

- The British and Irish governments will legislate for the accelerated release of paramilitary prisoners whose organisations are observing a ceasefire.

CHAPTER 15

Tribute to the People of Ireland

25TH ANNIVERSARY: 1987 STUDY

The year 1987 saw MRBI reach its first really significant milestone – 25 years in business. The company's tenth birthday, which involved a seminar at which three client case studies were presented to an invited audience of business executives and media people, is described in *Chapter 1*. In 1983, to celebrate the company's 21st birthday, we undertook a national, but somewhat limited, survey of Irish society, the report of which was widely distributed.

For our 25th anniversary, we planned something considerably more elaborate, in the form of an extensive national sociological survey, with the findings presented at three special receptions:

- the first for a wide range of clients and business executives;
- the second for the office and field staff of the company; and
- the third for army friends and colleagues.

The title of this study was "Éire Inniu: An MRBI Perspective on Irish Society Today (1987)", and the content was generated entirely by Áine and myself. It describes the Ireland of the time and addressed five areas of enquiry:

- **The Irish People**
  Our perceived characteristics and sources of influence on our lives.

- **Our Values**
  Importance of certain specifics for ourselves and for future generations.

- **Sunday Activities, Leisure and Sport**
  Interests and preferences.
- **The Irish Nation**
  Our expectation of reunification.
- **The Irish Language**
  Our ability to speak, and to understand the language as spoken on electronic media, and reaction to wider general usage.

The Irish People

In 1987, we saw ourselves as proud, patriotic, Christian and happy; but as somewhat dishonest, selfish, and lazy; and were concerned about ourselves and our country in equal measure. We also perceived ourselves to have been a less caring people than we were 20 years earlier.

The overall sources of influence on us 14 years ago were, primarily, the home and family; the media; and, to a much lesser extent, the Church, government and politicians. When measured in terms relating to six specific issues of the day, a number of variations were evident, and sources of influence on moral issues contrasted sharply with those of a material nature.

Issue	Main Influence	Some Influence
Marriage/Family life	Home	Church
Divorce	Church	Home
Abortion	Church	Home
Northern Ireland	Media	Politicians
Threat of nuclear war	Media	Politicians
Aid to the Third World	Media	Church

Table 15.1: Sources of influence on the Irish people

Our Values

We explored the values we held as a nation, in a number of different ways: What is important to us at a personal level? What do we value in the world around us? What do we want to pass on to future generations? The first approach involved respondents rating the importance of each of eight personal criteria.

Criterion	Important		Neither	Unimportant	
	Very	Fairly		Fairly	Very
	%	%	%	%	%
To be healthy	96	3	*	*	*
To feel secure	82	17	1	–	–
To have friends	80	18	1	1	–
To lead a full life	67	29	3	1	–
To have a job	71	17	8	2	2
To be respected	60	32	5	3	–
One's religion	61	26	8	3	2
To have money	47	44	6	2	1

* less than 0.5%

Table 15.2: Relative importance of specific values

Those participating in the survey then rated the extent to which they would miss each of six factors, if each no longer existed.

Factor	Would Miss		No Opinion	Would not Miss	
	Definitely	Probably		Probably	Definitely
	%	%	%	%	%
Trees in the countryside	70	21	4	4	1
Work	70	15	9	3	3
The Church	60	22	9	6	3
The gardaí	50	31	10	5	4
Television	34	31	12	14	9
The pub	16	22	13	19	30

Table 15.3: Factors the Irish people would miss

Finally, in the context of values, the interviewees were asked to state which of six aspects of life they would most like to pass on to their children (or to nieces or nephews, if more appropriate). In terms of first and second mentions, the positions, in descending order of preference, are given in *Table 15.4*.

Aspect	First Mention	Second Mention	Consolidation
	%	%	%
An ability to fend for themselves	39	25	64
A sense of morality	34	26	60
A skill or qualification	17	22	39
Property: home, farm, business	6	11	17
Experiences and memories	3	10	13
Money and investments	5	6	11

Table 15.4: Aspects the Irish people would most like to pass on to their children

Sunday Activities, Leisure and Sport

Each chapter in the report was introduced by an appropriate quotation, and Goldsmith's reference to the village on the morning of a sporting occasion was particularly apt in this instance:

> *How often have I blest the coming day,*
> *When toil remitting lent its turn to play,*
> *And all the village train, from labour free,*
> *Led up their sports beneath the spreading tree,*
> *While many a pastime circled in the shade,*
> *The young contending as the old surveyed.*

The leisure-cum-social interest measured in this section, related to the extent to which people took part in each of 12 specific activities on the Sunday prior to interview. The patterns are shown in *Table 15.5*.

Activity	%	Main Demographic Impact			
		Gender	Class	Age/Status	Location
Went to church	79	female		50+	rural
Read a newspaper	76	male	middle class	65+	
Watched television	74		working class	50+	urban
Went for a walk	45			young and single	urban
Went for a drive	43		middle class and farming		rural
Visited family or friends	38	female	middle class	up to 34	
Went to a pub	33			up to 34	urban
Had family or friends visiting	33	female		65+	rural
Spectator: outdoor sport	14	male		up to 49	rural
Played: outdoor sport	12	male		up to 34	rural and urban
Went to a restaurant	8	male and female		up to 34	
Played: indoor sport	5	male		under 24	Dublin

Table 15.5: What the Irish people do on Sundays

The Irish Nation

The question on the Irish nation related to people's expectation of when Ireland would be reunited. Respondents were presented with a prompt card that showed five time scenarios, and were asked which came nearest to their opinion. The 1987 situation is given in *Table 15.6*.

281

When will Ireland be reunited?	%
In 10 years	7
In 25 years	9
In 50 years	13
In 100 years	11
Will never be reunited	49
No opinion	11

Table 15.6: When will Ireland be reunited?

In 1987, half of the adult population thought that Ireland would never be reunited; a further 24 per cent expected it would take from 50 to 100 years, and no more than one in six (16 per cent) thought it would happen in ten to 25 years' time – quite a dismal prospect.

Those who were most pessimistic were younger electors aged under 34, living in Dublin and the surrounding areas and tending to be working class, while the most optimistic were rural elderly people aged over 65.

The Irish Language

The patterns covering our capability to speak Irish, to understand the language as spoken on television or radio, and our reaction to its wider usage are given in *Table 15.7*.

Those who claimed to speak the language fairly or very well (25 per cent) were very noticeably middle class (38 per cent), aged under 24 (38 per cent) and were living in Munster (29 per cent) and Connacht (27 per cent). The same demographic patterns held for understanding of Irish, while preference for its wider usage extended across all class, age and regional groups, at broadly the national average level of 47 per cent.

Spoken Irish: can speak it	%	Consolidation
Very well	7	
Fairly well	18	25
Very little	50	
None at all	25	75
Understanding Irish in the media		
Understand all of it	7	
Understand most of it	14	
Understand some of it	47	68
Understand none of it	32	
Preference for wider usage		
Like Irish used more widely	47	
No wish for wider usage	46	
No opinion	7	

Table 15.7: The Irish people's knowledge of and preference for the Irish language

Conclusion of the 1987 Survey

The foreword to the anniversary survey report stated that "Éire Inniu" represented a recognition by the company of the debt it owed to the people of Ireland and to Irish society generally, without whose co-operation no market research project could be successful, and it was very much in the nature of a tribute to the many who had contributed to MRBI's success story that the survey was conducted. The foreword said:

> *Éire Inniu will provide a benchmark against which future generations will be able to chart our progress as a people... and looking to the future, Éire Amárach represents a new challenge, as we reflect on our individual and collective roles towards the economic recovery, which is so crucial to our progress, and indeed survival, as a nation.*

THE 2001 SURVEY

Time has moved on. We are now half a generation down the road, and the Celtic Tiger economy is a five-year-old phenomenon. Although one can readily identify some of the changes that have taken place in our society, we decided to quantify and update the criteria of 1987, with some interesting but indeed not surprising results.

The Irish People: Perceived Characteristics and Values

In terms of how we now perceive ourselves, we are considerably more proud, more patriotic and happier than we were 14 years ago, and we also see ourselves as more hard-working, but significantly less generous and less Christian. Our view of ourselves hasn't changed in terms of being honest, but we certainly think we are now more hard-working.

We are fractionally more European and outward looking, and it seems reasonable to think that our somewhat increased concern for the country is related to the fact that we perceive society as less caring now.

Characteristic	1987	2001
Proud	85	90
Patriotic	70	75
Happy	68	74
Christian	68	63
Honest	58	56
Hard-working	40	51
Generous	66	46
European	47	51
Concerned for country	44	50
Interest in Irish affairs	73	71
Interest in world affairs	53	54

Table 15.8: Comparison of the difference in perceived values and characteristics of the Irish people (1987–2001)

While the society of the new millennium reflects many changes, the most significant and indeed the least surprising is that nearly 400,000 more people than in 1987 consider that we are a less caring society. The overall figure holding that view today is 62 per cent.

Irish people are	1987	2001	Difference
	%	%	%
More caring now	31	26	−5
Less caring now	48	62	+14
No opinion	21	12	−9

Table 15.9: Are Irish people more or less caring now than in 1987?

When questioned now about the overall sources of influence on our thinking and opinions, it is evident that the role of the home and family has increased considerably at the expense of the Church, which was in any event, quite low in 1987.

Factor	1987	2001	Difference
	%	%	%
Home and family	51	71	+20
The media (press and electronic)	30	19	−11
The Church	10	7	−3
Government and politicians	3	2	−1
None of the above	6	1	−5

Table 15.10: Comparison of influencing factors on the Irish people

However, this increase in the impact of the home appears to reflect a very general all-embracing type of influence, because when we explored the influences on specific issues, there was no significant increase in the role of the home on any of them. Similarly for the media, although its overall impact had dropped, on specific issues it still influenced the way we think in relation to Northern Ireland to the threat of a nuclear war and to aid to the Third World.

On the specifics of thinking about and forming opinions on divorce and abortion, one in four are still influenced by the Church, but this reflects a fall from almost one in two in 1987. Northern Ireland remains the domain of the politicians, and of course the media.

Factor	Home %		Media %		Church %		Politicians %		Don't Know %	
	1987	2001	1987	2001	1987	2001	1987	2001	1987	2001
Marriage and family life	58	62	7	5	29	21	1	–	5	12
Divorce	33	35	14	16	40	25	3	5	10	19
Abortion	28	32	12	15	47	27	2	5	11	21
Threat of nuclear war	8	5	51	40	2	1	22	20	17	34
Aid to the Third World	7	6	56	58	24	19	7	11	6	6
Northern Ireland	8	8	56	48	3	2	24	34	9	8

Table 15.11: Comparison of specific influencing factors on the Irish people (1987–2001)

Our Values

The comparisons on our values at a personal level show little change. We still want to be healthy and secure, living a full life with our friends. We want respect, money and a job, although we are marginally less concerned about having a job now than in 1987 – most likely because there are more jobs available. However, religion as a value has shown a marked drop of 11 percentage points (see Table 15.12).

On the broader issues in our world, the Church has again dropped significantly – down from 82 per cent who felt they would miss it in 1987 to 68 per cent today; and work has also dropped – 85 per cent would have missed it in 1987 while the figure today is 75 per cent. We haven't changed our thinking on trees, the gardaí or television, but there is a marked increase in the importance of the pub to us – surely a worrying trend in society. In 1987, 50 per cent of young people aged 18–24 claimed they would miss the pub, by 2001 the corresponding figure had grown to 85 per cent (see Table 15.13).

Factor	1987	2001	Difference
	%	%	%
To be healthy	99	99	–
To feel secure	99	99	–
To have friends	98	97	–1
To lead a full life	96	93	–3
To be respected	92	91	–1
To have a job	88	82	–6
To have money	91	88	–3
Religion	87	76	–1

Table 15.12: Importance of specific personal factors of the Irish people

Factor	1987	2001	Difference
	%	%	%
Trees in the countryside	91	89	–2
The gardaí	81	81	–
Work	85	75	–10
The Church	82	68	–14
Television	65	69	+4
The pub	38	51	+13

Table 15.13: Extent to which specific factors would be missed by the Irish people

When respondents were asked to comment on the six characteristics they would most like to pass on to their children, the first three – an ability to fend for themselves, a sense of morality and a skill or qualification – held their positions and are fairly close to their 1987 positions. Further down the line, passing on experiences and memories is positioned in fourth place – higher than in 1987; while passing on property is below its previous level and, as before, passing on money is in last position of the six (see *Table 15.14*).

Factor	1987	2001	Difference
	%	%	%
An ability to fend for themselves	64	66	+2
A sense of morality	60	55	−5
A skill or qualification	39	33	−6
Experience and memories	13	19	+6
Property: home, farm, business	17	14	−3
Money and investments	11	13	+2

Table 15.14: Characteristics that Irish people would like to pass on to their children

Sunday Activities and Leisure

The past 14 years have brought three very significant changes in behaviour within the 12 criteria that were applied in the two surveys.

Activity	1987	2001	Difference
	%	%	%
Watched television	74	77	+3
Read a newspaper	76	63	−13
Went to church	79	55	−24
Went for a walk or jog	45	48	+3
Went for a drive	43	43	−
Visited family or friends	38	43	+5
Went to a pub	33	33	−
Had family or friends visiting	33	30	−3
Went to a restaurant	8	20	+12
Spectator: outdoor sport	14	12	−2
Played: outdoor sport	12	12	−
Played: indoor sport	5	4	−1

Table 15.15: Activities in which Irish people participated on a given Sunday

The first is that some 24 per cent fewer (equating with over 700,000 adults) did not go to church on the Sunday prior to interview – in direct terms the figure dropped from 2.3 million to 1.6 million. The second major change is that 13 per cent fewer (385,000) read a Sunday newspaper, and the third notable point is that 12 per cent (or 355,000) more people had been to a restaurant on the previous Sunday, than had been in 1987.

The other less notable changes were that:

- 43% visited family or friends, an increase of 145,000;
- 48% went for a walk or jog, an increase of 85,000;
- 77% watched television, an increase of 85,000;
- 33% went to a pub, no change on 1987 levels; and
- 12% played an outdoor sport, no change since 1987.

The Irish Nation

At first glance, the figures relating to the reunification of Ireland suggest that we are more optimistic now, with 27 per cent expecting reunification within 25 years whereas, in 1987, just 16 per cent held that belief. However, that was 14 years ago, leaving just 11 more years to meet that expectation. The more interesting figure is the drop from 49 per cent to 40 per cent in those who think it will never happen.

Ireland will be reunited	1987	2001	Difference
	%	%	%
In 10 years	7	10	+3
In 25 years	9	17	+8
In 50 years	13	16	+3
In 100 years	11	8	–3
Never	49	40	–9
No opinion	11	9	–2

Table 15.16: Comparison of the Irish people's belief in the timescale for the reunification of Ireland (1987–2001)

The Irish Language

The figures for speaking and understanding the Irish language have shown a marginal improvement on both criteria. An increase of four points from 25 per cent to 29 per cent among those who claim to speak Irish very or fairly well is a promising sign, while 76 per cent now say that they understand some Irish as it is spoken in the media; this compares with 68 per cent in 1987. Finally, a majority – three in every five – now indicate a preference for wider usage of the language, compared with 47 per cent 14 years ago.

| | 1987 | | 2001 | |
| | % | | % | |
	Results	Consolidation	Results	Consolidation
Ability to speak Irish				
Very well	7		6	
Fairly well	18	25	23	29
Very little	50		47	
None at all	25	75	24	71
Understanding Irish used in different media				
All of it	7		5	
Most of it	14		14	
Some of it	47	68	57	76
None at all	32		24	
Preference for wider usage of Irish				
Yes	47		59	
No	46		28	
No opinon	7		13	

Table 15.17: Comparison in ability to speak and understand Irish, and attitudes towards the wider use of the language (1987–2001)

So, as a society in the new millennium, we appear to be less generous and caring; certainly less interested in the Church and religion; but happier, prouder and more into enjoying the fruits of our harder work.

CHAPTER 16

Smaointe Breise – Reflections

The outcome of our first political project, in April 1973, gave us a realisation of the value of market research in the political arena and considerable confidence in developing that part of the business. Over the next eight years, the company conducted 24 private political research projects, many of which made very worthwhile contributions to politics in Ireland. Some, of course, also delivered bad news, most notably the MRBI report to the FG/Lab government, prior to the 1977 general election (see *Chapter 2*). In those days, they didn't shoot the messenger, nor did they ban opinion polls! Mention of that election brings me back to John Meagher.

Shortly after our two companies were established in the early 1960s, John (of Irish Marketing Surveys) and I met for lunch once or twice each year. No one will be surprised to hear that these were lengthy affairs, at which everything, except our respective clients, was discussed. However, this occasion was slightly different. We were discussing the political situation and, having exchanged comments on the extent to which the media in general had been surprised at the Fianna Fáil landslide, John asked me if I had been surprised.

In the knowledge that MRBI had positioned Fianna Fáil on 51 per cent in our final campaign opinion poll, I answered *"not really"* – and asked him if he had been surprised. He smiled, looked at me, and repeated exactly what I had said and added, *"Are we trying to tell each other something interesting?"* It soon emerged that both of us were aware of the likely outcome for some time before the election, and that both of us had identified the final Fianna Fáil vote at 51 per cent. Although we never again discussed the details of that chat, I know that each of us took considerable satisfaction from the fact that we both realised that, technically and professionally, the two companies had come of age.

At that time, MRBI was handling approximately 80 commercial projects annually along with the political projects, and this pattern continued up to 1981–1982 – a period of considerable political activity, with three general elections in less than 18 months. Over the course of those elections, the company conducted five political research projects for the Irish Independent Group, all of which were published. Then, in the spring of 1982, we were approached by *The Irish Times*. The first *Irish Times*/MRBI opinion poll followed and, almost 20 years later, the series continues to monitor and provide analytical comment on political opinions across the nation.

Following the inauguration of the series, and the corporate high-profile that resulted from it, MRBI's commercial output increased significantly, while over the same period, the company has handled over 100 private political research surveys.

MISINTERPRETATION

One of the most common problems for opinion polling companies is the way in which figures are frequently misread or misinterpreted, mainly by people who have no direct relationship with the project. It is literally impossible to interpret opinion poll figures correctly, unless the actual questions, and the background, including comparable previous figures, are examined. The first essential in interpretation is to note the precise question asked and then to make oneself aware of the background – of when the research was conducted – and remember that the figures relate only to the day of interview.

Many observers frequently see the figures as predictive – this, too, is a misinterpretation. If the point is considered in any depth, it becomes apparent that opinion poll figures do not predict.

What would be the point of election campaigns and of all the media coverage of issues, if nobody ever changed their opinions? The quotation of the economist JM Keynes is very apt: "*When circumstances change, I change my opinion.*" The *Irish Times*/MRBI series of polls reflects these changes.

Another strange misinterpretaton is claiming that poll figures had been inaccurate because they were not identical to results of elections, when the poll in question had been conducted anything from a week to three months earlier. This claim implies that public opinion remains static in the face of lively political debate. I have known only one occasion over the past 20 years, when Fianna Fáil support did not move during the final two weeks before an election, and that arose during the 1992 general election campaign, when MRBI positioned the party at 40 per cent on two successive occasions. The party obtained 39 per cent on the day.

Another activity that never fails to mystify me, is why, having seemingly commissioned a private opinion poll for strategic purposes, the political party involved cannot keep the findings under wraps. Figures are invariably leaked to the media and made available to all and sundry, with the surprise element going out the window.

In a slightly different context, direct misinterpretation of figures also occurs and one of the most remarkable examples of this, which reflected some dubious mathematics, arose following the publication of an *Irish Times*/MRBI opinion poll in May 1984, relating to the New Ireland Forum. The question related to the holding of a conference to discuss the report of the New Ireland Forum, and the findings are shown in *Table 16.1*.

	Total	OUP	DUP	Alliance	SDLP	Sinn Féin
	%	%	%	%	%	%
Should be held	52	34	21	76	88	76
Should not be held	34	54	68	20	2	4
Undecided	14	12	11	4	10	20

Table 16.1: Should a conference be held on the "New Ireland Forum Report" (analysed by party support)?

At least three commentators, two of whom may have taken a lead from the first – inexplicably added the figures in columns 2 and 3 to conclude that 55 per cent of unionists in Northern Ireland were of the view that a conference should be held. It was assumed that 34 per cent of OUP and 21 per cent of DUP supporters equated with 55 per cent of unionists. The correct figure was of course the weighted average of the two, i.e. 29 per cent, but this inaccurate interpretation was consistently used in a number of interviews with government ministers and other politicians.

CRUCIAL OPINION POLLS

Of the ten research projects conducted by MRBI from February to November, in the lead up to the divorce referendum of 1995, the final two opinion polls on the 18th and 24th November (referendum day) for *The Irish Times* were, as far as Irish society is concerned, the most influential and crucial by far. Crucial and influential to the extent that, had these two polls not been commissioned, either the amendment allowing divorce would not have been carried or, alternatively, the High Court petition might not have been dismissed.

The 18th November poll figure for the 'Yes' vote was 51.7 per cent, the lowest level since the campaign started back in February, and it was apparent that, if the downward trend continued over the final week of the campaign, the amendment would have been defeated. Support for the 'Yes' vote had shown a continuous slide over the summer and autumn and, following the *McKenna* judgment of the previous day, the government press campaign had been discontinued. It was crucial, therefore, for the government that a serious and sustained effort be made to prevent a continuation of the downturn.

Although in the final government survey report on 13th November – 11 days before the referendum – I had recommended that credible speakers should take to the airwaves on behalf of the 'Yes' vote, I reiterated the point, when I saw the figures in *The Irish Times* poll of 18th November.

The outcome was that Taoiseach John Bruton, Minister for Health Michael Noonan and Minister for Equality and Law Reform Mervyn Taylor, each made a number of appearances on RTÉ television and radio and for the first time in the campaign, the 'Yes' vote stabilised, leading to the very narrow 'Yes' majority. While my initial recommendation certainly helped, the publication of the new figures in *The Irish Times* following the poll of 18th November, galvanised the government into immediate action. Had the opinion poll figures not been available on 18th November, there is a doubt whether the impetus or motivation would have been there for the speakers in the final week.

In the judgment of the High Court in November 1996, the summing-up stated that:

> ...*the undisputed poll figures showing the stabilisation in the 'Yes' and 'No' votes after the 17th November, when the*

government's press campaign ceased and was replaced by
radio and television appearances, offer dramatic support for
what would otherwise seem an improbable conclusion.

It is apparent, therefore, that had the two *Irish Times*/MRBI opinion polls of 18th and 24th November not existed, there would have been no evidence to show that the 'Yes' and 'No' votes had stabilised over the final week. In such a scenario, it is possible that the outcome would have been entirely different, and the petition banning divorce might have been successful.

A PLEA FROM A LESS FORTUNATE COLLEAGUE

Not all of the research was confined to political matters; much of it also related to serious social issues.

Dear colleague

I have ALS. I am confined to a wheelchair. I can no longer hold a pen to write. Each day my body betrays me a little more, but my mind is as active as ever. I am writing to ask if you could co-ordinate a survey in your country, and also if you could organise the necessary finance. At the last meeting of WAPOR in Toronto, I spoke with several colleagues about worldwide research on ALS (Amyotrophic Lateral Sclerosis). Can you help? Thank you.

Sincerely

Yvan Corbeil

This evocative and unusual letter, which I received in October 1988, from a WAPOR (World Association for Public Opinion Research) colleague in Quebec, resulted in the most fulfilling research project in which I was ever involved. The letter was convincing and dramatic and I couldn't but be moved by what Yvan Corbeil said.

Up until then I had never heard of ALS – or MND (Motor Neurone Disease) as it is known in Ireland and the UK. I responded without delay and told Yvan that MRBI would conduct the required research in Ireland, and would also finance the project. In time, he sent me the technical details, including a copy of the questionnaire, and specified that interviews be conducted with ten people in Ireland who had ALS. In the summer of 1989, I made contact with the Irish Motor Neurone Disease Association, which was then in its infancy, and met, for the first time, that wonderful person Eithne Frost. Eithne was a secondary teacher who had just taken a five-year career break to help build up the association. Ten years earlier in 1979, her husband, at 33 years of age, had died from MND and left her to support their two young children. Eithne gave me my first briefing, explaining to me that MND was a progressive degenerative disease of the central nervous system and that the lifespan from time of diagnosis was limited.

In 1989, there were 27 people with MND registered with the Irish association, and I immediately decided to broaden the survey to include all patients, and also to extend the questionnaire to include the specific requirements of the Irish association. We also extended the survey to include carers.

In designing the extensive questionnaire, we consulted with Dr M Hutchinson, consultant neurologist; Dr R Boothman, Department of Health; Dr G Dean, epidemiologist; and Dr C Barry, medical director CRC. In essence it included: introduction; health problems before diagnosis; duration of symptoms; experience of prompted list of symptoms; when first diagnosed; if told of MND; who diagnosed; most disturbing aspect; equipment now being used; future requirements; if communication aids used; house installations; movement outside home – nature and frequency; knowledge of helpful organisations and people; rating of helpfulness of professional people with whom in contact; knowledge of MND Association and newsletter; identity of special carer, and special help required; reaction to community care services; if ever in contact with toxic substances; illnesses of deceased relatives; and personal classification details. The questionnaire extended to nine pages and 24 people were interviewed in their homes.

The report contained the following conclusions.

- *There is a widespread lack of adequate counselling, and a co-ordinated approach between the MND Association and each relevant Health Board would meet this deficiency.*

- *The main source of support is the spouse or other family relative and there is a basic requirement for a co-ordinated carer's group. The initiative for this would appear to be with the MND*

Association, but it requires the allocation of special resources by the relevant authorities.

- *MND causes considerable financial demands on the families of patients, and a co-ordinated voluntary approach is necessary.*

- *The situation in regard to community care services is unsatisfactory, and the service is non-existent in many areas. The responsibility would appear to be with the Health Boards, each of whom will receive a copy of the report.*

- *Almost all MND patients require a wheelchair as the ailment progresses, and many also require walking frames, communication aids, respirators, home modifications and carers. The MND Association will continue to require considerable financial assistance on an ongoing basis and a higher priority in the allocation of resources by the Department of Health is indicated.*

Yvan Corbeil's specific requirement was extracted from the data and a special report sent to him.

The survey among carers – which primarily covered their observations on symptoms; on aids used; the nature of specialist help received; carer requirements; suggested sources of assistance and spontaneous comments on patient problems – was incorporated into the main report.

Copies of the report were sent to the Department of Health and to each health board, and I was invited to make a presentation of the findings to the AGM of the Irish Association in November 1990 and to an international conference on MND in Birmingham in 1991.

The MRBI report provided a practical focus for the Irish MND Association for the future development of patient and carer strategy and, while the main source of income was voluntary subscriptions, various governments have funded specific MND projects throughout the 1990s. Recently, for the first time, the government provided core funding for the association. After completing her five-year career break, Eithne Frost resigned from her teaching post in 1994 to take up the post of chief executive. She has since expanded the association to all parts of the country, and there are now 230 patient members in the association. She, and her staff of six, maintain daily contact with pockets of supporters and patients throughout Ireland, and I have maintained my relationship, as a patron of the association, ever since my first contact in 1989.

A number of well-known people have been struck down by MND; on this side of the Atlantic the late David Niven and Don Revie spring to mind. In the US, ALS is sometimes called the Lou Gehrig disease, after the well-known baseball player who also died from it; and, of course, Yvan Corbeil himself, whose letter I have never forgotten. In a number of respects, it changed my life.

BANNING OPINION POLLS

When, in late June 2001, Fine Gael produced an amendment at the committee stage of the Electoral Amendment Bill, which banned the taking – and also the publication – of political opinion polls during the final seven days of an election or referendum campaign, I had to ask if anyone in the party had done any real homework on the issue? Here, Fine Gael was supporting Fianna Fáil in government to enact legislation that would take Ireland to the same authoritarian level as North Korea and China, the only countries in the world that ban the taking of political opinion polls.

My mind went back to the general election of November 1982, when Garret FitzGerald took the party to its highest ever first preference vote of 39.2 per cent. I also recalled those talented analysts, Peter Prendergast, Sean O'Leary and the late John Boland who, in turn, delivered outstanding victories against all the odds, in the two Cork by-elections of November 1979; in Dublin North-Central in the general elections of February and November 1982; and in the Dublin West by-election in May 1982, all based on constructive use of MRBI research. Political amnesia appears to be a reasonably common commodity, not just confined to tribunals.

There appears to have been no technical or administrative preparation by either the government or Fine Gael, and the manner in which the amendment was handled by both was not only impulsive but was also immature. The glaring lack of understanding of the nuances of market and political research, which characterised the debate over the period of ten days when the matter was before the two houses of the Oireachtas, was obvious. In short, it was the greatest political mess voluntarily created by any government in my memory, and it remains a mystery why advice was not sought from a number of sources, before such an unprecedented decision was taken.

One of a number of woolly impressions which were created during that crucial ten days, was that it was never clear whether or not the government had taken legal advice on the constitutional aspect, specifically *Article 40.6.i°*, which guarantees the right of citizens to express their convictions and opinions freely. A similar amendment to ban opinion polls was withdrawn in 1991, reportedly for constitutional reasons; and, in two *Liveline* phone-in programmes on RTÉ radio in July 2001, the majority of the many electors who expressed strong objections to the measure were convinced that it was both unconstitutional and undemocratic. They saw themselves as losing a right that they had enjoyed for almost a quarter of a century.

This reaction by the electorate would almost certainly have converted to negative behaviour at the ballot box had the amendment gone ahead and advice from a sociologist would have alerted the government to this likely eventuality. Finally, advice from any experienced market research professional would have highlighted the existence of loopholes in the amendment, one of which was eloquently identified by Independent Senator Shane Ross when the matter came before the Seanad. In fact, the government had every reason to be grateful to Senator Ross since it was heading for a public relations disaster. Some overseas media had already directed ridicule in its direction, with one article saying that the Irish government had foolishly decided to take on the entire media, and the article concluded by saying that *"Mr Ahern declares he is not worried, but in saying so, he looks like a man who has just sat on a cow-pat."*

In fact, it was much worse since, in addition to the media, the market research industry was also targeted and most surprisingly of all – as already mentioned – the electorate saw itself as being within firing range.

The amendment was introduced immediately following the publication, on 27th June 2001, of a TG4/MRBI opinion poll taken in the run up to the by-election in Tipperary South, on Saturday 30th. Interviewing on the poll commenced on the 20th and ended on the 23rd, one week before the election. As of 23rd, MRBI showed Tom Hayes (FG) topping the poll with support in the mid-thirties, and a likelihood of being elected on the third count with transfers initially from Denis Landy (Lab) and, subsequently, from Michael Maguire (FF), which is precisely what happened in the election.

As soon as the results of the opinion poll were published, Fianna Fáil declared war on the market research industry, claiming that its candidate's chances had been seriously damaged, and I recall Noel Davern (FF) on television demanding that opinion polls be banned forthwith. Other Fianna Fáil mentors were less explicit and contented themselves with the admission that "*we have to blame somebody*". For some reason that escapes me, Fine Gael people were also unhappy since, within a day, the party had tabled the technically deficient amendment. Furthermore, the fact that both parties reacted negatively indicated a common deficiency in their respective abilities to analyse the figures constructively in their own interests. This had been done on numerous occasions in the past following the publication of *Irish Times*/MRBI campaign polls, and I recall one example.

In late October 1990, following the publication of the third *Irish Times*/MRBI poll in the presidential election campaign, Dick Spring telephoned and asked if I could meet himself and Ruairi Quinn. When we met he asked me to interpret the findings in the interests of the Labour nominee, Mary Robinson. At that stage, two weeks before the election, Brian Lenihan was on 44 per cent, down five points over the previous two weeks; Mary Robinson was on 36 per cent, up four, with Austin Currie on 20 per cent, up one. I took them through the report; elaborated where necessary, highlighting the trends, and particularly the transfer patterns, and answered a number of questions on strategy for the remaining weeks. The subsequent action on the ground as is now known, paid off, and Mary Robinson won on the second count, on Austin Currie's transfers.

The campaign opinion poll in Tipperary South in late June, provided a similar framework for any candidate or party who wished to avail of it, and a positive and constructive analysis, followed by a focused follow-through on the ground by Fianna Fáil, would have seen Michael Maguire survive to the third count, rather than being eliminated on the second. Of course, a similar positive response by Phil Prendergast and her supporters could have offset this.

This is one of the reasons why MRBI has provided copies of *Irish Times*/MRBI reports to all the main parties over the past 20 years. I recall a number of party activists regularly making contact following the publication of the polls – on behalf of Labour, Fine Gael and the Progressive Democrats – and in spite of the contradictory behaviour on the part of the latter two in supporting the proposed ban, I have no regrets that I responded positively on these occasions.

Many of the statements made in attempting to justify the proposal were ambiguous and, at times, misleading. It was never clear whether the spokesperson was unaware of the real situation, or was feigning ignorance. One very prominent speaker claimed *"the banning of opinion polls for seven days was much less severe than was the case in Europe"*. This statement was misleading in that it implied that opinion polls are banned in some European countries. Some countries have a limited ban on publication, but no country in the western world bans the actual taking of polls. However, government spokespersons did not differentiate between the two, and the aphorism *"banning opinion polls"* used by all speakers seemed to relate solely to banning their *publication*.

Not only would the proposed ban affect media interests, but it would also restrict parties and candidates from commissioning research in the run up to an election. To my knowledge – and I followed the debate very closely – only one argument was made to justify the ban on the taking of polls, and the point made was nothing short of ludicrous. The claimed justification was that *"it would be unfair to allow political parties to have the results of private polls and to withhold that information from the public"*. This patronising statement displays a total lack of understanding of the role of market research, including the conduct of private opinion polls.

For over 40 years, the market research industry in Ireland has been conducting thousands of confidential surveys for corporate clients in both public and private sectors, and not only has none of this commercial information ever been released to the public, but there is no logic whatsoever in saying that the public deserves, or even wishes, to see the figures. To claim that withholding the results of private opinion polls would be unfair looks rather lame when the public's perception of the government attempt to ban opinion polls was that it was depriving them of a constitutional right. In any event, very little opinion polling is conducted during that final seven days of election campaigns, and had the amendment not been thrown out by the Seanad, the material effect on the market research industry would have been negligible. Publication was, and is, a matter for the media and since a moratorium on political comment of one day already exists, the government would have been much better advised to have sought a consensus for an extension of the moratorium for up to one week – the moratorium to include the findings of opinion polls.

It is now obvious that the government had its own agenda. In railroading the amendment through the Dáil without either a debate or vote, the prospect of success generated a false sense of immunity from criticism.

THE MILITARY DIMENSION

The statement that market research was the "*commercial equivalent of military intelligence*" was my first intimation that a relationship existed between it and the army. However, on taking up my new career I soon realised that the affinity went much deeper than I had first understood.

I have observed that the principles of war and of marketing are identical, with military commanders – even in the changed circumstances of today's war zones – and marketing executives are constantly obliged to take account of as many as possible of the principles of surprise, concentration of effort, speed of action, initiative and control. Marketing and military plans continue to be based on reports of competitive disposition or, in the military context, enemy strengths, and movements. Reliable intelligence remains a fundamental prerequisite for the military man while today's successful marketing strategies are similarly based on relevant marketplace information, gleaned through market research.

All Army Cadet School graduates will have studied Liddle Hart's most famous book *The Other Side of the Hill* and, in the early 1960s in MRBI, the Liddle Hart philosophy was unexpectedly reintroduced to me. The late Matt Feehan, who had retired from the army a few years before me, was marketing director of Urney Chocolates, and was considering the idea of commissioning market research. He looked at me quite seriously and said, "*I want you to find out what's happening at the other side of the hill; we are launching some new products, and we want to take the high ground and apply the double envelopment.*" We were completely at one in our discussion of the information he required about marketplace and competitor activity, and the part which the MRBI research would play in his plan to launch two new chocolate bars, at different price levels. Although the similarity between the two professions has not always surfaced to the same degree, the realisation has been almost a daily experience for me.

My attachment to, and appreciation of, the education and training which I took with me from the army to the business world has never faded. It has given me considerable satisfaction to initiate and present two MRBI trophies to the officer and non-commissioned officer who obtain first place in the Artillery Young Officer's and Senior NCO's course each year.

Parallel to this, I maintain close personal contact with my early contemporaries from the military college. After many decades, we still hold an annual reunion where the post-dinner reminiscences echo Goldsmith's nostalgic description of the village preacher's battle-scarred visitor:

> *The broken soldier, kindly bade to stay,*
> *Sat by the fire, and talked the night away.*

2001 AND BEYOND

Finally, we look to the relatively recent past to get a few indicators for the future in Ireland.

These pages tell elsewhere that a considerable majority see ourselves as less caring today than we were a generation ago (see *Chapter 15*). However, the uncomfortable point about this is that it comes as no surprise; we can observe it every day. In fact, the research may understate the situation. We are not just less caring, we are manifestly a more violent society.

The dimension that impinges most seriously on political opinion polling, however, is the relatively recent tendency for many electors to claim that they intend to vote for particular parties, when the real situation is that they are no longer sufficiently interested in politics to bother voting at all. To date, it has not been possible to identify these people in interviews and, until this is possible, MRBI must continue to apply our new adjustment procedures to poll findings.

Also, in the political context, a comparison of first preference votes, between the 1981 and 1997 general elections, provides a firm indication of movements over the past 20 years. In first preference terms, and in spite of an increased total valid poll from 1.718 million to 1.789 million, Fianna Fáil has dropped six points and Fine Gael nine points over this period, while the Labour Party has had a marginal increase of 1 per cent and all Others combined, a significant increase of 14 points or 250,000 votes.

	General Election 1981		General Election 1997	
Electorate	2.275 million		2.741 million	
Total Valid Poll	1.718 million		1.789 million	
Turnout	75.5%		65.3%	
	%		%	
Fianna Fáil	45		39	
Fine Gael	37	82	28	67
Labour Party	10		11	
Others	8		22	

Table 16.2: First preference trends 1981–1997

In consolidated terms, over the entire period from 1981, combined support for Fianna Fáil and Fine Gael has dropped from 82 per cent to 67 per cent; the Labour Party has remained stable; and the Others combined has risen from 8 per cent to 22 per cent. The signs of increasing fragmentation are there and first preference figures in the next general election will provide interesting reading.

Since these figures cover a period of 16 years, there is every reason to expect that the pattern will continue for some time to come and that, in the next general election, first preferences will be distributed to a greater extent than ever before. The squeeze on the two large parties is clearly evident and, although I do not see a FF/FG coalition in the immediate future, the concept received considerable support in an *Irish Times/* MRBI poll in September 2000 (see *Chapter 10*). While I assume that many members of Fianna Fáil and Fine Gael would disagree with the viewpoint that there is little between the two parties in ideological terms, I feel that such a coalition will materialise, and the left–right divide in Irish politics will eventually become a reality. For my part, however, I remain a floating voter.

APPENDICES

Appendix A

A schedule of political events including *Irish Times*/MRBI opinion polls.

Appendix B

The satisfaction ratings and party support levels, measured on *Irish Times*/MRBI opinion polls. A graph showing the net party support figures (excluding the undecided) can be found after the index.

APPENDIX A

Chapter 2: Political Schedule (1973–1977)	
Date	Event
5th February 1973	Taoiseach Jack Lynch dissolves Twentieth Dáil
28th February 1973	General election: FG/LP government – Liam Cosgrave, Taoiseach
19th April 1973	MRBI survey: presidential election campaign
30th May 1973	Presidential election: Erskine Childers elected
25th June 1973	Erskine Childers inaugurated as president
17th November 1974	Erskine Childers dies
19th December 1974	Cearbhall Ó Dálaigh inaugurated as president
21st July 1976	Christopher Ewart-Biggs, British Ambassador assassinated
22nd October 1976	Cearbhall Ó Dálaigh resigns as president
3rd December 1976	Dr Patrick Hillery inaugurated as president
25th May 1977	Taoiseach Liam Cosgrave dissolves the Twenty-First Dáil
30th May 1977	First MRBI campaign survey
5th June 1977	Second MRBI campaign survey
9th June 1977	Final MRBI campaign survey
16th June 1977	General election: Fianna Fáil majority
5th July 1977	Fianna Fáil government – Jack Lynch, Taoiseach

Chapter 3: Political Schedule (1977–1981)	
Date	Event
1st July 1977	Liam Cosgrave resigns as Fine Gael leader
1st July 1977	Dr Garret FitzGerald elected Fine Gael leader
15th July 1977	Major MRBI survey: characterisation of electorate
July 1978–April 1979	MRBI survey: prior to European parliament elections
June 1979	European parliament elections
October 1979	MRBI surveys: Cork by-election constituencies
7th November 1979	By-elections: Cork City and Cork North-East
5th December 1979	Jack Lynch resigns as Taoiseach
8th December 1979	Charles Haughey elected Fianna Fáil leader
11th December 1979	Charles Haughey elected Taoiseach
January 1980	MRBI opinion poll
October 1980	MRBI survey: Donegal constituency
6th November 1980	By-election: Donegal constituency
8th December 1980	Anglo–Irish Summit: Taoiseach Charles Haughey and British Prime Minister Margaret Thatcher
14th February 1981	Stardust Disaster: Fianna Fáil Ard-Fheis postponed
21st May 1981	Taoiseach Charles Haughey dissolves the Twenty-Second Dáil
4th June 1981	MRBI opinion poll for *Irish Independent*
11th June 1981	General election: FG/Lab government
30th June 1981	Dr Garret FitzGerald elected Taoiseach

Chapter 4: Political Schedule (1981–1982)

Date	Issue
30th June 1981	FG/Lab coalition government – Dr Garret FitzGerald, Taoiseach
Mid-July 1981	Emergency budget introduced
27th January 1982	1982 budget – government defeated in Dáil vote
4th February 1982	MRBI opinion poll for Sunday Independent
13th February 1982	MRBI opinion poll for *Irish Independent*
18th February 1982	General election
9th March 1982	Fianna Fáil minority government – Charles Haughey, Taoiseach
23rd March 1982	1982 Fianna Fáil budget passed in Dáil
30th March 1982	Dick Burke (FG) takes up appointment as EEC commissioner
3rd May 1982	MRBI approached by *The Irish Times* for the first time
14th May 1982	First *Irish Times*/MRBI opinion poll in Northern Ireland
May 1982	Three MRBI opinion polls for Fine Gael: Dublin West by-election
25th May 1982	Dublin West by-election won by Liam Skelly (FG)
Mid-October 1982	Fine Gael/Labour government publishes the "National Plan"
21st October 1982	First *Irish Times*/MRBI opinion poll in Republic of Ireland
28th October 1982	Dick Spring replaces Michael O'Leary as Labour Party leader
3rd November 1982	Government defeated in a vote of no confidence
12th November 1982	*Irish Times*/MRBI campaign opinion poll
20th November 1982	*Irish Times*/MRBI campaign opinion poll
24th November 1982	General election: FG/Lab coalition – Dr Garret FitzGerald, Taoiseach

Chapter 5: Political Schedule (1982–1987)

Date	Event
14th December 1982	Dr Garret FitzGerald elected Taoiseach for second time
11th February 1983	*Irish Times*/MRBI opinion poll: post-budget and abortion
26th May 1983	*Irish Times*/MRBI opinion poll: abortion referendum
31st August 1983	*Irish Times*/MRBI opinion poll: final campaign poll
7th September 1983	Referendum: Right to Life – carried by 67% to 33%
28th January 1984	*Irish Times*/MRBI opinion poll: post-budget
3rd May 1984	"New Ireland Forum Report" published
10th May 1984	*Irish Times*/MRBI opinion poll: "New Ireland Forum Report"
14th June 1984	European parliament election
2nd October 1984	"Building on Reality"(government national plan) published
17th October 1984	*Irish Times*/MRBI opinion poll: national plan and divorce
19th November 1984	Chequers meeting – Taoiseach and British Prime Minister
5th February 1985	*Irish Times*/MRBI opinion poll: post-budget and political issues
11th April 1985	*Irish Times*/MRBI opinion poll: political issues
16th July 1985	*Irish Times*/MRBI opinion poll: political issues
15th November 1985	Anglo–Irish Agreement signed
20th November 1985	*Irish Times*/MRBI opinion poll: reaction to Anglo–Irish Agreement
21st December 1985	Progressive Democrats established
3rd February 1986	*Irish Times*/MRBI opinion poll: Anglo–Irish Agreement and Progressive Democrat Party
24th April 1986	Government press conference announces that the divorce referendum will be held
28th April 1986	*Irish Times*/MRBI opinion poll: divorce and political issues
18th May 1986	*Irish Times*/MRBI opinion poll: divorce and political issues
15th June 1986	*Irish Times*/MRBI opinion poll: divorce and political issues

Chapter 5: Political Schedule (1982–1987) – *continued*	
Date	**Event**
26th June 1986	Referendum: divorce – defeated by 64% to 36%
29th October 1986	*Irish Times*/MRBI opinion poll: political issues
December 1986	Single European Act and Extradition Bill passed
20th January 1987	Labour ministers resign from government
20th January 1987	Twenty-Fourth Dáil dissolved and general election called
23rd January 1987	First *Irish Times*/MRBI campaign opinion poll
3rd February 1987	Second *Irish Times*/MRBI campaign opinion poll
11th February 1987	Final *Irish Times*/MRBI campaign opinion poll
17th February 1987	General election for Twenty-Fifth Dáil – Fianna Fáil back in government

Chapter 6: Political Schedule (1986)	
Date	**Event**
September 1983–February 1986	*Irish Times*/MRBI polls: reaction to divorce
2nd April 1986	"Statement of Intent" published
27th April 1986	*Irish Times*/MRBI opinion poll: final stage of campaign
14th June 1986	MRBI survey for government
23rd June 1986	MRBI survey for Fine Gael
26th June 1986	Referendum: divorce – defeated by 63% to 37%
4th July 1986	Dr Comiskey, Bishop of Ferns, criticises the 27th April opinion poll in the Wexford People
7th July 1986	*The Irish Times* carries Dr Comiskey's comments
13th August 1986	MRBI writes to Dr Comiskey
26th December 1986	Reply received from Dr Comiskey apologising and undertaking to publish the apology
30th January 1987	MRBI responds to Dr Comiskey
27th March 1987	MRBI again writes to Dr Comiskey

Chapter 7: Political Schedule (1987–1992)

Date	Event
10th March 1987	Charles Haughey elected Taoiseach of Twenty-Fifth Dáil
11th March 1987	Garret FitzGerald announces intention to resign as Fine Gael leader
22nd March 1987	Alan Dukes elected Fine Gael leader
31st March 1987	Ray MacSharry presents the 1987 budget
3rd April 1987	*Irish Times*/MRBI opinion poll: budget and political issues
14th May 1987	*Irish Times*/MRBI opinion poll: Single European Act referendum and political issues
26th May 1987	Referendum: Single European Act – carried by 70% to 30%
2nd September 1987	Alan Dukes' Tallaght Strategy Speech supporting government
September 1987	*Irish Times*/MRBI opinion poll: political issues
14th October 1987	Government press conference announcing PNP agreement
6th November 1987	*Irish Times*/MRBI opinion poll: reaction to PNP and political issues
27th January 1988	Ray MacSharry presents the 1988 budget
2nd February 1988	*Irish Times*/MRBI opinion poll: budget and political issues
14th May 1988	*Irish Times*/MRBI opinion poll: Dublin millennium and political issues
6th October 1988	*Irish Times*/MRBI opinion poll: political issues
17th November 1988	Ray MacSharry replaces Peter Sutherland as EU commissioner
25th November 1988	Albert Reynolds appointed Minister for Finance
17th December 1988	Ray MacSharry appointed Commissioner for Agriculture in EU
26th January 1989	Albert Reynolds presents the 1988 budget
31st January 1989	*Irish Times*/MRBI opinion poll: budget and political issues
28th April 1989	Government motion on allocation for haemophiliacs defeated
25th May 1989	Taoiseach dissolves Dáil and calls a general election

Chapter 7: Political Schedule (1987–1992) – *continued*	
Date	**Event**
27th May 1989	*Irish Times*/MRBI campaign opinion poll
27th May 1989	Fine Gael and the Progressive Democrats announce a pre-election pact
9th June 1989	*Irish Times*/MRBI campaign opinion poll
15th June 1989	General election for the Twenty-Sixth Dáil – inconclusive result
26th June 1989	Twenty-Sixth Dáil meets – all three nominees for Taoiseach defeated
3rd July 1989	Twenty-Sixth Dáil meets again – no agreement on government
4th July 1989	*Irish Times*/MRBI opinion poll – reaction to Dáil impasse
6th July 1989	Twenty-Sixth Dáil meets for the third time – optimism but no government
12th July 1989	Twenty-Sixth Dáil meets – FF/PD coalition government agreed and elected
20th November 1989	*Irish Times*/MRBI opinion poll: political issues and other matters
1st January 1990	Charles Haughey takes over presidency of EU
31st January 1990	Albert Reynolds presents the 1990 budget
6th February 1990	*Irish Times*/MRBI opinion poll: budget and political issues
21st May 1990	*Irish Times*/MRBI opinion poll: European presidency and political issues
6th October 1990	*Irish Times*/MRBI opinion poll: political issues
11th October 1990	Tánaiste Brian Lenihan dismissed
3rd November 1990	*Irish Times*/MRBI opinion poll: political issues
7th November 1990	Presidential election: Mary Robinson elected
13th November 1990	Alan Dukes resigns as Fine Gael leader
20th November 1990	John Bruton elected Fine Gael leader
5th February 1991	Limited cabinet reshuffle – Brian Daly becomes Minister for Defence
16th April 1991	*Irish Times*/MRBI opinion poll: political issues
31st May 1991	Beef Tribunal established

Chapter 7: Political Schedule (1987–1992) – *continued*

Date	Event
18th June 1991	*Irish Times*/MRBI opinion poll: local elections and political issues
27th June 1991	Local elections: county and county borough councils only
10th October 1991	*Irish Times*/MRBI opinion poll: political issues and political standards
24th October 1991	Some Fianna Fáil members campaign for Haughey's removal as leader
11th December 1991	*Irish Times*/MRBI opinion poll: political and other issues
January 1992	Sean Doherty Press Conference: 1982 phone tapping
6th February 1992	Haughey resigns as Taoiseach and Fianna Fáil leader
11th February 1992	Albert Reynolds elected Taoiseach and Fianna Fáil leader

Chapter 8: Political Schedule (1990)

Date	Event
6th February 1990	*Irish Times*/MRBI poll: political issues and budget
1st May 1990	Mary Robinson's campaign formally launched
21st May 1990	*Irish Times*/MRBI poll: political issues
30th July 1990	MRBI/Fine Gael opinion poll: presidential election and general issues
29th September 1990	MRBI/Fine Gael opinion poll: presidential election
4th October 1990	Mary Robinson interview with Hot Press magazine
6th October 1990	*Irish Times*/MRBI poll: presidential election and political issues
15th October 1990	RTÉ Q&A programme with presidential candidates
22nd October 1990	MRBI/Fine Gael opinion poll: presidential election
31st October 1990	Brian Lenihan dismissed as Tánaiste and Minister for Defence
3rd November 1990	*Irish Times*/MRBI poll: presidential election
6th November 1990	Presidential election

Chapter 9: Political Schedule (1992-1994)

Date	Event
7th February 1992	Maastricht Treaty signed
10th February 1992	Charles Haughey resigns as Taoiseach
11th February 1992	Albert Reynolds appointed Taoiseach
24th–25th February 1992	*Irish Times*/MRBI opinion poll: political issues and abortion
5th–6th May 1992	*Irish Times*/MRBI opinion poll: political issues and Maastricht
8th June 1992	*Irish Times*/MRBI opinion poll: political issues and Maastricht
15th June 1992	*Irish Times*/MRBI opinion poll: political issues and Maastricht
18th June 1992	Referendum: Maastricht – carried
30th June 1992	Des O'Malley gives evidence to Beef Tribunal
13th July 1992	Beef Tribunal is adjourned
24th–25th September 1992	*Irish Times*/MRBI opinion poll: political issues and abortion
Late September 1992	Tensions develops between some Fianna Fáil and Progressive Democrat ministers in government
29th September 1992	Beef Tribunal resumes
6th October 1992	Further reported tensions between cabinet sub-committee and Progressive Democrats on wording of abortion amendment
10th October 1992	Dáil resumes after summer recess – all parties, other than Fianna Fáil, oppose suggested wording of the abortion referendum
27th October 1992	Taoiseach Albert Reynolds gives evidence at tribunal – describes Des O'Malley's evidence as "reckless and dishonest"
29th October 1992	Progressive Democrats call on Taoiseach to withdraw his allegation or dismiss Des O'Malley – tensions and disagreements continue
30th October 1992	Taoiseach repeats his claim that Des O'Malley was "dishonest" in the evidence he gave
31st October 1992	Progressive Democrats threaten to withdraw from government

Chapter 9: Political Schedule (1992-1994) – *continued*	
Date	Event
4th November 1992	Progressive Democrat ministers resign from government and government confidence motion defeated
5th November 1992	General election and abortion referendum fixed for 25th November
9th November 1992	*Irish Times*/MRBI opinion poll: voting intentions
17th–18th November 1992	*Irish Times*/MRBI opinion poll: voting intentions
25th November 1992	General election and referenda on availability of abortion, right to travel and information
4th January 1993	Pádraig Flynn appointed European commissioner
12th January 1993	New FF/Lab government – Albert Reynolds re-elected Taoiseach
1st March 1993	*Irish Times*/MRBI poll: political issues and budget
2nd July 1993	*Irish Times*/MRBI poll: political issues and reaction to the tax amnesty
1st October 1993	*Irish Times*/MRBI poll: political issues
23rd November 1993	*Irish Times*/MRBI poll: political issues and Northern Ireland (Articles 2 and 3)
15th December 1993	Downing Street Declaration signed
31st January 1994	*Irish Times*/MRBI poll: political issues, budget and Downing Street Declaration
30th May 1994	*Irish Times*/MRBI poll: pre-European election
30th May 1994	By-elections: Dublin South-Central and Mayo West
7th August 1994	"Beef Tribunal Report" published
22nd August 1994	*Irish Times*/MRBI poll: political issues and Beef Tribunal report
31st August 1994	IRA ceasefire
September 1994	Government disagreements arise over High Court presidency and the extradition of Fr Smyth
17th November 1994	Labour Party leaves government
17th November 1994	Albert Reynolds resigns as Taoiseach
18th November 1994	*Irish Times*/MRBI poll

Chapter 10: Political Schedule 1994-2001

Date	Event
19th November 1994	Bertie Ahern elected Fianna Fáil leader
25th November 1994	*Irish Times*/MRBI poll: general election not preferred
15th December 1994	New FG/Lab/DL coalition government – John Bruton, Taoiseach
8th February 1995	First budget of the new government
13th February 1995	*Irish Times*/MRBI poll: political issues, budget and divorce
22nd February 1995	Northern Ireland Framework Document signed
22nd May 1995	*Irish Times*/MRBI poll: divorce
27th July 1995	*Irish Times*/MRBI poll: divorce
30th September 1995	*Irish Times*/MRBI poll: political issues and divorce
4th November 1995	*Irish Times*/MRBI poll: divorce
18th November 1995	*Irish Times*/MRBI poll: political issues and divorce
24th November 1995	Divorce referendum and *Irish Times*/MRBI poll: divorce
16th February 1996	High Court petition
9th February 1996	Canary Wharf bombing – IRA ceasefire ended
4th June 1996	*Irish Times*/MRBI poll: political issues and Northern Ireland
25th September 1996	*Irish Times*/MRBI poll: political issues, EU and neutrality
30th November 1996	Michael Lowry resigns as a government minister
6th December 1996	*Irish Times*/MRBI poll: political issues and government resignation
28th January 1997	*Irish Times*/MRBI poll: political issues and budget
27th March 1997	*Irish Times*/MRBI poll: political issues and abortion
April 1997	McCracken Tribunal commences
5th May 1997	*Irish Times*/MRBI poll: political issues and the McCracken Tribunal
15th May 1997	General election declared: date fixed for 6th June
20th May 1997	*Irish Times*/MRBI poll: general election issues
28th May 1997	*Irish Times*/MRBI poll: general election issues
6th June 1997	General election and *Irish Times*/MRBI in-home survey

Chapter 10: Political Schedule 1994-2001 – *continued*

Date	Event
26th June 1997	FF/PD coalition government – Bertie Ahern, Taoiseach
July 1997	IRA ceasefire restored
10th September 1997	Dáil debates McCracken Tribunal report
27th September 1997	*Irish Times*/MRBI poll: political issues
11th October 1997	*Irish Times*/MRBI poll: political issues and presidential election
22nd October 1997	*Irish Times*/MRBI poll: political issues and presidential election
27th October 1997	*Irish Times*/MRBI poll: political issues and presidential election
30th October 1997	Presidential election: Mary McAleese elected
October 1997	Flood Tribunal established
5th November 1997	Ruairi Quinn replaces Dick Spring as Labour Party leader
12th December 1997	*Irish Times*/MRBI poll: political issues, budget and abortion
10th April 1998	Signing of the Belfast (Good Friday) Agreement
15th April 1998	*Irish Times*/MRBI poll: political issues and Northern Ireland
22nd June 1998	Referendum: changes to Articles 2 and 3 of Constitution passed
6th October 1998	*Irish Times*/MRBI poll: political issues
24th February 1999	*Irish Times*/MRBI poll: political issues
10th May 1999	*Irish Times*/MRBI poll: political issues
3rd June 1999	*Irish Times*/MRBI poll: pre-European election poll and political issues
3rd November 1999	*Irish Times*/MRBI poll: political issues – new adjustment procedures (voting intentions) used for the first time
18th January 2000	*Irish Times*/MRBI poll: political issues and budget reaction
14th June 2000	*Irish Times*/MRBI poll: political issues, reaction to O'Flaherty issue and FF/FG internal enquiries
22nd September 2000	*Irish Times*/MRBI poll: next election issues – coalition preferences

Chapter 10: Political Schedule 1994-2001 – *continued*

Date	Event
November 2000	The first in a series of eight constituency polls conducted for TG4
23rd January 2001	*Irish Times*/MRBI poll: political issues and budget reaction
31st January 2001	Fine Gael parliamentary party passes a vote of no confidence in John Bruton
9th February 2001	Michael Noonan elected Fine Gael leader
15th May 2001	*Irish Times*/MRBI poll: political issues and voting intentions in the Nice referendum
7th June 2001	Referendum: Nice Treaty – defeated by 54% to 46%

Chapter 14: Political Schedule – Northern Ireland

Date	Event
3rd May 1973	Northern Ireland Assembly Act passed
9th December 1973	Sunningdale Agreement signed
5th April 1982	The Prior proposals on a new Northern Ireland Assembly published
14th May 1982	Inaugural *Irish Times*/MRBI poll: Prior proposals
1st June 1983	MRBI opinion poll for The Irish News: the general election
9th June 1983	General election: Westminster
8th December 1983	MRBI opinion poll for the BBC: Northern Ireland Assembly and Forum
2nd May 1984	"New Ireland Forum Report" published
15th May 1984	*Irish Times*/MRBI poll: "New Ireland Forum Report"
15th November 1984	Anglo–Irish Agreement signed
27th May 1987	MRBI opinion poll for SDLP: South Down
11th June 1987	General election: Westminster
9th April 1992	General election: Westminster
15th December 1993	Downing Street Declaration signed
22nd February 1995	Framework Document published
22nd January 1996	Mitchell Report published

Chapter 14: Political Schedule – Northern Ireland – *continued*

Date	Event
23rd February 1996	*Irish Times*/MRBI poll: situation in Northern Ireland and Mitchell Report
1st May 1997	General election: Westminster
10th April 1998	Belfast (Good Friday) Agreement signed
14th April 1998	*Irish Times*/MRBI poll: Belfast Agreement
12th May 1998	*Irish Times*/MRBI poll: voting intentions on agreement referendum
22nd May 1998	Referenda on Belfast Agreement carried
2nd June 1998	*Irish Times*/MRBI poll: voting intentions in Northern Ireland Assembly election
16th June 1998	*Irish Times*/MRBI poll: voting intentions in Northern Ireland Assembly election
25th June 1998	Northern Ireland Assembly election
1st July 1998	First meeting of New Assembly – First Minister and Deputy First Minister elected
13th July 1998	Young Quinn brothers burned to death in arson attack
15th August 1998	Omagh bomb explosion – 29 killed over 300 injured
9th July 1999	*Irish Times*/MRBI poll: "The Way Forward" and other matters
29th November 1999	Nomination of 10 ministers to Northern Ireland Assembly
1st December 1999	Formal devolution of power

YEAR	1982	1982	1982	1983	1983	1984	1984
OPINION POLL DATE	Oct	Nov	Nov	Feb	Feb	May	Oct
Government	FF	FF	—	FG/L	FG/L	FG/L	FG/L
Taoiseach	CH	CH	—	GF	GF	GF	GF
Opposition Leader	GF	GF	—	CH	CH	CH	CH
SATISFACTION RATING	%	%	%	%	%	%	%
Government	20	—	—	35	35	28	28
Taoiseach	31	31	—	56	46	48	47
Opposition Leader	62	61	—	39	34	46	48
PARTY SUPPORT							
Core							
Fianna Fáil	36	39	—	36	32	37	43
Fine Gael	36	36	—	32	29	29	31
Labour	7	8	—	5	6	6	6
Progressive Democrats	—	—	—	—	—	—	—
Other	7	5	—	4	4	3	6
Undecided	14	12	—	23	29	25	14
Net							
Fianna Fáil	42	44	45	47	45	49	51
Fine Gael	42	41	39	42	41	38	36
Labour	8	9	9	7	8	8	7
Progressive Democrats	—	—	—	—	—	—	—
Other	8	6	7	4	6	5	6
Major Event		General Election November 1982				Northern Ireland Forum Report	

YEAR	1985			1986				
OPINION POLL DATE	Feb	April	July	Nov	Feb	Apr	June	Oct
Government	FG/L	FG/L	FG/L	FG/L	FG/L	FG/L	FG/L	FG/L
Taoiseach	GF	GF	GF	GF	GF	GF	GF	GF
Opposition Leader	CH	CH	CH	CH	CH	CH	CH	CH
SATISFACTION RATING	%	%	%	%	%	%	%	%
Government	28	26	24	34	23	27	25	22
Taoiseach	40	39	41	51	45	44	45	44
Opposition Leader	44	40	47	43	36	46	48	45
PARTY SUPPORT								
Core								
Fianna Fáil	42	42	45	44	36	41	45	40
Fine Gael	28	28	28	32	20	22	22	25
Labour	5	5	4	5	4	4	4	4
Progressive Democrats	—	—	—	—	21	15	13	13
Other	5	7	9	5	5	4	5	5
Undecided	20	18	14	14	14	14	14	13
Net								
Fianna Fáil	52	51	52	51	42	48	51	46
Fine Gael	35	34	33	37	23	26	25	29
Labour	6	6	5	6	4	5	5	5
Progressive Democrats	—	—	—	—	25	17	15	15
Other	7	9	10	6	6	4	4	5
Major Event				Anglo-Irish Agreement	Post PD established		Divorce Referendum	

YEAR	1987							1988		
OPINION POLL DATE	Jan	Feb	Feb	Feb	April	May	Nov	Feb	May	Oct
Government	FG/L	FG/L	FG/L	—	FF	FF	FF	FF	FF	FF
Taoiseach	GF	GF	GF	—	CH	CH	CH	CH	CH	CH
Opposition Leader	CH	CH	CH	—	AD	AD	AD	AD	AD	AD
SATISFACTION RATING	%	%	%	—	%	%	%	%	%	%
Government	—	—	—	—	39	31	29	40	42	36
Taoiseach	36	36	36	—	46	38	38	46	55	54
Opposition Leader	46	43	43	—	54	51	44	47	44	44
PARTY SUPPORT										
Core										
Fianna Fáil	40	40	40	—	40	32	33	35	43	42
Fine Gael	18	19	21	—	24	26	27	23	23	21
Labour	4	4	5	—	5	4	5	6	6	8
Progressive Democrats	12	11	13	—	13	20	11	11	8	6
Other	5	5	5	—	6	6	7	6	6	6
Undecided	21	21	16	—	12	12	17	19	14	17
Net										
Fianna Fáil	52	50	48	44	46	41	40	44	50	50
Fine Gael	23	24	25	27	27	33	32	28	27	26
Labour	5	5	6	6	6	5	6	7	7	10
Progressive Democrats	15	14	16	12	14	14	14	14	10	7
Other	5	7	5	11	7	7	8	7	6	7
Major Event				General Election February 1987			Post Tallaght Strategy			

YEAR	1989					1990				
OPINION POLL DATE	Feb	May	June	June	July	Nov	Feb	May	Oct	Nov
Government	FF	FF	FF		None	FF/PD	FF/PD	FF/PD	FF/PD	FF/PD
Taoiseach	CH	CH	CH		CH Act.	CH	CH	CH	CH	CH
Opposition Leader	AD	AD	AD		AD	AD	AD	AD	AD	AD
SATISFACTION RATING	%	%	%	%	%	%	%	%	%	%
Government	49	43	—	—	—	52	54	53	48	—
Taoiseach	67	—	—	—	51	57	56	61	59	—
Opposition Leader	48	—	—	—	69	52	41	41	36	—
PARTY SUPPORT										
Core										
Fianna Fáil	45	39	38	—	38	44	42	43	42	44
Fine Gael	21	22	23	—	10	7	24	20	20	22
Labour	6	7	6	—	27	24	8	9	10	9
Progressive Democrats	7	4	5	—	3	3	4	6	4	4
Other	4	6	8	—	9	8	6	7	8	6
Undecided	17	22	20	—	13	14	16	15	16	15
Net										
Fianna Fáil	54	50	47	44	43	51	50	51	49	52
Fine Gael	25	28	28	29	31	28	29	23	24	26
Labour	8	9	8	9	11	8	10	10	12	10
Progressive Democrats	8	5	6	6	4	3	4	7	4	5
Other	5	8	11	12	11	10	7	9	11	7
Major Event			General Election June 1989						Brian Lenihan dismissed	Presidential Election – Alan Dukes resigns

324

YEAR	1991				1992							
OPINION POLL DATE	April	June	Oct	Dec	Feb	May	June	June	Sept	Nov	Nov	Nov
Government	FF/PD	FF/PD	FF/PD	FF/PD	FF/PD	FF/PD	FF/PD	FF/PD	FF/PD	FF/PD	FF/PD	FF/PD
Taoiseach	CH	CH	CH	CH	AR	AR	AR	AR	AR	AR	AR	AR
Opposition Leader	JB	JB	JB	JB	JB	JB	JB	JB	JB	JB	JB	JB
SATISFACTION RATING	%	%	%	%	%	%	%	%	%	%	%	%
Government	54	44	29	28	45	45	47	48	41	31	—	—
Taoiseach	56	52	33	32	60	63	—	—	60	31	28	—
Opposition Leader	42	39	39	37	38	33	—	—	36	30	31	—
PARTY SUPPORT												
Core												
Fianna Fáil	44	38	36	35	46	45	43	43	42	33	34	39
Fine Gael	20	21	23	23	20	18	18	18	19	20	21	25
Labour	10	9	13	13	10	11	10	9	10	14	19	19
Progressive Democrats	5	6	6	7	4	8	4	5	6	7	5	5
Other	10	11	10	11	7	8	9	6	8	8	7	12
Undecided	11	15	12	11	13	10	17	18	15	18	15	—
Net												
Fianna Fáil	49	45	41	40	53	51	53	53	49	40	40	39
Fine Gael	23	25	26	26	23	21	22	22	23	24	25	25
Labour	11	11	15	15	12	13	11	12	12	17	22	19
Progressive Democrats	6	7	7	8	4	9	7	6	7	8	6	5
Other	11	12	11	11	8	6	9	7	9	11	7	12
Major Event			Move to replace Charles Haughey		Charles Haughey resigns Albert Reynolds Taoiseach			Maastricht Treaty Referendum	Beef Tribunal resumption		PDs resign from government	General Election and Abortion Referendum

YEAR		1993			1994				
OPINION POLL DATE	March	July	Oct	Nov	Feb	May	August	Nov	Nov
Government	FF/L	FF/L	FF/L	FF/L	FF/L	FF/L	FF/L	FF/L	FF/L
Taoiseach	AR	AR	AR	AR	AR	AR	AR	AR Act.	AR Act.
Opposition Leader	JB	JB	JB	JB	JB	JB	JB	JB	JB
SATISFACTION RATING	%	%	%	%	%	%	%	%	%
Government	22	30	34	42	49	43	38	49	—
Taoiseach	37	40	47	53	62	—	46	—	—
Opposition Leader	31	23	24	27	29	—	33	—	—
PARTY SUPPORT									
Core									
Fianna Fáil	34	36	37	40	43	38	34	28	39
Fine Gael	19	16	15	15	13	16	18	17	20
Labour	13	15	15	14	11	13	14	18	16
Progressive Democrats	8	9	7	10	10	5	5	8	5
Other	7	9	9	8	7	11	12	12	9
Undecided	19	15	17	13	16	17	17	17	11
Net									
Fianna Fáil	42	42	44	47	50	45	42	35	44
Fine Gael	23	19	19	18	16	20	22	21	23
Labour	16	18	18	16	13	16	16	22	18
Progressive Democrats	9	11	9	11	12	6	6	9	5
Other	10	10	10	8	9	13	14	13	10
Major Event					Post Downing Street Declaration		Post Beef Tribunal Report		Bertie Ahern elected Leader FF

YEAR	1995			1996		
OPINION POLL DATE	Feb	Sept	Nov	June	Sept	Dec
Government	FF/L/DL	FF/L/DL	FF/L/DL	FG/L/DL	FG/L/DL	FG/L/DL
Taoiseach	JB	JB	JB	JB	JB	JB
Opposition Leader	BA	BA	BA	BA	BA	BA
SATISFACTION RATING	%	%	%	%	%	%
Government	45	46	46	42	43	39
Taoiseach	53	54	54	56	54	53
Opposition Leader	69	62	57	57	52	58
PARTY SUPPORT						
Core						
Fianna Fáil	41	37	40	40	36	38
Fine Gael	20	19	21	23	20	20
Labour	13	13	10	8	10	8
Progressive Democrats	5	6	4	6	5	9
Other	9	6	10	9	7	5
Undecided	12	19	15	14	22	20
Net						
Fianna Fáil	47	45	48	47	45	46
Fine Gael	23	23	24	26	25	24
Labour	15	16	12	10	13	10
Progressive Democrats	6	7	4	7	6	11
Other	9	9	12	10	11	9
Major Event	John Bruton Taoiseach No election					

YEAR — 1997

OPINION POLL DATE	Jan	March	May	May	May	June	June	Sept	Oct	Oct	Dec
	FG/L/DL	FG/L/DL	FG/L/DL	FG/L/DL	FG/L/DL	FG/L/DL		FF/PD	FF/PD	FF/PD	FF/PD
Government	JB	JB	JB	JB	JB	JB	—	BA	BA	BA	BA
Taoiseach	BA	BA	BA	BA	BA	BA	—	JB	JB	JB	JB
Opposition Leader	BA	BA	BA	BA	BA	BA	—	JB	JB	JB	JB
SATISFACTION RATING	%	%	%	%	%	%		%	%	%	%
Government	50	53	49	54	57	—	—	62	55	55	65
Taoiseach	58	63	55	55	58	—	—	73	—	67	74
Opposition Leader	59	58	59	60	65	—	—	60	—	43	50
PARTY SUPPORT											
Core											
Fianna Fáil	38	37	36	36	36	—	—	42	42	42	44
Fine Gael	22	25	22	22	23	—	—	21	22	22	23
Labour	8	9	10	9	9	—	—	11	11	8	11
Progressive Democrats	8	7	7	6	6	—	—	2	3	2	3
Other	7	7	9	11	12	—	—	7	6	8	7
Undecided	17	15	16	16	14	—	—	17	16	18	12
Net											
Fianna Fáil	45	43	43	43	42	44	39	50	50	51	50
Fine Gael	27	30	26	26	26	27	28	25	26	27	26
Labour	10	11	12	10	11	8	10	13	13	10	13
Progressive Democrats	9	8	8	7	7	4	5	2	3	2	3
Other	9	8	11	14	14	17	18	10	8	10	8
Major Event						Election Day Poll	General Election June 1997				

APPENDIX B

YEAR	1998	1998	1999	1999	1999	1999	2000	2000	2000	2000	2001	2001
OPINION POLL DATE	April	Oct	Feb	May	June	Nov	Jan	April	June	Sept	Jan	May
Government	FF/PD	FF/PD	FF/PD	FF/PD	FF/PD	FF/PD	FF/PD	FF/PD	FF/PD	FF/PD	FF/PD	FF/PD
Taoiseach	BA	BA	BA	BA	BA	BA	BA	BA	BA	BA	BA	BA
Opposition Leader	JB	JB	JB	JB	JB	JB	JB	JB	JB	JB	JB	MN
SATISFACTION RATING	%	%	%	%	%	%	%	%	%	%	%	%
Government	73	68	52	51	58	46	55	60	48	43	58	59
Taoiseach	84	81	70	58	67	69	66	69	64	55	66	64
Opposition Leader	56	47	47	46	43	47	45	42	39	40	37	37
PARTY SUPPORT												
Core												
Fianna Fáil	49	49	39	38	43	38	39	40	36	34	38	39
Fine Gael	18	17	20	19	21	18	20	18	14	17	15	18
Labour	10	11	11	13	9	11	9	8	10	10	10	9
Progressive Democrats	3	2	3	4	2	3	2	3	3	2	3	3
Other	7	8	9	8	11	10	10	12	16	12	12	14
Undecided	13	13	18	18	14	20	20	19	21	25	22	17
Net												
Fianna Fáil	57	56	48	46	51	41	44	45	40	40	41	42
Fine Gael	20	20	25	24	25	25	28	24	19	24	20	24
Labour	11	12	14	15	11	17	14	12	16	17	15	13
Progressive Democrats	3	2	4	5	2	4	4	4	4	3	4	4
Other	9	10	9	10	11	13	10	15	21	16	20	17
Major Event	Belfast Good Friday Agreement			Sheedy Affair		Tribunal Revelations			Tribunal Revelations	Tribunal Revelations		

[Net figures based on new adjustment procedures]

329

A graph showing the net party support figures (excluding the undecided) can be found after the index.

INDEX